FIELD GUNS IN FRANCE

FIELD GUNS IN FRANCE

by

Lieut.-Col. NEIL FRASER-TYTLER
D.S.O., T.D., R.A. (T.A.)

Edited by
Major F. N. BAKER, R.G.A.
Editor of
Nan Shan and Port Arthur

To the glorious memory of the Red Fox Army

I WOULD like to assure the reader that I hold no brief for war. It is a horrid, hateful business at the best of times, but when at war one should wage to the best of one's ability. One of the chief enemies of efficiency is war boredom. A way out of this pervading morass of war slackness, brought on by boredom, can be found by taking the keenest possible interest in the killing side of war. It is only by working up a personal hatred against one's enemies that this can be done. Somewhere in us, deep down or near the surface, according to our natures, we have got that instinct to kill, and it only needs cultivation to make it a personal hatred against the enemy, by which means war boredom can be eliminated. The pitch slackness reached in the third battle of "Wipers" had to be seen to be believed.

N. F. T.

INTRODUCTION

THE following letters were written to his father by a Gunner Officer in France between November, 1915, and August, 1918. They are often merely records of trivial happenings, but they show what a very mixed business modern war may be—with its lights and shades, it tragedies and its comedies. When reading them one finds oneself insensibly entering into the spirit of the daily or nightly task or the adventure or hazard that is on hand. Many episodes are referred to in which others were interested, and it is hoped that perhaps friends may like to possess a record which in some cases unhappily refers to good soldiers "gone west".

In their original form the letters were oftentimes hurried, written under difficulties in dug-outs and makeshift accommodation—they were also occasionally disconnected, so in order to present a fairly coherent whole, the plan was adopted of grouping them so that the reader may obtain at a glance a general idea of the sector in which operations are being described, and its bearing on the whole. As the period during which they were written is usually divided into spaces representing phases of the War, it was found convenient to allot various groups of letters to these phases, and it is hoped that this would give the reader a means of "finding his bearings", as it were. Place-names and names of units have of course been added since the letters were written.

The writer was given command of a R.F.A. howitzer battery in October, 1915, and took it to France in November of the same year. He landed at Havre, and after some preliminary instructional work with another brigade, took up a position on the Northern bank of the Somme, which curiously enough was the "right of the line" so far as the field guns were concerned. This was the time when the front was fairly quiet and British shells scarce, but it includes an interval in January, 1916, during which the Germans made a very determined attack, capturing Frise and almost cutting our communications. (See first of maps at end, area marked A.) Incidentally this attack was one of the forerunners of the Verdun offensive. The spring of 1916 passed with the writer still in the same position, busily preparing his corner for its part in the great Somme offensive. This action commenced on the 1st of July, 1916, and prolonged its bitter combat well into November, when the battery and its commander were withdrawn and sent to a new position just South of Arras. (See first of maps at end, area B.)

There the unit remained until December, 1916, when reorganization resulted in the writer taking over an 18-pdr. Battery temporarily, being transferred eventually to an Army Brigade—but not leaving the locality.

In March, 1917, the line advanced on the heels of the retreating Germans, when the writer had his first experience of more or less open fighting. The German retreat was in the nature of a pivoting movement ; their right, resting in Arras to Vimy Ridge, being more or less stationary. This movement culminated in the battle of Arras, which commenced on the 9th April, 1917, and lasted till nearly the end of May. At its termination the writer and his unit moved Northwards by train to the Messines front. (See first of maps at end, marked C.)

They arrived there about the 25th May, and the remarkable Artillery struggle known as the battle of Messines Ridge was decided on the 7th of June. The counter-battery work on both sides was intensified to a degree previously unknown, and the writer's unit was "well in the scrap". On the evening of the battle (7th of June) the Army Brigade to which the unit belonged moved out, and eventually, after some days, reached the Ypres neighbourhood, where they rested for a few weeks.

Then began preparations for the Ypres offensive (see first of maps at end, marked D), a preparation very costly in casualties. The action proper started on the 20th July, the great infantry attack being launched on the 31st of that month. It will be remembered that there also our casualties were very heavy.

This great effort dragged along from August to November, and was a record for losses in the Artillery personnel, which in July and August were actually greater in number than those suffered by the Infantry.

In November the unit was chosen as the Depôt Battery of the Fifth Army Artillery School near Abbeville—a selection regarded as a great honour. However, as the Germans broke through at Cambrai a day or two after the battery had reached the school, the writer was hurried off to rejoin his brigade on the Cambrai front. (See first of maps at end, area E.) Here he became temporary O.C. of the Brigade, his Colonel being on leave, but the after-effects of gas encountered in the fighting at Ypres forced him to take the opportunity of recuperating at the Artillery School, where he was offered an appointment as Instructor and he remained in that capacity until the German offensive of March, 1918, opened.

INTRODUCTION

During the great retreat of the Fifth Army, he had many and varied experiences, and on the arrest of the German advance went back to the Artillery School, where he spent the summer—his actual fighting experiences over.

The letters dealing with the last phase of the War, when he was attached to the Military Section of the Supreme War Council at Versailles as D.A.A. and Q.M.G., have been omitted owing to lack of space.

F.N.B.

January, 1922.

PREFACE

The moril of this story, it is plainly to be seen:
You 'avn't got no families when servin' of the Queen—
You 'avn't got no brothers, fathers, sisters, wives, or sons—
If you want to win your battles take an' work your bloomin' guns!
                                                R. KIPLING.

IT is customary, I know, to write a few honeyed words of apology before inflicting on the public an autobiography or other personal work. But I may say at once that no such apology will be found here.

These letters were published to interest a few gunners, and anyone else who buys the work does so entirely at his own peril.

No glossary explaining technical terms is attached, and no reward is offered for any calculation of the number of times the pronoun "I" appears.

Neither have I attempted any moralizing about the many aspects of war, grisly, sordid or muddy though they be!

Because, after all, the sole *raison d'être* of Armies is obviously the enforcement of some policy supported by the threat of war in the background, and war itself is the employment to their fullest extent of the machinery of death already prepared. Hence "slay and spare not" should be the motto without question or comment, but with a feeling of thankfulness that the greatest war this old world has ever seen came at a time when, young and fit, one felt thoroughly able to take part in it.

I have attempted to give detailed views of microscopic portions of the front, very similar to the picture presented by the high-powered deer-stalking telescope with which I did most of my observing.

But I hope the reader will bear in mind that these letters remain practically in their original form, and hence I fear the heroism of the gunners and drivers has hardly received its due tribute.

In day-to-day notes such as these, mention may be made of some outstanding feat of valour, but the patience and endurance which, day after day, month after month, through long years of war, carried them undauntedly through endless summer days reeking with poison-gas and long winter nights surrounded by slime and miseries almost beyond description, is accepted without comment as a matter of course.

PREFACE

The batteries referred to were D/151 in 1915-16, and A/150 Army Field Artillery in 1917, both Lancashire batteries from the 30th Divisional Artillery. It is to that great fighting county, therefore, I owe my thanks for the stout-hearted men I had the honour to command, and good partners I found them in the game of killing the Hun.

N.F.T.

My most grateful thanks are due to Mr. Rudyard Kipling for allowing me to use his beautiful lines as chapter headings.

JANUARY, 1922.

CONTENTS

OUR INTRODUCTION TO WAR, NOV., 1915—JAN., 1916.
Letters.
1. From Larkhill to Havre—The Rest Camp—By Train to Doullens—Billets at St. Ouen.
2. In Action at Last—A Quiet Front—Taken for a Spy.
3. Aeroplane Bombs—The Weekly "Strafe"—Return to St. Ouen.
4. The Daily Round—Xmas—A Lecture on the Battle of Loos—Getting Ready for the Somme.
5. In Action near the Somme—Taking over the Zone—Chancing it across the Open.
6. Renewed German Activity—Digging In—Excursions into No Man's Land.

THE BATTLE OF FRISE, JANUARY—MARCH, 1916.
(See Map "A" at end.)
7. A Sudden Attack—Loss of Frise—We prepare to Retire.
8. In a Tight Corner—Awaiting the French Counter-attack.
9. The French Attack—Killing taken Seriously.
10. We change our Zone—Close Liaison with the French—In the Allied Front Line.
11. Sniping with 4.5 Howitzers—Lunch with Our Allies.
12. A Wood in the Marsh changes hands Four Times—Visitors to the O.P.

PREPARATIONS FOR THE SOMME, MAY—JUNE, 1916.
(See Map "A" at end.)
13. Leave—Casualties by Rats—An Abortive Hun Raid.
14. Every Minute of a Typical Day—Retrieving a Fallen Angel.
15. The French Invasion—Our P.P.C. Shell—An Old Etonian Dinner and its Sequel.
16. Our New Position—A Desirable O.P.—Fire in a Gun Pit.

CONTENTS

THE SOMME, JULY—NOVEMBER, 1916.
(See Map "A" at end.)

Letters.

17. Preparations during June—The Great Bombardment.
18. The Attack of the 1st July.
19. The Lull—We Advance—A Visit to Montauban—Trones Wood—The First Round.
20. A Close Call—Capture of the Second Line—Good Sport in the Front of Trones Wood.
21. The Loss of Delville Wood—Maintaining Communication with Trones Wood—Private Attack on Arrow Head Copse.
22. Observing from the French Front—A French Section in Trouble—My Birthday Feast—The Battle of the 30th July.
23. A Lucky Escape—We go out of Action at Last.
24. Idle Days by Quiet Waters.
25. The Somme once again—An Advanced Position—Mud.
26. The Shoot of a Lifetime—Good Killing—An Overworked 'Phone Line.
27. The Attack of the 12th October—Rainbow Trench after our Bombardment—Dawn Explorations—The Gueudecourt Saps.
28. Rain and Mud—More Front Line Observing.
29. Shell-hole Fighting—The Finger of Fate—Back to the Wagon Lines.
30. Rain and Mud—Mud and Rain.
31. Horsemastership in Mud—Idle Reflections.
32. Shutting up Shop on the Somme—A Comic Relief—A Wandering Sausage.

THE WINTER ADVANCE, 1917.
(See Map "B" at end.)

33. A Pale Pink War—Nursing a Quiet Parish.
34. The Hun Retires—Comedies of the Advance.
35. The R.A. attack Henin.

CONTENTS

THE BATTLE OF ARRAS, APRIL—MAY, 1917.
(See Map "B" at end.)

Letters.
36. The Battle of Arras—Capture of the Hindenberg Line—A Good Kill at Dawn.
37. Another Advance—Splendid Sniping—The Battle of 23rd April.
38. The Attack of 3rd May—Rifle Paralysis—A Scientific Kill.
39. The Hun Artillery Wakes Up—Two Days at Rest—Army Brigades and C.R.A.'S.
40. The Loss of "Mehal-Shahal-Hash-Baz"—Our last Fight at Arras—Telescope Reflections—Northward Bound.

THE BATTLE OF MESSINES, JUNE, 1917.
(See Map "C" at end.)

41. A Stormy Reception on the New Front—Casualties and Explosions.
42. A Well-staged One-Act Show.

THE THIRD BATTLE OF YPRES, JULY—OCTOBER, 1917.
(See Map "D" at end.)

43. The Curtain Rises on the Ypres Tragedy—A Fiendish Ten Days.
44. The Battle of the 31st July—Checkmated by Rain—More Stormy Times.
45. The Failure of the 16th August—A Hopeless, Endless Push.
46. Much Ado About Nothing—More Fighting.
47. Paris Leave—Miry Days.
48. The Attack on Houthulst Forest—We are Decimated by Gas—Our March to Fifth Army School—Our Short Stay There.

THE CAMBRAI PUSH, NOVEMBER, 1917.

49. A Forced March to Cambrai—Closing Days as a Battery Commander—Back to Fifth Army School.

CONTENTS

THE FIFTH ARMY SCHOOL, DECEMBER, 1917—FEBRUARY, 1918.

Letters.
50. At The Red Fox School.

THE RETREAT, MARCH, 1918.

51. With Fifth Army during March.
52. Re-equipping the Army—Many Changes.

TRAINING.

53. Interesting Work—Gas Trouble and Hospital.

LIST OF MAPS AT END OF BOOK

Map "A" of the Somme

Map "B" of the Battle of Arras

Map "D" and "C" of the Third Battle on the Ypres and the Battle on the Messines Ridge.

Map of the British Front

FIELD GUNS IN FRANCE

LETTER ONE.

ST. OUEN. (4th December, 1915.)

From Larkhill to Havre. The Rest Camp. By Train to Doullens. Billets at St. Ouen.

> Eyes of grey—a sodden quay,
> Driving rain and falling tears,
> As the steamer puts out to sea
> In a parting storm of cheers.
>   R. Kipling.

WELL, it is "Forrard away!" at long last, and very welcome too. We left Larkhill at noon, 30th November, reaching Southampton at 2 p.m., and in spite of the A.M.L.O. detrained and were on board within the hour.

I say in spite of this officer because as soon as our train stopped, he rushed up and ordered me to "fall in" the battery in two ranks. This done, he proceeded to mark off from the right the first twenty men, telling me to send them off at once under an officer to another ship. He was far too excited to grasp the fact that these 20 men happened to include three Nos. 1 and 10 drivers, who all had horses to look after. However, they marched smartly off to the shelter of the nearest pile of stores, under which cover they were dismissed, and a collection of gunners and surplus drivers took their place.

This incident was all the more humorous because we had been daily practising "entraining and embarking drill" according to the official notes, and every man knew his duties.

Otherwise everything was perfect, a big 5,000 ton boat, good accommodation for horses and men, and incidentally an excellent cabin for myself. We sailed at night and reached Havre at 6 a.m., but we did not dock till 3 p.m. Three batteries and an ammunition column were on board, so disembarkation appeared to take ages, but our Colonel was informed that the brigade had made the best disembarkation time for the past three months. We then had a $4\frac{1}{2}$ mile march to the rest camp, the last half-mile being up a steep road to the plateau above the town. It was a pitch dark night, but we soon had our lines down and the men turned in. Our incessant practice at Larkhill at rapid harnessing and unharnessing and the putting down of horse lines, proved of value this dark night.

Next day (Wednesday) the H.Q. Staff and two batteries floated over to "somewhere" (18 hours by train). We are due to leave on Thursday morning, so we had a nice idle day, looking at the horses and cleaning up: in fact the quietest day I have had for months.

We have not yet received our G.S. wagons, and marvellous to relate we moved up from ship to this camp with all our gear in the cook's cart. I fear this ideal state will not last long, and were our ammunition baskets examined "A" sub-section gun limber would produce a motley collection of my kit, socks, toys, spare mess gear, etc., which Hickey, my servant, has carefully packed therein.

We marched out of camp after breakfast, entrained at 11 a.m., and steamed off at 1.30, with two gramophones in full blast.

The interval at the station gave our four really good cooks an opportunity of serving up a hot dinner.

It took some trouble in England to make them good, but they have now learnt that their lives will be made unbearable unless they always carry dry sticks, etc., so on every move they are extraordinarily swift in getting their "dixies" into action.

We reached Doullens at 6 a.m.

As another battery in a train in front of us was occupying the only siding, we had two hours to wait, so we were able to get the men breakfasted at a very good Red Cross buffet in the station. Heartened by the hot coffee, the battery detrained with great speed, and from the moment the trucks entered the siding till the last vehicle marched out of the yard, only sixty minutes elapsed. From a report that was afterwards sent in to General Fry, of the 30th Division, we learned that the next best time to ours was 1¾ hours while the worst was 4½ hours. Let us hope that this may mean a good mark for D Battery.

Of course, the slow times were taken by units arriving at night, but the preparatory detraining drills at Larkhill proved of great value in quickening up things One has to unload the vehicles one truck at a time on to a tiny ramp, and take every horse out of the trucks by means of three old and rickety "ponts roulants", which are pushed from truck to truck—a heavy and tedious job. Contrary to all orders we had unharnessed, but it saved the horses 18 hours of discomfort.

Leaving the station at 10 a.m. we had a long 30-mile trek south-west to St. Ouen—a dirty little industrial town in a damp valley—getting into billets at 2.30 p.m. Macdonald (the senior subaltern) and the battery staff had gone on from the midday halt to find out all details re horse lines and billets.

It is such a pleasant rest getting out here. War in England was far too strenuous. Here one is nursed at every corner—"war made easy for beginners" with a vengeance ! We are all going up in turn to be attached to regular batteries in the line, for a few days "instruction in war". We leave on the 6th, and are going to join the brigade commanded by Colonel Seligman—a well-known gunner and formerly one of the smartest battery commanders in the Regiment.

Our first line wagons stay behind here, so we can safely cache our already large collection of illicit stores picked up on the journey by the battery scavengers. It is good to be the first unit at a station after a night of detraining !

LETTER TWO.

MAILLY MAILLET. (12TH DECEMBER, 1915.)

In Action at Last. A Quiet Front. Taken for a Spy.

Sons of the sheltered city—unmade, unhandled, unmeet—
Ye pushed them raw to the battle as ye picked them raw from the street.
R. KIPLING.

HERE we are in action at last, and, as I expected, life is an absolute rest cure, even for us coming up new, while the batteries that have been here since August take life very gently indeed! We left St. Ouen at 9 a.m. on Tuesday, 7th, and got into fair billets at Puchevilliers after a wet 17-mile trek. At 3 p.m., during the last few miles of the march, I heard for the first time the sound of guns in war. Next morning, Colonel Lyon, Edwards, who commands "A" Battery, myself, and respective staffs, rode on ahead to Mailly Maillet, where we were due to report at 11 a.m. in order to select our positions for our practice shoots.

The town is about 3,000 yards from the front line, but until one is within two miles of it, no trace of war is visible. Even round the town agriculture goes on more or less. The town itself is only slightly damaged, and plenty of shops are still open. We duly reported at 11 a.m. at Seligman's H.Q. in the main street. Our Adjutant had been in a frenzy for the last two days in case we should be late ; he takes war much too seriously, accusing me of being far too facetious about so grave a matter.

Punctual to the minute, our clattering, though hardly glittering, cavalcade drew up in front of the house, and all those who were not too overburdened with map cases, protractors, revolvers and glasses, leapt nimbly to earth and advanced to the office, where we were met by the only officer there !—a subaltern busily engaged drying his socks. We then had a look at our future positions in an orchard boasting excellent apples, and returned to lunch with the battery to which we were attached.

After lunch, while walking over to their battery, we actually saw some shells burst : apparently a rare sight on this quiet front.

The Hun started with rather high shrapnel bursts on a battery next door, about 200 yards from where we were standing.

FIELD GUNS IN FRANCE

Certainly on being for the first time under shell-fire, one experiences nothing but intense curiosity. But I fancy shell-fire is like riding to hounds ; one must have a really bad fall before one can say if one's nerve over a stiff country is good or not, and it is too early to say yet. Besides, high explosive is a treat in store for us. The guns turned up at dusk and were duly run into their holes, and so ended the day.

Next day, the 9th, was very wet, and not the sort to make us feel warlike, so we spent a busy day improving the men's billets, and making our mess a little less damnable.

The wall nearest the Hun is well sandbagged up, but the earth filling is pretty smelly. Three Generals came to look at us, but as it was raining they only stayed about five minutes. I met Ormerod (commanding the 148th Brigade of our division) who had ridden over from the next village. He was looking rather hot and angry because a shell had come through the mess window during breakfast and killed his horse and his Adjutant's as well. Hardly fair, for as long as we don't shell the Hun villages they are not supposed to shell ours.

I have now got a good four-poster bed in a well-furnished house (a bakery), the passages of which are filled with oat sacks and rats. Teddy Edwards (O.C. 1/151) sleeps on the floor in the same room. We have a stove, but the wood famine is rather acute. To-night we had to light it with a pair of corsets and a long wooden toy sword which we found in a cupboard.

Of course the "residenter" batteries live in the lap of luxury, but we being only trippers have to eke out a precarious existence as best we can.

On the 10th the rain continued to come down, so no one did anything beyond carpentry and improvements generally. However, as two days of inaction in a wet orchard was beginning to tell, I determined to indulge in my old pastime of finding my way across country in the dark, and with Maclean and Wilson (two subalterns) I started off to see if we could find an O.P. in the ruined village of Auchonvilliers, near the front line, from which we might be able to observe, instead of having to tramp three miles to our "tutor battery" O.P.

Half-way to the front line Maclean fell into a trench and twisted his ankle, so we had to leave him to wander home as best he could, while we went on and found what appeared to be an excellent front line O.P. in a ruined barn. The pastime of dodging Very lights when crossing the open near the Hun lines amused us greatly. On our way back we ran into a party of Royal Irish Rifles : they challenged us, and when we replied "Artillery Officers" they at once became most ferocious, and we soon found ourselves marching, surrounded by bayonets, to Battalion H.Q., which was at dinner when we arrived.

Some were for shooting us at sight, others for asking us to dinner. Fortunately, as we were very hungry, the pendulum swung in the favour of dinner and Irish whisky : chiefly because I was able to produce a most valuable piece of evidence as to our identity, viz., an unsigned indent demanding 50 yards of "canvas latrine" ! We soon discovered why our reply "Artillery Officers" had aroused so much ferocity. Ten days before a spy in gunner uniform had called on them on a bogus mission to examine and report on every bomb store on their front. This he did with great thoroughness, even testing the rate of burning of the bombs and then, having concluded by severely strafing one or two company commanders for their bad storage arrangements, he speedily but quietly vanished into Hunland.

The phone message confirming our identity came through soon after mess, and after a very cheery evening we got home by 10 p.m. to find our own people quite confident that we had been scuppered, as we had been away since tea. Of course we were much chaffed over the incident, but such occurrences are fairly common in this area owing to an acute wave of spy mania.

On Saturday afternoon, accompanied by a subaltern and the O.C. of our tutor battery, I rode out three miles to their O.P. Having left our horses in Mesnil, a much-destroyed village, we went up the slope by a trench labelled "Charles Avenue". From the forward slope of the ridge there is a wonderful panorama of the Hun trenches lying below. To the north, Beaumont Hamel and Grandcourt ; to the east, Thiepval and Courcelette : ugly places to attack they all look. I fired 40 rounds H.E., and duly registered various points. No one ever expects to see a Hun or to hurt anybody, the whole country being a maze of solid white lines of chalk trenches, and one might as well fire into various furrows of a 20-acre field with a shot-gun and hope to kill the one hare in it.

It was very interesting to watch from the O.P. one's first shell fired in war, to hear it come rumbling overhead, and to note where it would deign to burst, as everything had of course been worked off the map. We were told, however, that things went well, and after the frenzied anxiety of English practice camps, it was all complete bliss and peacefulness.

Several other Brigades were having spasms of activity all the afternoon, and there was much noise and fuss, but no reply from the Hun.

On Sunday afternoon everyone fired with great vehemence ; we started at 2.30, but as it soon after began to snow heavily and observation became difficult, we stopped at 3 p.m. and turned in to get warm.

While walking back to our billets, the Huns opened fire with extreme ferocity and incredible rapidity on an arable field to the right of the town, and shelled it hard for ten minutes, to the delight of the Town Band, which played appropriate airs of derision in the Town Square, there being the usual Sunday concert on. Anybody who can play attaches himself to the band when resting, and the noise is terrific if plenty of musicians happen to be out of the trenches.

After the hardships of fighting on the East Coast of England, the comfortable life out here is very enjoyable. I have had a bed every night since we left Havre. At the moment of writing the O.C. of "A" Battery is superintending drying clothes round the fire, while I, esconced in the four-poster bed, smoke a top-hole cigar.

The house is filled with flour sacks and army corps of rats fight like dogs under the bed all night, until reproved with a mess-tin filled with stones and tied to the bed-post, an effective and ever-ready missile.

I hope these trivial details will give you some idea of the happenings on typical aimless days in a quiet, but incidentally also one of the most enjoyable weeks in my life.

LETTER THREE.

ST. OUEN. (17TH DECEMBER, 1915.)

Aeroplane Bombs. The Weekly "Strafe". Return to St. Ouen.

WELL, we are back at St. Ouen again, and I must try to describe our last week at Mailly Maillet.

One morning, while we were working in our orchard an "Albatross" appeared and hovered over the town, to the intense indignation of four "Archies", who literally smothered the blue sky with their shrapnel bursts. Being a dead calm, frosty day, the puffs of white smoke hung about for a long time. Before going the Hun plane swooped down to about 6,000 feet and dropped two bombs. I heard them "whiffling" through the air. They landed close enough for us—on each side of the barn our men were billeted in. One was a dud, but the other blew a hole as big as a cart-wheel in the garden, and what was worse blew our signalling sergeant head over heels into the latrine pit! It was all rather a joke, and the men were lucky to see bombs, as the enemy so far has used them but seldom.

We generally carry out any shooting we have to do in the afternoon, as then the light for observing is at its best—so you can see we have a long day and very little to do. The regular brigade takes life pretty easily, and in their smooth-running batteries the officers have but little detail work to do.

The result is that many of their subalterns who have joined straight from the "Shop" know very little about the interior economy of their batteries. They step into the machine and glide along with a first-class B.S.M. and Q.M.S. behind them. Personally I would rather have my own older New Army subalterns, who went through the ranks of the early divisions, and having seen their battery grow up from the first days of wooden guns and twenty horses per battery, know every detail of the equipment and requirements of a battery and have quite a sound knowledge of gunnery too.

On the 14th the weekly big joint strafe came off. About ten batteries, from 18-pdr. up to 8-inch Howitzer were to engage the great Sand Redoubt in front of Serre from 10.15 till 11.30 a.m., so some of us, including our Colonel, went up to the front line to "spectate".

The communication trench, called "Roman Road", up which we went, was dry and boarded at first, but presently the boards ended and the mud began, and for the last 300 yards there was water over the knees and thick ice mixed with glue-like mud to struggle through.

Those who had scorned trench waders had a cheery time of it. I tried to carry the Colonel, but finally, on my getting stuck with the double weight, he had to take to the water. Eventually we reached a point about 600 yards from the redoubt, where the Colonel and I observed with comfort and safety from a disused machine-gun emplacement. The orderly officer was most miserable, being the complete soldier in boots, spurs and belt, and he got very ruffled when a sniper put a bullet within an inch of his back.

The bombardment duly took place and seemed to knock Hades out of the redoubt, the 8-inch shells fairly shifting the landscape. The parapet of the trench we were in was dotted with French soldiers' graves, as it was here that their big attack in June, 1915, took place.

On our way home Macdonald and I visited the cemetery. Rows of corked whisky bottles, with names, etc., inside mark the graves, until they can be replaced by the wooden crosses. We stayed while a padre read the service over a man buried that morning, a short service somewhat interrupted by the German reply to our shoot. For fifteen minutes there was one continuous roar. When the Hun does deign to reply, his effort is certainly short and very concentrated.

Next day two of the subalterns were having their trial shoot, so I had an idle day beside the fire in the telephone dug-out, playing with the yellow kitten that haunts the place and repeating the orders as they came down from the O.P. to the sergeant-major, who passes them on to the guns by megaphone. On the 16th our rest cure came to an end, and we had to go back to make room for the other half of the brigade.

The gun teams turned up at the chilly dark hour of 6 a.m. in order to be clear by dawn. There happened to be a dense mist, however, so our early start was all the harder to bear.

Without informing Brigade H.Q., who were already worked up to a frenzy over the movement of the batteries, I left the column to Macdonald's care and trekked off alone, and did the two days' march in one, reaching St. Ouen by 3 p.m. the same afternoon—a long ride.

On my arrival, I got orders to take over the brigade, or rather the greater portion of it, with no adjutant and a reduced brigade staff! General Elton, our C.R.A., met me, and cheerfully said: "I am glad you came back early, as the Corps C.R.A. is coming on the

20th, and you must get the building of the harness shelters and cinder standings, etc., started in all the units by then."

Fortunately our horse lines require very little work, as we have got the entire battery in a huge factory yard, with good accommodation for men and harness.

In the evening of the next day the battery turned up all complete after an absolutely uneventful march.

LETTER FOUR.

ST. OUEN. (9TH JANUARY, 1916.)

The Daily Round. Xmas. A Lecture on the Battle of Loos. Getting Ready for the Somme.

Do ye wait for the spattered shrapnel ere ye learn how a gun is laid ?
R. KIPLING.

SINCE I wrote last, we have had a busy time, and hard work back here after our holiday in the line is very trying to the temper. On our return life became one eternal round of Brigade fatigues, and one's own battery ceased to exist. It melted away on brigade fatigues. As we had no horse standings, etc., to make for ourselves, we lent up to sixty men per day to the other less fortunate units, and finding so many is a big tax on a battery. Having promised to complete the cinder and chalk standings for the Brigade by the 1st January, life became a regular slave-driving hustle. However, we evolved a sort of loading drill, which enables a G.S. wagon to be filled with cinders from the slack-heaps in $2\frac{1}{2}$ minutes, so the work got done somehow.

My days were taken up riding round the various units, planning shelters and standings, endless office work, constant parley with the Engineers on the question of material, besides having to cope with a deluge of "Red-hats" and "Blue-hats", who inspected guns, men's feet, horses, kitchens, according to their respective breeds. However, in spite of it all we have had a great Xmas. Thanks to the untiring efforts of the "Dinner Committee", a really first-class show was produced, complete with decorations, roast pork, barrels of beer and other luxuries, and the dinner was followed by a most successful concert. The C.R.A. and his staff came in for a few minutes, and healths were drunk.

I think it rained every day during the last fortnight of the Old Year, and the black slush round the horse standings and watering places in this damp valley gets deeper and deeper. New Year's Eve passed uneventfully, except that I finished the last hour of the Old Year by holding the most wonderful poker hands !

At this time, some hints about our immediate future began to filter in.

We hear we are going to take over a piece of the line at once: great news, indeed, as so many units are kept for months at the base doing a further period of training. Our division will be on the extreme right of the British sector, on the northern bank of the Somme. Judging by what one is told at Divisional H.Q. and by "gup" with officers from that Sector, our new front will lack the peaceful atmosphere of Mailly Maillet ! The Maricourt salient appears to be something like the Ypres one, and all the roads, even as far back as Bray, are under shell-fire, so we will at least see life, and "things" may some day happen down here. The Guards Division is coming south, and Lord Cavan is going to command the XIV Corps—Stormy Petrels !

On the 3rd, Colonel Lyon inspected the brigade—a sort of farewell inspection, as from now onwards we are to be attached to an 18-pdr. Brigade, so we will be with the 149th Brigade under Colonel G. Stanley (Lord Derby's brother—you will remember him in the Grafton country in old days).

Thanks to our good billet in the factory, guns, harness and men were looking clean and the horses fit, the thin ones having done well on five feeds and four waterings per day, combined with steady exercise.

Next day Edwards and I went into Amiens by train, and spent the time chiefly in eating and shopping, and in a short visit to the Cathedral, which certainly is wonderful in its perfect proportions. The beautifully carved doorway is all sandbagged up now as a protection against air raids.

Needless to say at lunch in the Hotel du Rhin I ran into an Old Etonian, A. P. West (Black Watch), from m' tutors.

One evening a few of us went over to Vignacourt for a lecture on the Battle of Loos, given by Colonel Tudor, R.A. The hall was filled with generals, among whom was General Wattie Ross, and he asked me to come over and lunch at his place.

It proved to be an interesting lecture, some of the points made being that wire-cutting should be done by trench mortars and not by guns, that a three or four day bombardment is usually quite enough to stupefy the first system of trenches, that the limitless objective is too much to attempt, and units should have their definitive objective to capture, consolidate, and hold in the successive stages of the advance, so that the inevitable ebb in front of a strong counter-attack may be checked immediately, and finally, that communication trenches must be very wide.

The 8th was chiefly spent in packing up for our move, and since my kit and the officers' mess outfit has increased so much of late, I decided that a two-wheeled cart must be got hold of somehow. The country round here is too respectable to think of "acquiring" such an article by any other means except purchase, so, laden with some of my Poker winnings of the previous week, Maclean and I scoured the country far and wide, and at last found and purchased a useful two-wheeled cart for 160 francs—a stiff price—but the seller having only one arm and the Medaille Militaire, we did not grudge it to him.

Within twenty-four hours the trap was all complete with harness and hood, the latter made from a railway wagon cover. Our horse lines being next the railway station, tarpaulins and covers constantly get blown by the wind out of the goods yard into our Q.M.S. stores !

To-day I rode over to Vignacourt, where General Leckie (G.O.C., R.A., 14th Corps) picked me up, and we motored over to lunch with Wattie Ross. General Leckie, who knows him well, says he is the most blood-thirsty and daring General in the Corps, and keeps his brigade chock-full of the spirit and joy of slaughter. One of his latest ingenious ways of worrying the Hun is to arm his night patrols with spiked clubs, a silent form of death which has something mysterious and nerve-racking in its effect on the enemy.

LETTER FIVE.

VAUX VALLEY. (20TH JANUARY, 1916.)

In Action near the Somme. Taking over the Zone. Chancing it across the Open.

ON the 10th we at last shook the dust—or rather the mud—of St. Ouen from our feet, and, together with "B" Battery (Major Kirkland's) marched off and joined the column comprising our future group (the 149th R.F.A. Brigade) a few miles beyond the town. The column was long and the roads very congested, so it was a slow march into Talmas, where we billeted for the night. We have got a good deal of transport this trip, a three-ton lorry, two G.S. wagons, a cooks' cart, and a new trap. But with two days' forage and a lot of extras in the way of boards, posts, and a quantity of our patent wooden nosebags, it was all full. We continued the trek next day in glorious sunshine to Pont Noyelles. Luckily our place in the column was second, so our horses were unharnessed and feeding before the tail entered the town. The battery cooks continue to do good work. Thanks to the boxes of coal and tar-soaked wood which they always carry on the march, they are able to get their dixies into action over a hot fire with the least possible delay : thus waiting for "dinners up" after stables is obviated. Wednesday, 12th, was another glorious day, and fortunately very misty, so there was less chance of getting shelled on the roads. All the battery commanders left their batteries soon after starting, and joining our Colonel at Sailly we rode on through Bray, reaching Susanne at noon, where we all separated and made our way by map to our respective future battery positions.

I had a cheery lunch with the outgoing battery (a six gun one) in the Maricourt Valley, and afterwards walked across the hill to Vaux Valley, which is to be my future home. At present they have a section there, that is two guns only, so we will have plenty of work enlarging it into a four-gun position.

Returning to Susanne I found my horses and rode back to Bray, meeting Macdonald and our transport coming through the town. During daylight they only allow single vehicles down the big hill on the west of the town, so all the batteries had been halted to wait till dusk, and the transport only was allowed to filter forward. To our great joy we found that we had been allotted a really good wagon line on the river (Somme), between Bray and Cappy. Quite a little town in itself, with covered sheds for horses, harness rooms, huts, old cottages, and above all excellent water-troughs. Moreover, as it was empty, we were able to take possession at once, instead of having to flounder in the mud of the Bois des Tailles while the outgoing batteries were pushing off.

Soon after dusk I met the Battery on the main road, and taking the one gun destined to go into action that night, we set out again. We reached our destination without mishap, although "B" Battery just in front of us met trouble in the shape of enemy 5.9's, and had some casualties.

Our position is a little valley 600 yards from the Northern bank of the Somme. Our companions there are the 9th Siege (6-inch Howitzer) Battery, whose guns are practically next door to our gun-pits. On arrival their Captain (Capt. Riley) gave me dinner and temporary quarters in a wonderful dug-out belonging to the O.C. (Major Grinlinton) who is on leave. It is quite 20 feet deep in the chalky rock, and has a second exit coming out 30 feet away. Except for the rats, it is as dark and silent as the grave. All the Siege Battery dug-outs were tunnelled by a French 150 mm. battery, who were here over a year, and the valley is named after them "150 mm. Valley".

Owing to the lack of accommodation for the first few days, till the 19th, I lived up here myself, the subalterns riding as far as Susanne each morning and then walking up.

On the 14th, the day after our arrival, I went up with Lieut. Heseltine, in command of the outgoing section, to the main O.P. It is a very handy one. Only a ten minutes' walk from the Battery, through Vaux Wood, and situated on the crest of the precipitous hill just above Vaux village, it displays a wonderful panorama of Hunland. In the far distance Mont St. Quentin, standing up on a high ridge ; lower down, the factory chimneys of Peronne ; to the right the French outpost village of Frise, forming a dangerous salient ; to the left, and facing the O.P., the enemy village of Curlu ; and further left still the British front line post in the beautiful old Moulin de Fargny, while everywhere in the foreground is the great Somme Marsh, which forms our only protection, as we have no trenches or wire between us and the Hun. We spent part of the morning registering our gun on a ruined shrine, which made a very good zero point. Various targets were pointed out to us also, and we worried an enemy working party with a few rounds.

At 1 p.m. the Hun dared to fire five rounds into the sacred village of Vaux, hitting the cook-house of the Infantry Battalion head-quarters. On hearing this grave news our Group H.Q. ordered us to fire as many as two rounds into the equally sacred village of Curlu, which we promptly did, smashing the corner of their head-quarters. A curious war. Here we find two almost untouched villages in the respective front lines, and they are only 1,500 yards apart! However, there will be all the more to slay and destroy when our muzzles are really taken off.

The afternoon was spent learning the country as seen from another O.P. nearer the river, and watching the almost continuous shelling of our trenches near Maricourt.

In the evening I went into Susanne to see the Engineers about material, calling at Group H.Q., and after dining with Kirkland at "B" Battery got back home. A longish circle for a pitchy dark night, but my love for night walking has not diminished, and it teaches one to find the way across country better than anything else. If ever we come to open warfare again it will be a very useful accomplishment.

Next day we spent in exploring yet another O.P. and in learning the lie of the land; it meant getting to the front line near Maricourt—a walk of at least $1\frac{1}{4}$ hours. The phone wire runs down the front line, so one is able (in theory at any rate) to talk to the battery from any point. We tried some shooting at the Hun front line, which ran within 50 yards of ours. This is not as risky as it sounds, because owing to the curve of the trenches the old shell trundles up "No Man's Land" almost parallel to the enemy trenches for quite a long distance. Therefore it is "line" we have to attend to—a comparatively easy thing—so a "short" round does not necessarily spell disaster.

Our few shells brought on a sharp reply from a 77 mm. "whizz-bang" battery, which made us beat a hurried retreat into the nearest dug-out. At the critical moment, while diving down the trench towards the shelter, one of my great feet, clad in trench waders, got wedged between two duckboards. Two would-be V.C. signallers, however, emerged from the dug-out and gallantly pulled me in—all somewhat helpless from laughter.

All day long, in fact, the Hun had spasms of intense hate against our trenches; indeed, ever since the 9th of January his artillery has been extraordinarily active. No one knows what started it. Certainly a lot of heavy guns have been brought up to this sector lately; whether it is merely to frighten a new division, or whether it presages an attack along the river, the dividing line of the French and ourselves, is impossible to say—*Nous verrons*. But it is tiresome, and there have been many casualties, especially in Susanne. We continued to work our way, often through knee-deep mud, down the big hill as far as the Moulin

FIELD GUNS IN FRANCE

de Fargny on the Somme, which is the extreme right-hand point of the British trenches. On the front of our battery there are no trenches, only detached posts facing the marsh. From the Mill we went up to a listening post on the famous bluff, a chalky precipice known as Le Chapeau de Gendarme. The post is only 26 yards from the Hun post above it, and ours is roofed with thick wire netting to prevent Brother Boche throwing in banana skins or other tokens of "Kultur". Our way home should have been up the muddy front line trench, a long, tiresome trudge. However, along the base of the hill there runs a delightfully hard road leading into Vaux, and of course in full view of the Bluff.

The infantry assured us that it was impossible to show one's nose on it in daylight, but now the setting sun was making splendid shadows, and I felt certain that an old stag, had he been on the Bluff, would not have spotted one on the road, so we walked serenely down (200 yards apart I may add) and not a shot was fired at us. The Manchesters in Vaux village were somewhat surprised to see us arrive like gentlemen by the road.

However, the Hun did have one whack at us after all. There was a stairway trench leading from the wood on the crest into the village, up the face of Vaux hill. This we climbed, taking a short cut across a field on the summit, which was still in full sunlight. Within a minute a whizz-bang landed within twenty yards of us. Afterwards we discovered he kept a gun laid on this point!

LETTER SIX.

VAUX VALLEY. (26TH JANUARY, 1916.)

Renewed German Activity.   Digging in.   Excursions into No Man's Land.

> D'you say that you sweat with the field-guns ?   By God, you must lather with us—'Tss !   'Tss !
>
> R. KIPLING.

SINCE my last letter the Hun has been hard at it. Any believer in the rumour of a weakening of the Hun should have been here during the past ten days : he has been steadily blowing up the whole country, Susanne and Bray included. One of our worst days was Saturday, the 15th. On that day the last gun of the outgoing section was due to leave at 9 a.m., and the Hun gave us eighty-eight rounds of 5.9 in salvoes, but luckily all were just over, otherwise there would not have been much left, as each crater is seven feet across. He kept it up intermittently all day—a good farewell to the Section, which during its stay from July, 1915, till 1st January, 1916, had scarcely seen one shell-burst in this little glen. In spite of the Hun being so busy, we scarcely replied, and so have had time to get on with our two new gun-pits, and, above all, with the various tunnel dug-outs which we have started in front of the guns on the opposite bank of the valley.

Many of the gunners being miners, we are able to plan most elaborate dug-outs, which with inexperienced men would mean risking being buried alive with the roof collapsing. On the first day of the tunnelling, I found one of my regular R.H.A. sergeants had the idea that the miners should be relieved every ten minutes—an idea born of drill book theories on intensive effort by untrained personnel. You can imagine the feelings of these tough nuts who have been accustomed to swing a pick for two hours on end without turning a hair ! As we have been doing but little firing, I have spent every day away from the battery, learning by heart the maze of trenches round Maricourt and all our outposts in Vaux and Royal Dragoon Wood. I also made the acquaintance of the four companies of the 10th Manchesters in front of us.

FIELD GUNS IN FRANCE

On several misty mornings I had long wanders into No Man's Land; there is nothing like these expeditions to teach one the lie of the country.

On Sunday, the 23rd, I had quite an interesting morning in the mist. Having gone to the O.P. and found observation hopeless, I went down the steep slope into Vaux by the stairway trench to call on "C" Company of the Manchesters and then on past their forward post into the marsh, and eventually got within 400 yards of Curlu Village. The only incident worthy of note was flushing a very noisy flock of ducks—which stirred into action an erratic machine-gun somewhere in front of me. But the walk taught me quite a lot about the geography of the paths and causeways of the swamp, which will be useful if ever the Hun tries to attack across it. From the O.P. it is impossible to tell which is solid ground and which is swamp. Besides making these excursions, we have been very busy getting our numerous telephone wires into really first-class order, and we have plenty of them, to three O.P.'s, to three Infantry Company H.Q., to Group H.Q., and to Kirkland's "B" Battery. You may remember Colonel Long's recipe to keep his horses fat and well—"I look at them" : the same applies to telephone wires, and by personally examining now and then every inch of the wire, one secures a very high standard of efficiency out of the linesmen who patrol the system. Although we are so close to our Allies we see very little of them, as the Somme, 800 yards on the left flank of the guns, divides us from them, and the first bridge is at Cappy, near our wagon lines. The southern side of the river is much steeper than our bank, consisting as it does of a long steep ridge extending from Cappy to the bend of the river beyond Frise. It is covered with trenches, which have been very heavily strafed all this week. Hun trench mortars have also been very active the last few days, and on the 24th I had to go down again to the Mill to try and locate an especially annoying one, as the map square reference as given by the infantry was somewhat vague.

It is always a tiresome walk to that spot down a disgustingly muddy trench, and, moreover, while going down the hill one is sniped at frequently from the Bluff. On my return to the O.P. I fired five rounds at the gentleman who had frightened me most on my walk. One shell spoiled his pet sniping hole which I had located, but as it was not the first, I fear he was safe in some deep dug-out long before it burst.

LETTER SEVEN.

VAUX VALLEY. (30TH JANUARY, 1916.)

A Sudden Attack. Loss of Frise. We prepare to Retire.

ON the 27th the day broke shrouded in dense mist, enabling us to get on with the work, which, thanks to the "planes" and occasional shells, had not progressed as quickly as we should have liked. Sheltered by one of the fogs of war, people were prancing about in No Man's Land, trying to see themselves as others saw them. An Infantry officer (2nd Royal Scots Fusiliers) with his sergeant and servant, went over to the Hun trenches and returned with a twenty pound bomb (trench mortar). He saw no Huns, however.

In the morning I went into Susanne and called at group headquarters, where I happened to meet our Artillery General (General Birch) and the Divisional Artillery Commander (General Elton). By harping on the old theme "to replace damage of shell-fire," I managed to annex from the Engineers 40 railway sleepers and about three thousand sandbags.

We are certainly blessed with good weather this month—to-day it was glorious, and there was quite a lot doing. We started the morning with a few rounds at some fellows who were loafing outside a wood, and then, at 10.30 a.m., following an arrangement with the Infantry (2nd Royal Scots Fusiliers), we proceeded to knock out a very aggressive machine-gun. It was situated within fifty yards of one of our saps, which, unfortunately, was directly in our line of fire. There was, moreover, a steep valley behind it which made ranging difficult. Our plan was for the Infantry to evacuate the sap, and at a pre-arranged signal fire was to be opened. The first shot, by extraordinary good luck, was a direct hit on the emplacement; everything appeared to go up at once. Having got my line, I chanced the rest, and slipped in half a dozen more without loss of time—a most enjoyable and successful shoot. The Infantry reported the machine-gun "gone west", and were very grateful. They appeared to have had a rough time at night from that gun. Before lunch we began to get odd doses of shrapnel on to the guns, but it was not until the end of lunch that the band really began to play, and then, from 1.30 to 2.50, we got it in salvos from at least two batteries (4.2-inch and 5.9-inch), 80 per cent. of the shells being from the 5.9-inch battery. I got the men safely across to the opposite side of the little glen, where they sat under some trees and watched the fun. Except for two unfortunate incidents, the episode would have been quite amusing. One man got a nasty wound behind the shoulder, so we had to take him up to the Infantry dug-outs about 200 yards up the glen ; and the cook of the Siege battery got knocked out completely and fell into his fire ; I think, however, he was quite dead before being burnt.

Wilson and I flitted between our Army on the bank and the telephone "dug-out", continually asking for permission to retaliate, and answering inquiries as to our health from other batteries, who were wondering what was up. It was all over by 2.50 p.m. None of our guns were hit, although some parts of the wood looked as if a tornado had swept through it.

At 9.15 p.m. we had an alarm of gas, so "helmets on" we stood to night lines. The panic lasted about an hour. When everything seemed quiet on the front, we turned in.

At 6 a.m. on the 28th a devil of a din began, and the first 5.9-inch (H.E.) shell landed behind my shelter, and made me finish shaving on the staircase leading down to the telephone dug-out. Between 7 and 8 a.m. shells poured into us ; about 7.30 we lost touch with the Group, our O.P. and other batteries, the lines being cut to pieces by a perfect avalanche of shells. About 8.15 a.m. I thought I smelt something, and in ten minutes we were choking with weeping gas. Fire slackened by about 9.15 a.m., when the men got their breakfast out of the cookhouse by rushing across between shell-bursts. Somehow or other a cookhouse always seems to be in the stormiest corner.

Lines to the O.P. were smashed as quickly as I could get them mended, and on hearing heavy rifle fire on our front I opened a rapid rate of fire with all four guns on a registered point. We observed either by the Siege battery Observing Officer or our own, using whichever line happened to be unbroken at the moment.

At 9.30 a.m., for the fifth time, I sent three men to mend the Brigade line ; they found ten breaks, and somehow managed to live and work through a perfect inferno of shells, getting it mended as far as Susanne by about 11 a.m. But how they ended up alive beats me ! One of the three went right through to Susanne Chateau, a building which was half-destroyed and crammed full of gas. There he found Group H.Q. empty, and on his returning to the nearest point from which he could get through to the battery on the wire, I gave him a message describing the situation, and told him to pin it on the door. However, he eventually found the C.O. and delivered the message personally.

All this time we were choking and firing and spitting in our valley. Truly the fog of war was all around us! Neither we nor the 6-inch people next door had any orders or news of what was going on.

This very heavy shelling continued without a break until 12 noon. Really one ceased to worry about it—the perpetual din was so terrific. One did not hear shells coming, and with the struggling for breath through the gas, one simply could not be bothered to duck—sheer weariness—not courage.

At 1 p.m. it started again, both "weeping" gas and H.E., and by 2 p.m., the grassy slopes looked like ploughed fields. The attack appeared to open about 3 p.m., when our front line trenches were smothered by shrapnel up to 3.45 p.m. I felt I must open fire at any cost, for it certainly looked as though the Hun was attacking on both sides of the river. The O.P. line, having been mended for the twentieth time, was working well, so we kept up a decent rate of fire, and in spite of heavy shell-fire, orders were got through clearly from O.P. to dug-out, and thence by megaphone to the guns; luckily, too, no one was hit at that time.

We shot hard and were shelled hard until dusk, then peace. Tea and a wash-up followed, and afterwards I went off to Susanne to try and get some news from the group head-quarters.

Things seemed to have been pretty warm there, nothing but ruins and "weeping" gas. The few people about seemed to be chiefly occupied in being sick, and I soon followed suit, discarding my tea, and had to have water over my head at a dressing station. Then I went to the castle, which was half in ruins and still being hit occasionally. There I found Colonel Stanley, our Group Commander, and his adjutant in their cellar, which was absolutely filled with gas. There were various rumours that the Hun had carried a good many trenches, but no definite news. I returned to the battery about 7.30. About 8 p.m. I fired a few rounds into the village of Curlu at the request of the Manchester Regiment: the result was sharp retaliation from the Hun.

About 10 p.m. I became somewhat anxious about our right. The wires, being cut, were no help, though really one had long given up expecting orders and simply had to paddle one's own canoe, being just able to keep in touch with our own Infantry by orderlies. About 10 p.m., all being quiet on the British front, and pretty noisy on the right (across the river), I determined to pull two guns out of their pits and put them in the strip of wood which cuts the valley in half. From there they were pointing almost over my other two guns. Desperate work it was, under a nasty fire, but we got it done and fixed up by 11.30 p.m. It proved to be worth the trouble, for hardly had we finished

FIELD GUNS IN FRANCE

when we heard that the Huns had advanced, and we were ordered to fire at a certain point, which, had we not already moved, would have been an impossibility.

At 4.15 in the morning (29th) we heard that the Huns had taken Frise, and were still advancing. The day broke very misty, so we were able to consolidate our new position, and everything remained more or less quiet until 11 o'clock, when the fog lifted. While the fog held I was making bridges with sleepers across some trenches on our left, and planning the best way for the men to man-handle the guns back. In this job we intended to join forces with the Siege people, as our line of retreat by road looked like being completely cut. We also decided on the place for a final stand if the worst came to the worst.

As soon as the fog lifted things began to hum, lots of shells and gas on our position, and also on Susanne, and soon all four of our guns were at it—two shooting in a nearly opposite direction to the other two. Thanks to the incessant work of our linesmen, the phone communication kept good, and by 2 p.m. we were at one and the same time engaging four different targets : two guns shooting by map under group orders on to the French front, and two under the battery forward observers. Towards dusk, things began to look nasty on our front, and we had rumours that the Hun was massing to attack, so we had to stop helping the French and ran the guns back to their old positions. On Group Head-Quarters confirming this news we went to "gun-fire" on the German front line, every yard of which I had registered in the past fortnight. The range was rather close for us, 2,300 yards only. As the Siege got the same orders as we did, there was a devil of a shindy for just over an hour, from about 6.30 p.m. to 7.50 p.m. The Hun sent it back pretty hot, but no one was hit, and it did not put off the gun layers, as not a round was short, luckily, because our trenches were only 100 yards from the German lines. The men have had a rough time, working practically without rest for two days, namely, from 10 p.m. on the 27th to 8 p.m. on the 29th. At 9 p.m. two officers of the 65th Howitzer Battery, R.F.A., which had been rushed up with many others to reinforce, appeared out of the darkness. I showed them the only possible position, and one stayed with me while the O.C. (Captain Pask) went back to fetch the battery, which arrived about midnight. We managed to find an empty dug-out for the four officers, and the Siege found room in their tunnels for the men. All night long one was bombarded by queries on the phone, this sort of thing : "Had I seen the supports for the Manchesters?" "Did I hear of an 18-pounder battery wandering in the neighbourhood?" "Was it my water cart destroyed by a shell in Castle Road ?" and other tiresome conundrums. While the 65th Battery was unlimbering they lost a few horses, but it was not till 3 a.m. that the Hun really woke up, and he then gave it us pretty hot until 4.30 a.m. It was too noisy to hope for sleep, but I was so tired that I did not bother to leave my shack, although it was at the top of the bank. Luckily the only three shells that fell within ten yards were duds, and they settled with a tired sigh into the grass of the bank.

The 30th dawned with a quiet morning and more dense mist, which helped the other battery to get well under cover, covered up with branches. Nothing was known about the developments on our right, but we thought that the Huns could see right down our valley from their newly-captured position. At 2 p.m. the Infantry reported a grand target just across the marshes, where it appeared there was unloading of timber and construction work going on. However, my guns having been put back into their original pits, I could not engage this target, and the 65th Battery were too done with their long trek up to help. So I borrowed two of their guns, the telephonists managed to get some sort of phone connection through to the extreme salient, which was a destroyed factory, and, thanks to the mist, we were not spotted cutting across through the open. We did some killing, but it was too misty to observe easily, so we stopped firing and sent the men home to reel up the wire.

When they were gone I did a bit of stalking into the marsh, getting within ear-shot of the Hun in the village of Frise. Why is it one always forgets to take a rifle on these expeditions? However, it was so foggy that I should have had no chance of slaying, although I got quite close to them and could hear them talking and hammering, and evidently making themselves quite at home in their newly captured village. We had a peaceful night, which lasted until 2 a.m., and then came the usual heavy shelling until dawn.

Next day we did a lot of shooting at the request of the Infantry, and after dinner I went to Susanne to get any orders about the expected counter-attack due the next day. The place still stinks with gas. I asked the Engineers to improve my bridges behind our guns, as they may still be necessary if the counter-attack is unsuccessful.

LETTER EIGHT.

VAUX VALLEY. (6TH FEBRUARY, 1916.)

In a Tight Corner. Awaiting the French Counter-attack.

WE are still waiting for the French counter-attack, and hoping that it will relieve the pressure on the Valley. We are indeed in an extraordinary position—Rat-Trap Valley, as kind friends outside the trap call it ; but we are all very happy, and the bridges are practically made, so that things do not look quite so hopeless as they did on the 30th January. A number of batteries have come up to reinforce the line, at least thirty French 75 mm. batteries and any amount of big guns. We, also, have sent up a prodigious mass of guns, many of which are the very heaviest (mothers and grandmas) (8-inch and 12-inch Howitzers). The preparatory shelling for the counter-attack started on the 2nd, and has been increasing in violence ever since, night and day.

Our happy valley is, I regret to say, becoming very unhealthy. We enfilade and "backfilade" the Hun trenches, and, judging by the way it replies, it seems to annoy him. The canvas mess hut has got all its talc windows shot out and its sides riddled ; my shack on the top of the bank is also getting draughty. Sooner or later I shall have to leave it. Unfortunately one cannot break the gunnery law about the danger angle without suffering. We are all firing into each other's faces with H.E. shells and a very delicate fuse and prematures have been rather frequent. We had one particularly unlucky one ; the shell exploded at the muzzle, three splinters came back through the shield and unfortunately wounded fatally the layer and two other men of the gun detachment ; what was even worse, however, was that six of the Siege battery gunners were slightly wounded.

The Valley is now ridiculously crowded with guns, twelve being sited only eight to ten yards apart, forming two sides of a square, and when we all get to "gun-fire" together it is pretty noisy. At night the scene is even stranger, twelve aiming post lamps all mixed up together, twelve guns lit up, three megaphones bellowing orders, and a real fine Dante's Inferno of gun flashes.

On Saturday, the 5th, the luck that we have been having ran

out, and we had a bad ten minutes. I was up at the O.P., as we had been busy firing all the afternoon, and suddenly, at exactly 4.30 p.m., three German batteries opened simultaneously on us (two 5.9 and one 4.2 battery), and in about four minutes had put about one hundred shells right into the battery position. My right section and the siege battery got it worst; it was a real bad show, dug-outs, gun-pits, and everything swept away in those four minutes.

Wilson, the subaltern on duty at the guns, had a wonderful escape, being blown down the telephone dug-out staircase; two men were killed and three wounded beside him. Fortunately we got a doctor up within an hour, and had no trouble getting the wounded men back to Susanne. The Siege battery officers, who had been out since 1914, tell me they cannot ever remember having had such a continual heavy shelling as we have had during the last ten days.

LETTER NINE.

VAUX VALLEY. (18TH FEBRUARY, 1916.)

The French Attack. Killing Taken Seriously.

THE perfect weather that we have been having is still going on, and we are getting busier every day. I have had my revenge for our heavy losses on Saturday, 5th, having at last got leave to go for the village of Curlu. By careful observation we had got all the billets and cookhouses marked down, and the times when they were occupied noted, so we had some very successful kills.

It would be impossible to exaggerate the scene of destruction and havoc all round the guns. All the big trees splintered, the bushes cut down, the little wood merely a tangle of roots, debris from dug-outs, bent galvanized iron sheets, clothing thrown up into the trees by the force of the explosions—in fact, one hopeless jumble of destruction. The only things left are the old guns (two of which show scars) and my shanty, which still stands serenely on the top of the bank ; I sleep in it no longer, and merely use it as a storeroom for kit. This perpetual shelling makes one wonderfully quick of hearing and very agile. Beside each gun-pit, and at intervals across the valley bottom, we have dug ten foot deep narrow trenches, with head cover across the centre. It is wonderful how one gets to know whether shells are going to land harmlessly a hundred yards over or are coming right on to you, when there is nothing for it but a headlong dive to safety.

We are told that things are going well, and duly tell the men so, but the fat muzzles of the Siege guns swing round a bit more each day to the rear, and our battery, which shoots straight forward, had a target at only 1,800 yards to-day. But it is all wonderfully interesting, and anyone who thinks this war is dull should come to this sector. From the O.P. there is a most marvellous bird's eye view of the battle. Owing to our curious position it can see right into German and French trenches, and it is thrilling to watch an attack being launched. On Monday (the 8th) the French attacked at 1 p.m., with the intention of recapturing the Bois de Vaches. For three days and nights they had never ceased shelling the wood, and the fire reached the intense stage at 12.30 noon. With my telescope I could see the French forming up for the attack, and the Germans crouching in their trenches trying to get cover from the barrage. Once the attack started it was difficult to say what was happening. From an onlooker's point of view little groups of men appeared to be wandering aimlessly in every direction, but the German reply made it difficult to observe accurately through the smoke of bursting shells. We heard afterwards that they had captured about half the wood, making an advance of a few hundred yards, and taking 400 prisoners.

Food is becoming very difficult to get, but luckily the rations are good. The civilians have long left Susanne and are now evacuating Bray, which used to own four shops, so we have to send the whole way back to Corbie to replenish our stores.

You asked me in your last letter to explain how, if our trenches are ten to twelve feet deep, people ever get out of them. I really don't know! The idea of anyone wanting to get out of a trench is such an original one that round here no preparations have been made to execute so unusual a move. Owing to the Hun having shelled severely Vaux village, I am now allowed to shell Curlu whenever I like. As a continual shelling only drives people into their deep funkpits, I have adopted the method of sudden "coups," i.e., four rounds at a quarter-second interval at odd times of the day and night. This we have done for nearly a week, and to-night the artillery group woke up to the idea and said that I was to start doing it, and offered me an 18-pdr. battery to work with.

We had a gorgeous killing yesterday. Macdonald saw 30 men go into a barn, which we had already accurately registered. We fired one salvo; one shell went right through the roof and blew out the ten-foot-high doors from inside. Several men ran out and many doubtless remained inside, as the shell must have burst right on top of them. We then tried the old trick of waiting for 15 minutes, which allows time for people to gather round the scene of a shelling, actuated by motives of curiosity or desire to help the wounded, after which we opened simultaneously with the 18-pdr. battery and fired fast for two minutes.

Every day the same turmoil continues across the river. Now and then the French gain a few hundred yards, but the line sways backwards and forwards, and it is difficult to find out the exact state of affairs. Sunday, 13th, was a particularly busy day for barraging: from 3.30 to 6 p.m. the firing was terrific. The French were going to take a few centimetres of ground after dark, and this was the tuning up for so great an advance! The Siege guns next mine fired 630 rounds in that time, so you can imagine what the combined din was like. We had no casualties, but the other batteries were not so fortunate. On the 16th it started to rain, and it has now rained without stopping

FIELD GUNS IN FRANCE

for four days. One is continually muddy, even in bed, and undressing varies according to how Fritz behaves. If all is quiet, breeches off; moderately quiet, breeches on, with sandbags round one's legs to prevent the mud from the breeches wetting the bed; if very troublesome, boots and breeches on, and completely swathed in sandbags!

As it now takes eight horses and sometimes ten to get the water cart up to us, you can imagine that we are economical with water, but we are all very happy and entirely free from any visits from the Staff. No one from the outside world has come to this valley since the 26th January.

More "moralizings" about war. You know how plenty of people go out hunting and really take no interest in the hunting itself. It is the same out here. One comes across only too many people who quite forget that the essence of war is to kill. They seem quite content to sit in their trench, or gun-pit, according to their profession, and grumble at being shelled; then when it is over make no attempt to take revenge. By hard thinking and hard work some new scheme can usually be devised, or a crafty plot hatched, to the end that a few more Huns may be wiped out. It often requires a lot of work, but the result, with any luck, justifies the trouble and risk taken. On the 18th, for instance, we had a most enjoyable time shooting out a machine-gun wedged on the side of the Chapeau de Gendarme (The Bluff), and only 25 yards from our listening point. A shell had never been fired at it before. Wilson, a telephonist, and a machine-gun sergeant, the latter to point out the exact spot, remained in the listening post while the remainder of the garrison retired to a safer spot. By means of linking up seven telephones I got through to Wilson, and from the O.P. directed the fire as near as I could to the point: then Wilson took charge for the final delicate corrections and successfully blew up the machine-gun and its emplacement, luckily without hurt to himself or his men.

LETTER TEN.

VAUX VALLEY. (29TH FEBRUARY, 1916.)

We Change our Zone.   Close Liaison with the French.   In the Allied Front Line.

SINCE my last letter many changes have been taking place. It was very nearly a case of Napoleon's maxim, "Order, counter-order, disorder," but luckily, although there was plenty of the former, there was not too much of the latter.

Our division was due to go out to rest, and the Renfrew T.F. Battery were to relieve us. I spent the 19th and 20th showing their O.C. round, and, having a large surplus of ammunition, strafed all the Hun's most tender spots for his benefit : the enemy heavy-weight menagerie seemed, however, to have cleared off, and we evoked no serious response.

On the 21st my right section went back to Corbie, and the Renfrew Battery took over the section's guns, I being left in command of the composite Battery until Friday, when the relief should have been complete.

Early on Thursday, 24th, however, everything was changed, as the 65th Battery was suddenly ordered to leave, and I had to take over their interesting job of co-operation with the French artillery, my targets being all across the river. As winter had started with a vengeance on the 22nd, I spent a cold day with Pask, lying on the lip of a disused mine shaft studying his zone, which was just visible at intervals between blizzards of snow and hail.

My right section trekked back in a hurry from Corbie with two new guns, and I secured two more from "B" Battery of my Brigade, as they were going out to rest.

By 9 p.m. that night all the changes were over, and I had handed over my old guns and position to the Renfrews and opened shop in my new one. It was a typical night move, complicated by mud so deep that it needed fourteen horses to move each vehicle, and a blinding blizzard to add to the gaiety of the scene. I was very sorry to lose my "dug-out" companion, Pask, one of the best.

Next day (Friday) it snowed viciously all day, and gave one a chance of settling down to the new job. I at once determined to have private telephone line to the French R.A. Head-Quarters, as the old method of communication through many British and French exchanges was too cumbersome. In the morning I crossed the river and went to the chateau at Cappy and found Commandant Lotte, commanding the Northern French Artillery group (2nd Colonial Division) ; I already knew his Staff Captain, Captain Legendre, and his A.D.C., Duboit, so we soon had the details of the proposed new line fixed up. They gave me a first-class lunch of five courses in a cellar, and we then went over to visit a 75 mm. Battery commanded by Captain Noir, who of course popped off numberless rounds to show off the working of his beloved guns. By dark that day my army of telephonists had got the line established, nearly 5,000 yards long, but as clear as a bell. The French seem very fond of using the phone : they constantly ring me up at odd hours of the night and day, often merely for a chat. My telephonists are busy learning French.

Nominally I am attached to a new British group, but they d(not worry in the least about me or my doings, so I just go my own sweet way and report after action.

On the 28th Wilson and I had an interesting day in the French front line, with Commandant Lotte and his staff. Meeting them at the footbridge across the river at Eclusier, we first went up to a Battalion H.Q. about 1,000 yards behind the French front line, and spent some time with the Infantry C.O. in his dug-out, looking at maps and drinking the inevitable "eau de vie." From there we went on to the famous Bois de Vaches, which has been changing hands repeatedly for the last three weeks. It used to be quite a feature of the landscape, a fair-sized wood chiefly of fir, standing on the top of the ridge above the river ; but to-day only forty jagged stumps about twenty feet high mark its site. The ground is very broken, a maddening country to get a good general view of, a maze of mounds and little corries very different from what it appears to be from my O.P. From the latter the ridge looks quite smooth, and the irregularities in the terrain do not appear, explaining why one sometimes sees both sides walking about with apparent impunity in the open during an attack, and making the whole thing appear so aimless.

The whole wood is a criss-cross of trenches or connected shell holes, no regular system of trenches having been evolved. In its place we find merely frenzied scratchings wherever each side happen to find themselves at dawn. The French fire trenches are packed with men, very different from the solitude of our front line, but one must remember that they have no protecting wire up yet.

The infantry in the line were Colonials and had all seen active service in Cochin China. They were a tough but rather dirty-looking lot, and altogether the front line was in a very messy state, and as they had had a bit of a show at dawn one realized the truth of the saying : "It isn't what the eye sees but what the feet walk upon that matters." An absurd feeling, of course, as though the poor devils could feel one walking over them ! They were a cold-blooded crowd. I noticed one Boche half-buried in the parapet and the men using his feet to hang their water bottles on !

On our way home we called at a French O.P., and I was able to watch our own guns firing across the river towards us, and thus saw the effect of the shells on the various targets that I had told my battery to engage at pre-arranged hours. This form of registering by firing rounds at pre-arranged hours, is rather a hobby of mine, and frequently saves one having to run out miles of wire just for the purpose of registering one hidden point.

The range and line can be altered at different stated times, and it is thus possible to get quite good results for registration purposes.

LETTER ELEVEN.

VAUX VALLEY. (9TH MARCH, 1916.)

Sniping with a 4.5 How. Lunch with our Allies.

MORE changes took place on the 30th. The Renfrew Battery and the other batteries of the 18th Division were brought out of the line, leaving us alone in the valley to cover with our four guns both the British and the French fronts, a zone of 140°.

It was a busy four days and we had any amount of shooting, but having to man so many O.P.'s taxed the signallers to their utmost. It is fortunate that we have as many as seventeen telephonists. However, on the 3rd a new battery (O.C. Captain Armstrong) appeared and relieved us from looking after the French zone. They had a bad day for their arrival, biting cold and constant snowstorms.

On Sunday, 5th, it was as cold as ever, nevertheless a padre turned up and held Holy Communion for quite a big congregation in one of the deep dug-outs. Immediately afterwards I went up to the O.P., and I think I added three fresh scalps to my tally. Owing to the sunshine on the snow the light for observing was perfect, and I saw the heads of three Huns on the Bluff. They were watching the Mill very intently as they stood under a sheet of corrugated iron which decked the trench, their elbows on a sleeper. I fired No. 2 gun, as it had that spot for its night line, and the round burst a little way to the flank. They ducked down, and I naturally did not expect to have another chance at them. To my surprise, after a few minutes they reappeared and continued to observe from the same point. I ordered "20 minutes more left repeat," and breathed a silent prayer to Fate to guide that shell. Off went the old gun; at the last moment they heard the shell coming and down went their heads, but it was too late. The shell burst at the bottom of the trench and everything went sky-high, the sheet of iron, the sleepers, and half the parapet. Sic transit !

We are very fortunate in having our main O.P. within ten minutes' walk of the guns through a charming wood, instead of having an hour's journey up a water-logged trench. This means that we can relieve our observers four or five times a day, so that while they are there, the telescopes are in action the whole time and the observers do not become stale.

That afternoon Susanne was subjected to a rather severe strafing, so in reply our battery and three siege batteries were ordered to open simultaneously on the village of Maurepas at 5.30 p.m., for three minutes.

Despite the long range, which makes our loading slow, we got off fifteen rounds per gun in that time.

Another sniping incident occurred a few days later. Two German staff officers were the target this time, but alas, they escaped—let us hope to find later a worse fate!

They suddenly apppeared in the open, walking up the road which leads to the ruined shrine which forms the zero line for my guns, and reaching the shrine proceeded to calmly study a map.

They heard the first round coming, and fell flat on their faces in the mud, the shell bursting just over. They then had to run for 500 yards across the open while I pursued them with three more rounds. In his panic one fell twice, and they were last seen clambering over their chevaux de frise wire on the skyline. After that most distressing incident—remember they were staff officers—I linked up my O.P. with that of John Nunn, who commands A/149, 19-pdr. Battery, as with my good telescope we are always seeing suitable targets for their shrapnel.

Winter ended about the 6th, and we have had a succession of glorious spring days.

On the 7th I had promised to take Capt. Armstrong over to lunch with the French and make their acquaintance, but I couldn't get off till late, having to wait all the morning for General Leckie, who didn't turn up. However, in spite of the delay, when I galloped over to Cappy I found thirty-six oysters waiting for me, with the usual cheery crowd of French gunners round the table.

The oysters were followed by pâté de fois gras, veal and chicken mousse, a young roast pig, and Rumpelmayer's chocolate cake, washed down with Graves, some excellent Pontet Canet and champagne, then eau de vie, a very good cigar and perfect coffee.

The extra luxuries were accounted for by one of the staff having just returned from Paris leave.

After a most hilarious lunch, though I personally felt like an inflated frog, we mustered energy enough to stroll over and see a friend of mine, Captain Vieux, at his battery near the Chateau.

We took possession of one of his guns and fired it off with great rapidity—an international gun detachment of officers! and then I persuaded the whole party to come over to our side and see our happy

FIELD GUNS IN FRANCE

home. After so large a lunch I had no desire to ride or walk, so we got hold of a battered old car which used to belong to the Chateau and Vieux, Dubois, Armstrong and I drove in triumph in it to Susanne. No vehicles are supposed to go beyond the turn in daylight, but as I said before we had "dejuened" extremely well, so ignoring the road-blocking sentry, we charged down the road, in full sight of the Huns across the river, the old car clanging like a smithy shop and bucking over the crump holes in the road with asthmatic grunts from every cylinder.

We eventually ran into a mud pool and stuck fast near Royal Dragoon Wood, so we dismounted and bolted for the shelter of our narrow valley, as the Hun was shelling the country-side rather hard. He was not after us, and the car particularly, but the shells would have hurt just the same.

After tea we showed off our guns and fired a few rounds with a picked gun detachment to impress our visitors. Anyway, the dial sights were duly admired, as they appeared so expensive compared with the cheap-looking sight on the 75 mm. Great interest was shown, too, in the panoramic view we have of the German front line, a view not always appreciated by us, the inmates of the valley, for the Hun has in return practically a bird's-eye view of us.

I saw them off at dusk. By some miracle the Hun had not spotted the car on the road, and it was untouched : with the help of the team out of our watercart, which fortunately appeared at the right moment, the car was dragged to terra firma, and they went off. Vieux really did admire our horses and harness, and I must say they are looking pretty fit and clean.

Our own Colonel (Lyon) has taken over the group at Susanne temporarily, and has been over to us and to our O.P. frequently. He often came to observe the effect of the various group "hates" which he is fond of organizing. They are great fun, and are very effective. Usually three to five minutes' intense fire from a group of batteries on one spot.

I say effective, not that one knows the result of our shoot as regards casualties to the Hun, but effective as regards "morale".

One knows only too well that a sudden concentrated burst shakes one far more than thrice the number of shells spread over a long period. Talking of shells, after all the bumping we have had with really big stuff, I find one gets quite blasé and indifferent to Hun shrapnel from their whizz-bangs (77 mm.). Foolish, perhaps, but quite true. Of late there has been a lot of activity in my old playground, the marsh, and it almost looks as if the Hun was going to be tiresome there some day.

6.3.16.

Just a line to enclose this note before I lose it. Rather an interesting note to keep for after days.

The gift referred to was a box of McIver shortbread. What a courteous old-world touch about the letter as compared with what one would get from a Britisher !

Monsieur le Capitaine,
    N. FRASER-TYTLER,
        Batterie D/151.
MON CHER CAMARADE,
    Je suis confus de votre gracieuseté ! et je vous remercie bien cordialement de votre delicate attention.

Je regrette sincèrement votre changement d'affectation qui survient au moment liaison était bien assurée. Je suis convaincû que nous entretiendrons également de cordiales relations avec la batterie nouvelle.

J'irai certainement vous voir sous peu, accompagné du Capitaine Le Gendre ; nous vous préviendrons la veille. Vous nous ferez toujours un très grand plaisir quand vous pourrez venir nous voir à Cappy. Notre table n'est guère luxueuse, mais—à la guerre comme à la guerre ; si le menu n'est pas exquis, vous pourrez toujours être certain de la cordialité des convives à qui vous inspirez une réelle sympâthie.

Veuillez croire, mon cher Camarade, a l'expression de mes sentiments affectueux et devoués.
                                    R. LOTTE.
        Commandant 2nd Colonial Artillery Division,
                  sous Section Nord.

LETTER TWELVE.

VAUX VALLEY. (22ND MARCH, 1916.)

A Wood in the Marsh Changes Hands Four Times. Visitors to the O.P.

PERFECT weather continues, though it is still cold at night. Our division is being relieved again, but to our joy we still remain here, and I have spent three long days taking round Generals, Colonels, and B.C.'s, explaining the country from the O.P., and helping to find positions for a host of incoming batteries.

Owing to our long stay in this position we have become the patriarchs of the valley, and show-men of the country and purveyors of information to all and sundry. Our zone having extended at times from Maricourt, in the north, to Herbecourt, south of the Somme, we can pride ourselves on a certain knowledge of the country.

It is a fascinating land, in spite of the Hun.

The other night I sat up on the hill above the marsh till after midnight with a director, trying to spot the flash of an advanced Hun battery in Feuillères.

The scene was wonderful. A glorious frosty night—squadrons of ducks quacking away in the mist-cloaked marsh—the never-ending rise and fall of Vèry lights in a great half-circle around, and the occasional distant "knocking" of a machine-gun.

There is one M.G. artist to the north of us who regularly plays a few bars of the "Policeman's Holiday" with his gun. You will realize that it needs a really artistic finger on the trigger to produce a tune!

The C.R.A. of the incoming Division (18th) is General Van Straubenzee, a scientific gunner who keeps things very much tuned up. I mentioned in my last letter the Hun's activity in the marsh region: on the 11th the Colonel of the 18th Manchesters came to tea and recounted the story of his marsh troubles and anxieties.

The terrain is certainly curious. From Vaux village a narrow causeway runs out terminating in our block-house; then follows a series of plank bridges across canals till a small wood called Knolly's Point is reached, where our outposts lie out at night, withdrawing to the block-house by day. Beyond that is No Man's Land, consisting of marsh and wood right across to Curlu.

That very night the fun started. At 6 p.m. the Hun opened a heavy bombardment on Vaux Wood and our portion of the marsh. We replied vigorously till 8 p.m., when the infantry informed us that the outposts had been driven back to the block-house, breaking down the bridges as they retired.

Except for occasional spasms of activity the night passed quietly, though the Hun was within 1,300 yards of the guns.

Next morning there was perfect peace on both sides till midday, the whole country being wrapped in dense mist. Hitherto we had always regarded Knolly's Point as an impossible place for any British gun to shell owing to its position under the steep Vaux hill, and I think the Hun thought the same, too. However, I was ordered to shell him out if possible, and we found that by using a range 500 yards lower than that which was supposed to clear the bank in front of the guns, we were able to lob over shells (charge 1) to within 80 yards of our block-house. Of course every now and then I, at the O.P., would hear a terrific explosion at the guns as a shell burst prematurely, having hit some hard branch, but shells are made to be exploded and no one at the battery got much damaged. Major Lupton (18th Manchesters) and a very intelligent scout sergeant were in my O.P., and the latter pointed out the sandbag breastwork which the Hun had erected since his arrival.

We gave the tiny wood a real good hammering, demolished the breastwork, and caused a big explosion (a bomb store).

Nunn's 18-pdr. Battery also fired, their difficulty, however, being to clear the trees above my O.P. Many shells, indeed, burst on the trees above, and the O.P. roof was entirely covered with debris; nevertheless this battery also managed to shell the wood. It was very curious, having one's target 400 feet almost perpendicularly below the O.P.

The infantry were preparing to retake the wood at 6.15 p.m., so for 15 minutes beforehand we fired incessantly. The attack, however, was much delayed owing to difficulties in repairing the bridges, but as the Hun commenced shelling the wood soon after, it proved that he had already evacuated his position.

About thirty of our scouts eventually swam and waded across, re-occupied Knolly's Point, and had a hot scrap in the marsh near Curlu. At dawn the next day I went down to our block-house, and then to the recaptured wood beyond it. It is rarely indeed in war that the gunner sees the result of his own shells within ten hours of firing

FIELD GUNS IN FRANCE 61

them. Several satisfactory dark patches were to be seen, also one very dead corpse—almost a direct hit it must have been. In addition, a glorious mixture of gear was scattered around. Rifles, cigars, a telephone, Thermos flasks, twenty steel snipers' shields, Vèry light pistols, steel cupolas for dug-outs, hand grenades, and any amount of small-arm ammunition, together with thousands of a most superior Hun type of sandbag, made of grey calico with strong web handles so that they can be used for carrying up ammunition or rations. I took two to keep clean clothes in.

Despite the soft ground our shells seemed to have detonated beautifully, and I only found three that were duds. The Hun must have intended to remain permanently in the wood, or he would hardly have brought so much heavy gear of every description.

On the 14th the Hun sluiced the whole neighbourhood badly, and we had a busy time replying on various Hun villages. Three of our horses were hit coming up with rations, also two men at the battery.

Owing to the arrival of more Howitzer batteries my zone no longer extends to the trenches by Maricourt, which saves many a weary plod through the mud, besides the upkeep of a mile and a half of telephone wire. Thanks to the good light for observing of late, we have been able to continue steadily in the rôle of universal providers of targets for the 18-pdrs. and Siege batteries. There's no telescope half as good as mine in all the O.P.'s, and we have been lucky in being able to spot a good deal lately.

A lot of French officers came over to tea on the 15th. We fired our guns for them, picked primroses, and were truly rural for the whole of an idle afternoon.

On the 20th our Divisional Infantry went back to rest, and I spent the day "liaising" with the incoming battalion, the East Surreys, a real good lot, and on the very first night we had an example of what they could do.

A terrific hate started at 2.30 a.m. that night and lasted for six minutes, then about 150 Huns attacked the same old wood, when the two machine-guns did a lot of good work till they both jammed. Our men then retired to the block-house, and the Hun sat in the wood. There was still a patrol out in the marsh, so the O.C. would not let us fire. However, at 4.30, two of our platoons crept across the single plank bridges, deployed in the marsh, and then charged with the bayonet, retook the wood, slaying four and capturing one. Quite a successful little show.

Since then all has been peaceful. More visitors have turned up at our O.P., one being General Leckie, who spent the morning with us.

Among others were Captain Noir, a French Battery commander, and Dubois, the A.D.C.

Noir wanted to shoot at things on our side of the river in return for the help Armstrong's Battery had given the French, so I gave him some targets—Curlu included—and a "barrage line" across the marsh in case of another marsh attack.

LETTER THIRTEEN.

VAUX VALLEY. (10TH MAY, 1916.)

Leave. Casualties by Rats. An Abortive Hun Raid.

I HAD quite a good journey back from leave, and met many friends on the boat. The Battery victoria and my horses were waiting for me at railhead when I got there in the afternoon. On my way up to the guns I stopped at the wagon lines for tea and found the horses all looking very fit. Thanks to the fishing tackle Colonel Lyon had given me, the men had been catching quite a lot of pike, the largest being an eight-pounder.

I got up to the guns by dinner-time; it's nice to be back home again! The country looks very lovely, and the wood is a mass of spring flowers in bloom, as of course everything is so much earlier than in England.

Wind was dangerous for gas the first night, and we had false gas alarms until 3 a.m., which gave me an opportunity of wading through the mass of official papers which had accumulated during leave.

Macdonald had done wonders at the work on the new gun-pits, and at the O.P. The latter really is a wonderful place now; everything has been lowered into the crest of the bank about 14 feet, and we now have a conning tower with circular slits on the lip of the cliff, then a tunnel to the telephone dug-out, and behind that a bedroom with two bunks. As they are rather dark, the latter rooms are lined with white calico, but in the O.P. we used green rot-proof canvas. The canvas is stretched over expanded metal sheets. The place is really "5.9 proof" and so comfortable, alas, that we fear it must mean we move shortly, when another will reap the benefit of our labours. We have in addition deepened the telephone wire trenches.

Two days after I got back I had a vile attack of "flu", but we were too short-handed to take much notice of it, two officers being away and Maclean being laid up with a poisoned arm, the result of having been fiercely attacked during the night by great rats and badly bitten while asleep. He declares that it was not a rat, but the vixen that lives in our bank and whose runs connect with our various tunnel dug-outs. Talking of animals, the country is full of partridges, rabbits and foxes. The latter are to be seen in the day-time far more than in England. I saw one catching mice the other day between the German first and second line trenches.

By the end of April, thanks to good weather, we had completed the four new gun-pits and moved the guns into them. They are good pits with over 10 feet of solid head cover on the roof, and quite "5.9" proof, like our O.P. What a change it will be if we ever get any open fighting this summer, and how it will contrast with our present mode of working with gun-pits and aiming posts lit by electric light, and the O.P. lined with maps, telescopes, switch-boards, and a maze of wires leading to every quarter of the line!

The gun-pits had their baptism of fire on the very first night. At 1.5 a.m. a desperate enemy strafe started and the Hun managed to raid our trenches at two points. They were soon thrown out, however, and as all our batteries were then firing on their S.O.S. lines in No Man's Land, very few Huns got back to their trenches: our infantry had hardly a casualty. The Hun, of course, gave our valley its fair share of H.E. and weeping gas in return, but we were none the worse. Our deep telephone trenches also stood us in good stead, as in spite of the terrific shelling not a wire was broken, and throughout the night the Infantry Battalion H.Q., whose wires were all gone, had to make use of ours.

LETTER FOURTEEN.

VAUX VALLEY. (18TH MAY, 1916.)

Every Minute of a Typical Day.   Retrieving a Fallen Angel.

THE battle of Frise had proved that a river formed a bad dividing line between two Armies, in that liaison was thereby made so difficult, consequently the French are now taking over the sector between the Somme and Maricourt. To do this they are sending their famous 20th Corps (the Corps de Fer). The first swallow of the blue-clad invasion arrived a short time ago in the shape of a solitary 75 mm. gun and a subaltern, by name Salandere.   The gun assists the Howitzer battery in enfilading the Hun trenches, and is in action quite close to us ; so Salandere messes with us and sleeps in a dug-out next to mine.

We are to move over to the right, and are fortunate enough to have been allotted gun-pits already made in the Maricourt Valley ; they are excellent 5.9 proof gun-pits. It will be a great saving in labour for men and horses.

The Guards entrenching battalion has moved down into the Bois des Tailles behind Bray, and Major Ellice, of Invergarry, is in command, his adjutant being Kemes Lloyd. Both have been over once or twice to lunch, and afterwards of course they visited the great O.P. Quite a show-place nowadays. Another change that is taking place is that our Howitzer brigade is to break up and we will be "D" Battery of the 150th Brigade, commanded by Colonel F. A. Dixon ; General Geoffrey White has arrived as our Divisional C.R.A. I went over to Head-Quarters the other day to pay my respects to him, and met there General Noël Birch (R.A., Fourth Army).

The last fortnight has on the whole been very quiet. I had one interesting day, however, getting a trip in a 'plane, my object being to look at our newly made gun-pits from the air, and to see some of our targets which lie over the ridge. On firing coloured lights from a Very pistol the battery engaged pre-arranged targets, but it was a squally day of thunderstorms and hail, making observation very difficult. The Hun anti-aircraft guns always get very fussy when a plane starts firing lights; apparently they think it is a signal for something desperate to happen. As I have got very little news I will try to describe in detail every minute of an average quiet day, taking yesterday as an example, from 9 p.m. to 9 p.m.

9.0 p.m. Arrival of Water Cart and Cook's Cart, with Mail and Rations. The usual amount of paper to be sent back to the Adjutants. Enter the Sergt.-Major with a list of stuff sent up and the unserviceable gear to be sent down.

9.15 p.m. Salandere, the French subaltern, looked in chiefly to poach from my O.P. report book a lot of rather exciting things seen during the day, Hun reliefs and transport movement, in order that he could phone them to his Colonel. He rarely observes himself.

9.30 p.m. Inspected night lines of the guns and then to bed.

10.0 p.m. Urgent phone message from Group, "How many men can I send to baths at Chipilly to-morrow at 9 a.m." Answer 5.

10.15 p.m. Phone message from Group, "The French are going to have a gas test at 9 a.m. to-morrow, so disregard noise."

10.45 p.m. Very urgent message from Group, "The baths at Chipilly are indefinitely closed."

11.48 p.m. Hear a certain amount of Hun shelling down near the Mill lasting for two minutes.

11.51 p.m. Hear Captain Nunn's 18-pdrs. spitting back.

Midnight. Half the world talking at once on the phone and presently my call goes and the voice of the Adjutant announces that the crowd at the Mill were not content with 18-pdr. retaliation, as they have been strafed with 4.2's. Would I fire, and, if so, what at? I replied that with my present stock of targets on hand I could offer a nice line, viz., the top of the Bluff, and as that was only 100 yards from the Mill our people would hear the noise and feel braver. The Adjutant agrees.

FIELD GUNS IN FRANCE 67

12.1 a.m.   Phoned to the telephone exchange, "Left section action." The second telephonist on duty megaphones the order, the sentry switches on the left section electric installation, and the guard stirs up the detachments. No. 3 gun is already on the target, No. 4 gun is switched on to it, the tap is turned on for two minutes, and then back to bed.

12.6 a.m.   From bed ring up Adjutant and report execution. He says, "If the Hun strafes the Mill again repeat the dose."

12.7 a.m.   Phone to exchange for the N.C.O. of guard, and give orders for a repeat dose if the Hun re-opens.

1.5 a.m.   Awakened by a desperate row down by the Mill and loud megaphone squawks from both sides of my dug-out. In less than 45 seconds gun-fire is opened, and after two minutes back to bed and asleep by 1.10 a.m.

2.45 a.m.   It was my morning to do the dawn gas "stand-to." The N.C.O. of the Guard wakes me, but as the wind is right he dismissed the men and remain in bed myself.

6.0 a.m.   Enter Hickey with shaving water, and I get up and write out reports.

7.0 a.m.   Breakfast.

7.30 a.m.   Depart with the Sergt.-Major, a No. 1 and 13 men to our future position. About fifteen minutes' walk. Start the men on a trench between the mess and the guns. Call on Paul, the O.C. of the Battery at present occupying the position. Find him in bed. Collect a drink and then back to plan a big ammunition pit, about the only thing needed in the position.

9.30 a.m.   Returned to Paul's mess and look at the papers while he wrestles with returns.

10.0 a.m.   We both decide to pay a call on Colonel R. K. Walsh, commanding the 2nd Royal Scots, in front of us. About half an hour's walk takes us there. Find him in his office and discuss various things not connected with war and finally I ask him how his Company at the Mill was after last night. To my disgust I find that they had quite forgotten to report our kind retaliation to their Head-Quarters, so said I would not fire for them again for ages and ages.

11.0 a.m. Look at Hunland from a very pleasant trench 250 feet above the marsh, a glorious view of water, hills and marsh.

11.30 a.m. Reached Vaux Wood, showed Paul the O.P., and then to the Battery, exit Paul.

1.30 p.m. Relieved the Sub. at the O.P. Salandere turned up, and I explaned the zone for his future information.

3.0 p.m. Not a shot was being fired and things were hot, dull and sleepy, so suggested stirring up the Huns on this side of the river; back to his O.P., where we lay on a sunny bank while he sprayed the Hun front line with his 75 mm. gun, which seemed to cause considerable annoyance.

3.30 p.m. to 5.0 p.m. Returned to my O.P. and watched nothing till 5 p.m. Heard three rifle shots and saw 20 anti-aircraft shells, but no other firing. Discussed the dullness of life with various other O.P.'s over the telephone.

5.0 p.m. The Sergt.-Major relieved me at O.P.

5.30 p.m. Tea and many envelopes marked "Urgent," "Secret," or "Very Urgent," containing such important matters as "Now that it is summer, 'frost coats' must no longer be drawn."

6.30 p.m. Called on Colonel Johnson at his Battalion Headquarters a few hundred yards from us.

7.30 p.m. Dinner, and so endeth a very average day.

One amusing incident has happened lately. Two German aeroplanes were brought down by one of ours in a scrap above Curlu, one falling in the Hun lines and one just in ours. Both caught fire at a height of about 4,000 feet, and the observer of the first one evidently felt uncomfortable and got out. His machine-gun preceded him and fell undamaged in our wood, while he himself came down on his back 100 yards from the Mill, but in No Man's Land.

The Hun evidently thought that he was carrying valuable papers, for he at once started shelling the body and fired 40 rounds to try and break him up, but were only partially successful. All that night they kept a machine-gun trained on him, and owing to the bright moonlight our three attempts to retrieve the body failed.

Next morning I met Colonel Walsh, and we spent three hours endeavouring to devise a way of getting him in. My scheme for using some of my strong pike tackle proved impracticable, as he was already fixed in some old wire, and one could not have pulled him through it. Eventually we both crawled out to within 25 yards of the body ; it needed careful crawling, as the Hun was very much on the look-out. We devised a route for the rescue party that night, and arranged that if the machine-guns re-opened I was to fire also. We got back to our trenches safely, and had a good lunch at his Head-Quarters. If either of us had been hit, it would probably have annoyed the powers that be, since it was hardly our proper job. The night was cloudy, however, and the body was got in all right, but only just in time, as a German patrol arrived on the scene also. In the end, after all the fuss, no papers of any sort were found on the body—or remains, to be exact.

LETTER FIFTEEN.

BOIS DES TAILLES, BRAY. (5TH JUNE, 1916.)

The French Invasion. Our P.P.C. Shell. An Old Etonians' Dinner and its Sequel.

WE are back at rest for one day before moving to our new position in the Maricourt valley. Since last writing on 18th May, the French have been gradually taking over the line between the Somme and the South edge of Maricourt, and I was left till the very last to act as showman of the district to the newcomers—a solitary khaki relic in a sea of blue.

During the last three weeks I have talked more French than English, and daily provide lunch and information for French Generals, many of whose names you must often read in French communiqués. My servant, Hickey, tells me he heard an infantryman on passing the mess remark, "That must be an Officers' 'estaminet,' as there always seems to be such a crowd in there drinking." And we certainly do seem to have had visits from every Battery commander of the two newly arrived divisions, which, by the way, belong to the famous 20th Corps (Corps de Fer). It has been very interesting seeing so much of the inside life of the French Army. We had very little firing to do for them, so, left in peace, we had time to get on with the work of preparing our future position.

I must now tell you about the result of the last shot fired from Vaux Valley. The day before we moved, while returning to the O.P. after lunching with the infantry, a British 'plane started flying very low over the marsh. The Huns as usual opened a brisk fire at him with rifles and machine-guns, and I could see some old friends of mine in the swamp being specially active. It was a curious little strong point on a narrow bank, with water on every side of it, and a few days before I had fired some sixteen rounds at it without effect, every round being "short" or "over" in the water.

I rushed down the trench leading to our O.P., shouting to the signaller "No. 2 gun, action, target 11, Fire," to the consternation of the two wrens nesting in the trench-wall. I could see the M.G. and the two snipers beside it still firing away. Off went the gun, and by great

FIELD GUNS IN FRANCE

good luck the first and only round was absolutely "bull's-eye". A glorious detonation and the whole show, iron sniper shields, timber, etc., went up together.

I then phoned to an 18-pdr. battery to get them to spray the spot with shrapnel later in the afternoon, on the chance of catching any inquisitive ones.

On the 4th June we completed the evacuation of our position, and moved back to the Bois des Tailles behind Bray—I say completed because the process had been going on for several days beforehand. We had already shifted about 30 tons of ammunition to the new position, besides 40 G.S. wagon loads of material and gear, a very mixed collection, including railway sleepers, arm-chairs, corrugated iron sheets, 8 tables, timber, kitchen ranges, and a grandfather clock—Heaven knows where the latter came from! And a short six months ago all our gear was moved in a cook's cart! Group H.Q. were rather anxious for me to stay with the gun in order to see them safely out, but as it was the great 4th of June I reminded them that I was due to chaperone General White into Amiens for the Fourth Army Old Etonian dinner. General Rawlinson was M.C., and I think Dick Sutton, his A.D.C., was responsible for the bunderbust, which was excellent. One hundred and sixty-eight were present, so hosts of friends met, and it was really a very cheery evening.

The Red Gods of War, how they delight in contrasts! While racing back in the General's comfortable car, we saw the eastern sky suddenly lit up with countless gun-flashes and Very lights, and heard the roar of an intense bombardment. It was a big raid which our division were carrying out at 11 p.m.!

On arriving at R.A. H.Q., we drank the health of the General's and Lanyon's D.S.O.'s, the news of which had just come in (Lanyon is our Brigade Major). I then motored back to the Bois des Tailles, where I eventually located our new wagon lines. More healths there in the Sergeants' Mess, this time in honour of a D.C.M. that had been awarded to one of the telephonists, Ryding, for getting news back to Group during the Frise show. He is a dauntless kid of 18, who has invariably been my follower on any particularly intricate enterprise.

Three of the guns arrived safely, and the fourth being stuck in a ditch, Macdonald had taken a fatigue party back to dig it out. On retiring to the bed made up for me in his well-equipped tent, I remember hitting out several candles with the *Tatler*; one of the candles must have fallen still burning on the floor, as presently I awoke to find the tent blazing around me. "Guard turn out" was the only thing I could think of to yell. A general rush to the rescue, led by the Q.M.S. in his shirt (he thought someone was stealing his stores), several with gas masks, who took the smoke to be gas—in fact, excellent salvage work on the part of everybody. The "salved" proved to be my worthy self and all Macdonald's kit.

With a chilly damp dawn Macdonald returned from his labours to find his beautiful tent in ashes, and me wrapped in a bed-bag in the subaltern's tent murmuring sleepily the self-evident truth, "Macdonald, I have burnt your tent!"

Dined with Ellice on the 5th in the Guards' Mess, which is quite close to our wagon lines, and lunched to-day at R.A. H.Q. with General White in order to meet General de Rougemont, who, now that Gallipoli is over, is temporarily out of a job and is doing a Cook's Tour of the front.

To-night the guns go up to their new home, and our brief two-day rest is over.

LETTER SIXTEEN.

MARICOURT VALLEY. (19TH JUNE, 1916.)

Our New Position. A Desirable O.P. Fire in a Gun-Pit.

I WROTE last during our short rest at the wagon lines. Well, on the night of the 6th June, helped by my Irish subaltern, Maclean, I moved the guns up to the new position in Maricourt Valley. Despite the short distance, the journey took from 7 p.m. to 10.30 p.m. The densest "Mansion House" traffic is nothing to the congestion on the Bray-Susanne road nowadays ; guns and wagons, timber lorries by the hundred, S.A.A. carts, water carts, French country carts, Zouaves, Turcos and British and Indian cavalry, unite to form one seething mass. Although the gun-pits are made, we have a good deal yet to do : altering the pits to make them face our new zone, and especially in the tunnelling work at the O.P.

In order to facilitate communication seven or eight batteries are using the same disused trench for their O.P.'s. Out of this trench each pair of batteries has tunnelled a narrow T-shaped passage, which has to be negotiated for about 25 feet on hands and knees. The head of the T forms the double O.P., consisting of two vertical 15-foot shafts, terminating at ground level in an iron dome. When, already covered with the slime encountered during the journey through the tunnel, the observer struggles up the iron steps in the tiny shaft and eventually reaches the little seat in the top, he discovers that he is now "all mud"—the shaft being nearly as sticky as the tunnel. John Nunn (A/149) shares my tunnel, and the telephonists sit at the bottom of the shaft and pick up the things I drop. In spite of all our precautions to hide the slits and the domes, I fear they look painfully obvious when viewed from our front line.

Imbert Terry and Fullerton are two other tenants of these "very desirable O.P.'s."

Except for one or two vicious spasms, things might have been peaceful. One of these spasms occurred on the night of the 13th. At 11.40 p.m. a tremendous roar commenced, as every Hun gun along the whole front sprang to life simultaneously in a beautifully timed opening ;

a moment later a man dashed into my dug-out to say that No. 4 pit had blown up!

Gum-boots, steel hat, gas mask and electric torch were ready to hand, and in 30 seconds Maclean and I were doing an unpleasant 1000-yard sprint through the mud to the guns. I am not sure which was the worst, the Hun shells that were coming pretty fast all round, or the scalp-raising blast of the French 75 mm. guns behind us, their shells only just clearing our heads by a few feet.

No. 4 pit had not as yet blown up, but I thought it would very soon do so. There were some 1,500 shells stacked in or near the pit, and it already resembled a furnace, with flames shooting 3 feet above the roof.

Anticipating the S.O.S. signal which came through soon after, three guns started "gun-fire," while Maclean organized a party to try and save the burning gun. A chain of men was formed, and they passed up shell boxes and sandbags full of mud to Maclean and two other men who stood at the entrance to the pit. The gun-charges were stacked in piles of 40 all round the pit, and when the fire reached them, they exploded pile after pile and added fuel to the furnace. One man was pulled out dead, killed by the shell that had started the fire, and gradually the gun and the stacks of shell were covered with a coating of mud and slime. That done, they attacked the flames on the roof and walls. To add to their troubles, another shell entered the pit opening, actually hit the trail, knocking the gun sideways, and then by some miracle burying itself in the platform without exploding. By degrees the fire was got under control, though the shells and gun had become so hot that they could not be touched. Every leather fitting on the gun was of course destroyed.

We had a good many other shells into the position, but no more casualties. The telephone dug-out got a direct hit on its roof with a 5.9, but withstood it with hardly a tremble.

We continued this slogging match till 1.30 a.m., when the din died down, and we stopped firing and so to bed again by 2 a.m. What wonderful good fellows Lancashire men are in a real "rough house"!

The names of Maclean and the two men with him have been sent up, and I hope they may get something for their gallant conduct, which saved the complete loss of the gun.

The result of all the uproar was that the Hun reached the French trenches at two points, but it proved to be merely an ordinary raid, and they were speedily kicked out.

LETTER SEVENTEEN.

MARICOURT VALLEY. (30TH JUNE, 1916.)

Preparations During June. Each Day of the Great Bombardment.

> Not where the squadrons mass,
> Not where the bayonets shine,
> Not where the big shells shout as they pass
> Over the firing line.
> R. KIPLING.

BEFORE this letter is posted the great attack will have been launched, so I am able at last to describe some of the hectic preparations that have occupied us all this month. I will then add some more in diary form about each day of the great bombardment.

As I mentioned before, the French have taken over the small sector between Maricourt and the Somme, which our battery and two 18-pdr. batteries formerly covered. To-day there are no less than 424 French guns and Howitzers packed into the little salient, and as we have increased our guns in nearly the same proportion, you can imagine the congestion of batteries in this valley. From Maricourt back to Susanne, all along the bottom of the Valley, row after row of batteries, and often brigades, can be seen, in lines one behind the other about 200 yards apart.

The whole of May and the first half of June was spent in frenzied efforts to be ready. It was literally a race against time, and I don't think the people at home realize the stupendous preparations that a "show" entails. The whole face of the country has to be altered, and altered, if possible, without the Hun spotting it. New roads everywhere, frequently of solid timber to take heavy traffic in wet weather ; new trenches all over the place—some of the new communication trenches running back as far as three to four miles owing to the great depth of the salient we are in.

Then in suitable localities behind the front line, trenches had to be dug to provide assembly places for Brigades forming the second wave of the attack. These positions consist of a labyrinth of trenches 10 to 12 feet deep, roofed with wire netting and grass to escape aerial observation ; besides all this the country is covered with a network of telephone trenches, deep narrow slits with about 20 cables in each.

When one is looking down from Maricourt towards Susanne the valley resembles one vast circus, with hundreds of motor-lorries, carts, timber wagons, caterpillars dragging big guns, convoys of trench store wagons going to forward dumps, often hundreds of the French trench mortar bomb carts—curious little vehicles like one-horse sulkies—and strings of anything up to 300 pack mules or horses bearing French S.A.A. All this in a place where four months ago not a single G.S. wagon was to be seen in daylight.

The traffic certainly is extraordinary, and our wagons often take six hours to do the seven-mile journey from the wagon line to the guns.

France ought really to be enlarged for this type of fighting. There honestly is not 100m for all the different kinds of dumps of engineers' stores, food and ammunition, and particularly trench mortar bombs. The latter especially take up a lot of ground, and as it is quite impossible to get the thousands of aerial torpedo bombs under any sort of cover, so they have just got to take their chance in the open. Each of the French battery positions looks like a busy anthill, as about 150 French Territorials are allotted to help each of their batteries to get dug in. I wish we could occasionally get infantry help like that for ourselves.

I will now start giving a daily account of our doings right up till the first of July.

22ND JUNE. A busy day making final preparations. In the afternoon all the battery commanders of the right group were called to a conference. Immediately after that was over, Colonel Stanley, who commands the group, came back with me in order to present the D.C.M. ribbon to Gunner Ryding, one of the telephonists, for which ceremony the Battery paraded in a quite unrecognizable state of cleanliness.

23RD JUNE, FRIDAY. This was "T" day. After lunch, Gregory, another Howitzer B.C., and I went to meet Col. Poyntz, of the 2nd Bedfords, in order to inspect certain Hun machine-guns which he wished us to remove before his raid on "V" night. I suggested that he should point them out first from my O.P. As bad luck would have it, just as we were going to the O.P. the Huns started firing salvoes of 5.9's right on to it. However, by making rushes between the salvoes we reached my tunnel entrance, and all seven of us crawled in. It was pitch dark, one of the previous shells having upset the only candle.

FIELD GUNS IN FRANCE

In order to ease the intense congestion of packed humanity, I told Macdonald (who had come up for a day's holiday from wagon line) that he should crawl up the emergency exit tunnel. The next salvo came, one shell blew in the mouth of the emergency exit and the blast sent Macdonald on to me and me backwards on to the Colonel. At the same time another shell exploded near the main entrance, causing the last two officers, who were only a few feet in the tunnel to make desperate efforts to push further up. "Those in front cried forward, etc." with a vengeance. By this time I was helpless with laughter. Imagine seven of us on our hands and knees in a narrow tunnel, rather damp and very dark, all pushing towards the centre ! The next salvo blew in the top of Nunn's O.P., which let in more light, however. By this time all evinced quite an uncalled-for dislike for my O.P., so we all backed out singly and escaped in rushes down the trench. We then proceeded to the comparative security of the front line, and planned the destruction of the many Hun machine-gun emplacements.

24TH JUNE. "U" DAY. The great and eagerly expected "U" day commenced with the simultaneous fall of a row of thirty tall elms, which lined the route nationale. Their destruction was necessary to clear the field of fire for certain 75 mm. batteries. By 10 a.m. the bombardment was in full swing, and the unbelievable din which we were to have night and day for the next week commenced. The 4.5-inch Howitzers and many of the siege guns were not shooting on this, the first day, and so, after a morning spent in final inspections, I went down to the front line in the afternoon to study our zone.

The front line parapet was lined like the dress circle at a theatre, with the 18-pdr. people all busy wire cutting. Naturally, in the face of such a fire no Hun sniper dared to show his head, and as the Hun artillery had not yet replied we spent a very cheery and useful afternoon. Going back to the battery I passed through the grounds of Maricourt chateau : the noise there baffled all description. About thirty light, medium and heavy trench mortar batteries were in action near the chateau, and being in the apex of the salient, they were all firing at once in three different directions. Certainly the most wonderful thing in a big show is the stupendous noise thereof. We do night firing the whole night through on various special points, and besides the usual routine firing there was on most nights a big joint show. On "U" night, for instance, there was a gas discharge on a wide front, as the wind was very favourable.

In order to cover this discharge, on the stroke of 10 p.m. every French and British gun simultaneously opened at gun-fire. It was a marvellous sight to watch the Brigade of French 75's just behind us, twelve guns close together firing about fifteen rounds per gun per minute. Within five minutes the Hun S.O.S. rockets were going up all round the salient, and what with the heavies searching their back areas and approaches, and the heavy gas discharge, his losses must have been heavy.

25TH JUNE. "V" DAY. A dull and cloudy day, and the bombardment more intense than ever. On either side of our guns is a French 12-inch Howitzer Battery. Their guns are old-fashioned mortars, firing a shell about 40 inches long. One can see the projectile from the time it leaves the gun. The shell seems to climb at a very steep angle, and when about half-way on its downward path it gradually becomes invisible.

As a battery we have only a 200 yards' frontage of the Hun trenches to fire on daily, and the 18-pdr. batteries have an even smaller allotted frontage on which to cut the wire. As it was the night of the Bedfords' proposed raid we reserved our fire till the early evening, and then fired continuously on to the area where the Hun machine-guns were. The raid itself came off at 11.15 p.m., preceded by a very intense bombardment. They took one prisoner, and had a very happy outing with no serious casualties.

26TH. "W" DAY. We got in a lot of heavy shooting during the morning, including one concentrated strafe on German's Wood. It was certainly the noisiest day since the beginning of the bombardment. Every order to the guns has to be written on slips of paper, it being absolutely impossible to make anyone hear the spoken word. The Hun commenced to reply hotly ; until then he had been ominously quiet, and what with frequent prematures the valley became pretty unhealthy.

In the afternoon I went down to the front line with Wilson in order to engage a portion of our zone which was difficult to see from our O.P. However, we had not been shooting long before some of our very heavy Howitzers started a combined shoot on the Hun front line. It was a wonderful sight to see these huge shells bursting 300 yards in front of us, with detonations like earthquakes and smoke of every colour, black, white, grey, yellow and brown, rising often hundreds of feet in the air. However marvellous as a spectacle, this show did not conduce to accurate observation of our own small stuff, but by firing salvoes I was occasionally able to pick out my own bursts.

About three o'clock the Huns started to reply in earnest, and things became very sultry. We all got hit by some splinters, and Gunner Ryding had a wonderful escape, a razor-like splinter 15 inches long grazing the back of his neck and embedding itself in the clay wall of the trench behind him. Communication soon became very difficult, the din being now indescribable. By 4 p.m. the wire was cut in many places, so I retired to my O.P. to continue the shoot from there. On arrival there I found that Lowe, my O.P. subaltern, had gone off with four fractured ribs : a shell exploding near the O.P. had blown him down the 15-foot shaft, and although his fall was broken by the telephonist's head, he managed to hurt himself pretty badly.

Having finished the shoot, I called at the collecting station to bid him good-bye. He appeared to be quite comfortable. The dressing station, 30 feet below the main road, was wonderfully quiet and restful. The night passed with its usual bombardment, while the French indulged in some fancy stunts, and their 75's were chattering like machine-guns all night.

JUNE 27TH. "X" DAY. Cold, with heavy rain all day. Hunland is changing aspect very fast now under the intense bombardment, all the little well-known woods are disappearing, and the Hun trenches have become merely one vast shell-ploughed field. Artillery gets curious targets nowadays. I spent three hours in thinning a blackthorn hedge round the Briquetterie, a rather important spot : it proved to be a tiresome and difficult shoot.

JUNE 28TH. "Y" DAY. The heavy rain continued all the morning, and the country is rapidly becoming nothing but a slimy bog. We heard that the great "Z" day has been postponed, as it would be quite impossible to attack over the ground in its present state. To-day has been rather an unfortunate day, as there were several bad prematures all round us, which caused many casualties, and, besides, the enemy shelled Maricourt very severely.

JUNE 29TH. "Y2" DAY. A cloudy day, but as no more rain has fallen the country is drying up fast. The only outstanding incident in the day was a smoke discharge on a seven-mile front, preceded by a very intense bombardment of one hour. It was a wonderful sight; every smoke candle was lit simultaneously, and as far as the eye could see a solid wall of smoke about 50 feet high moved over the Hun trenches. The night passed with two more gas discharges, one at 10.30 p.m., the other at 12.30. Both were accompanied by the usual barrage.

JUNE 30TH. "Y3" DAY. Thanks to the high wind the country is really dry again. In the morning the Hun started another "hate" at our group of O.P.'s, and completely demolished the one belonging to Terry, also knocking in the top of Nunn's. Luckily there were no casualties, however. In the afternoon we heard that the next day was to be the great "Z" day. One can't help wondering if the Hun has any surprise devilry in store ; he has been suspiciously quiet on the whole, but, of course, as the whole line is strafing he may think that it is only a bluff on this sector. At 10 p.m., when I was in bed, an orderly brought me an envelope containing the news of the zero hour (7.30 a.m.). Everything I can think of is ready, so there is nothing further to worry about. Whatever happens, especially in the ill-fated O.P., you will know that I have had the best nine months which could ever be crammed into a life-time. To-night the dug-out is fairly rocking with the roar of the bombardment, and when phoning to Head-Quarters I had to smother my head and phone under the bed-bag before I could hear a word.

LETTER EIGHTEEN.

MARICOURT VALLEY. (2ND JULY, 1916.)

The Attack of the First July.

> 'Tis war, red war, I'll give you then,
> War till my sinews fail.
> R. KIPLING.

THE 1st of July opened with a glorious though very misty morning. Dense belts of fog were hanging in the valleys, and only the tops of the hills were to be seen. After an early breakfast at 4.30 a.m. and a final inspection of the guns, I went up to the O.P., and by six o'clock the other three battery commanders and their F.O.O.'s had also turned up, and the party for the great spectacle was complete.

All night long the bombardment had continued, but at 6.25 a.m. the final intense bombardment started. Until 7.15 a.m. observation was practically impossible owing to the eddies of mist, rising smoke, flashes of bursting shells, and all one could see was the blurred outline of some miles of what appeared to be volcanoes in eruption. At 7.20 a.m. rows of steel helmets and the glitter of bayonets were to be seen all along the front line. At 7.25 a.m., the scaling ladders having been placed in position, a steady stream of men flowed over the parapet, and waited in the tall grass till all were there and then formed up; at 7.30 a.m. the flag fell and they were off, the mist lifting just enough to show the long line of divisions attacking : on our right the 39th French division ; in front of us our 30th division ; on our left the 18th.

The line advanced steadily, scarcely meeting any opposition in the first three lines of trenches. Every point was reached at scheduled time, so the automatic artillery barrage was always just in front of the infantry. At 9 o'clock we could see our flags waving in the trench behind German's Wood, and by 8.20 the formidable Glatz Redoubt was captured, an advance of 700 yards with very little loss. This redoubt had been submitted to a terrific bombardment, and the infantry reported that the maze of strong points, machine-gun emplacements, etc., had all been swept away, and that the trenches were crammed with dead. By 8.40 a.m. we had captured Casement Trench, and from there a dense smoke barrage was created with a view to hiding the advance of the second wave (90th Brigade), their objective being Montauban village. They went across in perfect formation up to Glatz Redoubt ; there they made a short pause, and then continued the attack and captured the whole village of Montauban by 10 a.m., establishing our line on the north side of the village, overlooking Caterpillar Valley.

Between 10 and 12 noon there was a lull in the operations, and then came the capture of the Briquetterie, preceded by half an hour's intense bombardment. During all this time the country was dotted with little parties of prisoners, each with an escort of two men—one Tommy behind to whip up the laggards, while the one in front was usually surrounded by a crowd of prisoners, all eager to show him the quickest way back to safety and food in our lines !

After the mist lifted the light for observing was perfect. I had of course my own glass, and also a 7-foot monster recently arrived from the Lady Roberts' Telescope Fund, and every detail showed up with the utmost accuracy. There was no Hun shelling, and gradually people emerged from their tunnels and sat on the top of the shafts till it felt quite like a "point to point" crowd. On the whole we had a very delightful day, with nothing to do except send numerous reports through to Head-Quarters and observe the stupendous spectacle before us. There was nothing to do as regards controlling my Battery's fire, and any fresh targets were dealt with by one officer, who sat all day in a dug-out by himself, with map board and battery watch before him. All orders were written on slips and sent by runners to each gun. Another officer was with the guns, while the third remained with me ready to go forward if necessary, and also to supervise the visual signalling arrangements in case our cable was broken.

In the afternoon the Hun shelling increased slightly, but he appeared to be completely demoralized, and, for the moment, shaken out of his wits. After dinner I went round to "swop lies" with the Brigade Commander of the 75 mm. batteries just behind us. He said he had been twice at Verdun, but even there he had never seen such an intense bombardment. Delicious coffee, plus Benedictine, always adds to the pleasure of an evening visit to this hospitable officer.

We were sitting, cups in hand, on the bank, when we saw three French gunners trollying down the little railway line which runs through all the positions. Just as they were passing us a single stray shell landed exactly on the trolley, which simply dissolved away! Some more men of their battery then collected any scraps they could find, putting them into different sandbags, amidst heated arguments as to which was the proper one, etc. I saw one man snatching a foot away from another, shouting : *"Vasy donc, sâle tête, que fais-tu-la, J'en suis bien sûr que ce n'est pas Jean qui porte les chausettes jaunes."* A gruesome yarn, I fear !

The night was troubled by constant futile Hun attacks, so we fired practically all the time. I went to the O.P. at 3 a.m. and found things were then quiet. Later I was relieved by one of the subalterns, but before returning to breakfast I could not resist taking an hour's holiday and running down to the old German front line. There is a wonderful fascination in walking on ground lately shelled by one's own guns. In this case, however, scarcely a trace of the outline of the trenches was left. I could have picked up numerous souvenirs, but as they are always heavy to carry and invariably get lost sooner or later, I refrained.

By this time the Hun was again shelling rather severely, so as I didn't wish to become a casualty while joy-riding, I hurried back to the Battery and a most enjoyable breakfast.

The remainder of the day proved to be dull and uneventful.

LETTER NINETEEN.

IN A MARICOURT ORCHARD. (10TH JULY, 1916.)

*The Lull.   We Advance.   A Visit to Montauban.   Trones Wood.
The First Round.*

SINCE writing to tell you of the great 1st, we have moved our guns forward about 1,500 yards to this orchard on the northern side of Maricourt.

It was high time to make the move, too, as we were being enveloped in the advancing tide of "sausages", heavy Howitzers and other appurtenances of the rear.   Besides, life was becoming very dull from want of something to do.

I can't help comparing this great Somme attack to a man who tries to knock in a post with a sledge hammer which is far too heavy and unwieldy. Collecting all his energy he deals one mighty blow successfully, but from the sheer weight of his sledge he has to rest for several minutes before repeating the blow. Contrast that with a gang of navvies, dealing without a check a rain of shrewd blows each from a different quarter. How easily the post goes home.

The Hun never expected the attack to extend so far south as this sector, and, judging from accounts of prisoners, he was in an indescribable state of confusion on the night of the 1st and 2nd, when a determined further attack might have captured Trones Wood, Guillemont, and even Longueval, together with the Hun second line of defence.

Criticism, however, when one knows so little is very useless, so instead here goes for a description of our doings since the 1st ; as I said before, life since then has been a comparative rest cure compared with the previous four weeks.

The 2nd and 3rd were gloriously fine, and there was nothing to do except lie in the sun on the top of the O.P. and read what *Le Petit Parisien* had to say about the *Emotion à Londres*. There was practically nothing to observe. Our division took Montauban on the 1st, and on the night of the 2nd two battalions captured Bernafay Wood, so we held everything up to the skyline, with the exception of Trones Wood.

Bernafay Wood is about 1,000 yards long by 350 wide, composed of dense undergrowth and a hopeless tangle of brushwood broken by the bombardment. It was known to contain many short disconnected trenches, each with a garrrison of about a dozen men. So it meant a rough night's work with the bayonet, every one losing touch with his fellow.

However, by 11 p.m. the Wood was ours, and the various counter-attacks through the night were repulsed.

Before we moved forward on the night of the 6th, our valley had got out of range of the Hun field guns. The other signs of our advance were the fleet of 16 sausages which seemed to hang right over the gun-pits, and the brigade of 75's with their noses cocked high in the air, no longer blowing one out of the Mess with their blast when firing.

The Hun shelled aimlessly and not very fiercely all day and attacked on most nights without success : at least the S.O.S. rockets went up frequently, often for a false alarm. Each battery keeps its guns laid on the microscopic portion of the front it is responsible for protecting, and on the S.O.S. rockets going up a dense curtain of shell drops within 30 seconds.

We, being Howitzers, have, of course, many other night jobs, such as tickling up roads, railways, dumps and villages. Our infantry had very little house-to-house fighting in the ruins of Montauban, and the prisoners captured there were half-starved, as during the bombardment hardly any rations had reached them.

One Hun, however, did put up a great fight. From a hidden hole beneath a pile of masonry, he sniped away for thirty-six hours, killing at least seven of our infantry. Everything possible was tried to shift him, but fire, water, smoke candles and packets of bombs all failed. Finally the Engineers removed the whole mound with gun-cotton, so one never knew the secret of his dug-out or how he kept alive so long. A stout fellow!

We hear now that our division (30th) is the only one that performed the whole of its allotted task absolutely up to schedule time, and at a very low cost in casualties.

As a battery we, too, have been lucky, only losing one subaltern, two N.C.O.'s, and two telephonists.

My old friends the French 2nd Colonial Division have done very well south of the Somme, and we heard that by the 4th their African cavalry were within 4 kms. of Peronne. Despite their greater advance they have not captured as many prisoners as the French XXth Corps north of the Somme. However, I remember during the Frise show they were very economical in the number of prisoners taken:

they must believe in my creed that "The only good Boche is a dead Boche."

On the evening of the 5th we got orders to advance, and when the teams came up soon after midnight we moved forward and wedged ourselves into a tiny orchard-garden. It needed a good deal of wedging too, as there were batteries on either side of us, and our garden was only 60 yards long and 15 broad, with deep trenches on three sides, and a tiny narrow deep lane the only means of approach.

Luckily the Hun was not shelling near us, or else the move would have been an expensive one. However, by 5 a.m., we had got the guns there and plenty of ammunition beside them, and the next day, the light for observing being good, the guns were registered on the south end of Trones Wood.

Friday, the 7th, was a very wet day, so as things were idle at the guns Maclean and I went forward to study the Hun second line over the ridge, as seeing the country with one's own eyes certainly helps in unobserved shooting. On the way we went past German's Wood, over Glatz Redoubt into the village of Montauban. In the *Petit Parisien* of the 2nd July was the glowing headline:

"FOUR FAIR VILLAGES OF PICARDY LIBERATED FROM THE INVADER."

One of them was Montauban.

In the pleasant wars of by-gone days possibly lace-capped old ladies would have been sitting at the porch of their homes, waving their knitting needles to each passing "liberator" while the children gambolled on the lintels or wherever children ought to gambol. To-day this village at all events is not a pleasant place; it is almost impossible to trace the line of the streets, hardly a wall higher than a few feet still stands, and all around reeks with the indescribable stench of stale high explosive and unburied remains: the distilled spirit of death brooding over the whole hamlet.

During an extra heavy rain-storm we sheltered in a dug-out, formerly Battalion H.Q. of a Bavarian unit. The room was filled with papers and books, and it was interesting to read their typed reports of the effect of our bombardment up to the 26th June: after that, words (on paper) seemed to have failed them.

Later on we went to the northern edge of the village, and looking across Caterpillar Valley had a fine view of the promised land. How green and free from shell-holes it all looked! A long grassy slope led up to Longueval, a long pretty little town which was quite untouched, and behind it loomed the dense mass of Delville Wood.

We were back at the guns by 5 p.m., well smothered in mud from head to foot. How pleasant war in Napoleon's day must have been when they seemed to fight a desperate battle lasting a day or less, then during the next three weeks sat in a café of the captured city clinking their long spurs while they toasted fair ladies !

On the morning of Saturday, the 8th, at 7.20 a.m., we began a long bout of firing which went on till 3.30 p.m., on Sunday, with, for objective, the capture of Trones Wood. The whole of the day passed in a series of terrific bombardments directed at that accursed place. At first things did not go well, but by 1.15 p.m., we had captured the southern half of it, and by 6 p.m. the whole wood appeared to be in our hands, which brought our men within 500 yards of the German second line.

But all was not over then. At 11 p.m. the Hun made a strong counter-attack, preceded by an hour of intense bombardment. At the same time he deluged Maricourt and its neighbourhood with tear gas, and after severe fighting, succeeded in retaking a great part of the wood.

Confused fighting went on all night, culminating in another great bombardment between 4 and 5 a.m., when we regained some of the lost ground. Even the French words—*"Une lutte acharnée"*—fails to describe what a hell on earth wood-fighting in a pitchy black night can be.

LETTER TWENTY.

FAVIERE TRENCH. (17TH JULY, 1916.)

A Close Call.   Capture of the Second Line.   Good Sport in front of Trones Wood.

> Ubique means you've caught the flash an' timed it by the sound.
> Ubique means five gunners' 'ash before you've loosed a round.
> R. KIPLING.

IN my last letter I described the first round of desperate fighting for Trones Wood on the 8th and 9th. There were endless attacks and counter-attacks; bombardments and counter-bombardments by night and day until the morning of the 13th, when there was a lull before the final struggle that night.

I forget how many times the centre of the wood changed hands, but we never quite lost our hold of the southern end. The wood used to show up as a dense compact mass on the skyline, but after the appalling shelling it has got it is now only a tortured collection of stumps. The hostile gun-fire has been gaining in severity each day; every night we have tear gas and incendiary shells all round the village, and by day heavy shells of every calibre, even up to three 17-inch.

Our luck held good all the time we were in the orchard. Once, just after a gun had been pulled forward to permit improvements to its platform, a 5.9 landed plumb on the empty platform. Another time three gunners had a fairy-tale escape. Our dug-outs are merely little scratchings in a bank under a hedge, and on this afternoon I heard a dud land in the bank. On investigation I found it had gone through ten feet of earth (in the bank) into a dug-out where three men were lying; it passed over one man's back, slightly bruising his ribs, and came to rest with the fuse touching the clay of the far wall. Three scared men crawled out of their hole very speedily, and I looked and saw lying there a silvery 5.9-inch shell, polished by its passage through the earth.

No observing was possible for days, as all the skyline was in our hands, and our only target the middle of Trones Wood, so we used to go forward by turns to study the Hun second line. On the 11th

I sent Wilson and Macdonald to see if it would be possible to establish an O.P. in the north end of Bernafay Wood. They had a tough day. It took them three hours to reach even the middle of the wood, hampered as they were by incessant shell-fire, the heavy going and the impossible tangle of broken tree stumps. While working their way up a sap, they noticed a movement in a pile of about thirty bodies—chiefly Hun—and found one of the Manchesters, wounded in five places, who had been lying in that charnel house for three days and nights. The journey back to the south side of the wood, the search for stretcher bearers and the return journey to the wounded man, took another five hours' hard labour. On their arrival they found that the sap had been hit twice again by shells, and a tree had also fallen across the man, but luckily without crushing him. He was quite cheery and thanked them. Good luck to him! It was by that time so late that Wilson and Macdonald had to return without reaching their objective.

The morning of Thursday, the 13th, saw a pause in our firing, a lull before the great attack on the second system of enemy trenches, though before this attack could be launched Trones Wood had to be taken. At 5 p.m., with redoubled fury, we commenced shelling the centre and north end of Trones Wood, and at 7 p.m. our infantry advanced and succeeded in taking it at last. We continued bombarding the zone beyond the Wood until 1 a.m., but the enemy attempted no counter-attack. Soon after midnight we got orders that at 3.25 a.m. the 18th Division were to attack and capture the second line, and that the preparatory bombardment was to last for five minutes only. Accordingly, at 3.20 a.m., the whole world broke into gun-fire. It was a stupendous spectacle—the darkness lit up by thousands of gun flashes—the flicker of countless bursting shells along the northern skyline, followed a few minutes later by a succession of frantic S.O.S rockets and the glare of burning Hun ammunition dumps. Our fire continued at a rapid rate till 10.30 a.m., when we got news of the capture of the objective, and soon after, on the skyline west of Montauban, we could see the silhouettes of cavalry and horse artillery moving forward, a thrilling sight after the weary round of trench warfare.

Our orders to advance arrived at 5 p.m., and as our guns were not to move before dark, we were able to make some preparations at our new position, where we still remain. It is a loathsome spot on a flat plain, just beyond the third row of Hun trenches and about 200 yards east of the Briquetterie road. The ground is a succession of huge shell craters, which make the task of getting the vehicles up one of the utmost difficulty. It was a dirty night's work, as the area was being heavily shelled all the time, and for two hours we were absolutely blinded by a terrible dose of tear gas. The wagons had to make three trips apiece to get the ammunition forward, and despite the blinding gas, the drivers drove magnificently in and out of the 10-foot deep craters. In spite of all our difficulties we were well installed in our new position by 3.30 a.m. of Saturday, the 15th, and without any casualties, which was wonderful: the battery next door to us lost fourteen men killed, and also had some wounded.

During this hectic move, I got orders to lay a wire at once to Arrowhead Copse in order to commence wire cutting in front of Guillemont at dawn. Wilson started off in pitchy darkness with four signallers and three miles of wire to try and find the spot. However, he telephoned to me at 3 a.m. to say that the said copse was in enemy hands, and that he was settling down to observe from the S.E. corner of Trones Wood. At dawn he managed to get the guns registered, but the Hun shelling was so terrific that it was impossible to keep a line intact, although we had seven men at work on it, and at 2 p.m. Group H.Q. recalled all F.O.O.'s and we got orders to shoot by the map, but even so we lost two good men.

As we are again the right-hand British battery, the French infantry in support are beside our guns, and on our arrival I succeeded in bribing a party of them with a 100 "Woodbines" to dig a tiny dug-out for me on the firestep of their trench, roofed with three sheets of galvanized iron. The one bright spot about our position is the possession of two deep Hun dug-outs, in which the bulk of the men can sleep in perfect safety, and anything which saves labour and economizes energy is a blessing, particularly as the men were pretty beat after fifty hours of non-stop firing and digging.

One heard on all sides that it was impossible to keep a line going to Trones Wood, but unobserved shooting is very dull, and often, I fear, very ineffective, so accordingly, early next day, Sunday, the 16th, I started off with four of our best signallers, my intention being to relay the line up Faviere Valley, so as to secure, if possible, observation from the Trones Wood front line.

After about six hours' hard work we got a line carefully laid to our most advanced point, and then began one of the most amusing twenty-four hours I have ever spent. You know that when hunting one sometimes feels there will be a good run, so this day I felt we were going to have good luck and a successful kill. My first act was to locate a new enemy trench, very shallow and full of Huns; I sent down the map reference to the battery, telling them to engage it and if possible not to hit me, as I was lying out in a shell-hole in front of our line, and the target was barely 150 yards further on.

A really good "target" is only too often wasted, being merely frightened away instead of destroyed, so in order not to alarm the Hun I registered the trench with the minimum number of shells, and then, having informed Group, I also registered the 18-pdr. batteries of our brigade. It was a rather ticklish job shooting other people's batteries so close to our lines. That done, I phoned the officer at the guns to arrange a zero hour in five minutes' time, and then speedily crawled into a safer hole to watch the last act of the drama.

The trench meanwhile was as crowded as ever with quite unsuspicious Boches. Then down came the curtain. It was glorious to hear the shells of four batteries all at "gun-fire", swooping down close over one's head and to see the havoc they were making in the trench, a great portion of which we enfiladed. That wonderful story in the "Green Curve" came to my mind, and after four minutes of "gun-fire" I rang down to the guns, "It is enough." That diversion over, I registered my own guns and the 18-pdrs. on other good spots, leaving one 18-pdr. from each battery to tickle up the trench with occasional rounds. While all this was going on, the news of my shoot appeared to have caused a mild panic at Divisional H.Q., as according to their information my target was in British hands. Endless questions began to come down the phone as to whether I was quite certain they were Germans. I replied that as their principal pastime had been sniping at my head (until I pasted them), I had strong reasons for believing them to be the enemy.

The afternoon was a busy one, as Group sent down a mass of targets for me to register the different batteries on. Owing to the incessant Hun shelling, communication was difficult, and during the idle intervals while the wire was being repaired, I was able to move about and examine the country. How different it all is from the neat, orderly manner of fighting in pukka trench warfare. From a flank, during one of my explorations, I spotted some Huns in a trench leading directly into our front line : no one had noticed its junction with our trench, as the entrance was blocked with debris. The Hun also seemed unaware that his front door was open, and I joined the infantry in a most successful and amusing bombing stunt up the trench, establishing a blocking post half-way along it. During another tour I met a most energetic infantry brigadier, and we spent an enjoyable hour crawling round together.

Towards evening the rain came down in torrents, but I managed to borrow an overcoat from the body of a fairly clean-looking Hun officer who was lying near. The sunken road (our front line), leading below Maltz Horn Farm to the S.E. corner of Trones Wood is literally paved with dead Huns.

Having fired the various batteries right up to dusk, I decided not to return to the guns, so the telephone, my signallers and myself, passed the night comfortably under a tarpaulin. One of my reasons for staying away from the battery was that the infantry were rather expecting a counter-attack, and the sight of a gunner telephone seemed to hearten them ; for many hours, however, genuine communication with the guns being impossible, a loud bogus conversation down the useless phone had a heartening effect.

The next morning, just before dawn, the game began afresh with some shooting at Hun ration parties. For this purpose I used two of the 18-pdr. batteries, and a little later on, when the mist cleared, we had a second joint slam at the trench we disturbed so the previous day, and had another successful kill. Presently Maclean joined me with a relief of telephonists, and we had a succession of good targets till 10 a.m., when our line broke down for the umpteenth time. I then wended my way down Faviere Valley to the guns for a few hours' sleep, intending to return about midnight to my new and happy hunting ground at the corner of Trones Wood.

LETTER TWENTY-ONE.

FAVIERE TRENCH. (22ND JULY, 1916.)

The Loss of Delville Wood. Maintaining Communication with Trones Wood. Private Attack on Arrow Head Copse.

THE newspapers give pretty gruesome accounts of the appalling carnage round Trones Wood, so I need not enlarge on it: I spent six days out of the last seven observing from the front line at that place, and I can assure you the accounts are not exaggerated. It is a hot spot, and the Hun appears to have reinforced his artillery greatly, and fairly pours in shell; weeping gas and poison gas unite with the most appalling stench from the heaps of dead to form a combination very trying to the temper, especially when one is struggling to speak down a line which is being cut to pieces every ten minutes either by shell-fire or by the frantic digging of the infantry in their attempts to patch up a nightmare of a trench. The only balm is being able to see one's own shells really doing execution.

Soon after midnight on the 18th I went up to the Trones Wood sunken road to relieve Maclean. Dawn brought its usual harvest—a ration party falling an easy prey—then as the morning wore on the Hun shelling steadily increased, developing into a most terrific barrage, chiefly directed against Delville Wood. Early in the afternoon the enemy attacked and retook the greater portion of that wood. Our wire held fairly well, so it was possible to keep Group informed and to shoot five or six batteries on various good targets round Guillemont station. It was dirty work, however, as our corner was choking with gas. In the afternoon I handed over to Macdonald.

Returning to Group H.Q. at Maricourt, I got caught in the enemy barrage on the back areas, so it meant a stormy passage. Arrived there, I collected two reinforcements, one being a new subaltern, the other a promise from the colonel of two signallers from each battery in the Group to enable me to keep up the Trones Wood line. This line is the only means of communication with the front line that the division has got, but it is of course an expensive luxury and needs eight to ten men continually mending it—and my signallers were naturally becoming slightly tired !

Musson, the new subaltern, is a rancher from Central Argentine, a real good tough sort, and above all keen, but he could not have chosen a worse moment to arrive. It was a case of duck and dodge all the way back to the guns, and the cruellest blow of all was yet to come. Thirty minutes before dinner a 5.9 landed near our kitchen, and the cook went "looney" from shell-shock. After rushing wildly about he went to ground in a covered-in sap. No one could get him out. I tried to coax him out by crawling in with a biscuit, a sergeant grasping my legs to pull me out in case he bit me. Eventually we had to take the roof off, and he was tied up and sent off in a passing ambulance.

Hickey saved the remnants of our dinner and finished the cooking, though everything was covered with earth by the same shell which had done for the cook, or rather for his nerves.

This shell-shock is a funny business: no one can quite explain why it affects some and not others. I would describe the feeling as a severe "knock-out" blow on both sides of the head at once, and, having been twice during the last few days half-buried by 5.9's bursting on the parapet, I can claim a practical knowledge of it.

The night passed with the usual shelling, attacks, and false alarms, combined with the never-ceasing Hun firework display. However, for a change there was no gas-shelling. Before dawn on the 19th Wilson went off with the joint army of linesmen and relaid the line. He also posted linesmen in pairs in safe holes every 500 yards; thanks to this, the line held good all day, or, to be exact, was continually cut but as quickly repaired.

It is much less expensive to use a lot of linesmen, each pair being responsible for a small section. They get to know the danger spots in their section, and are not so likely to get into trouble as a pair of men working on the entire length of the wire.

Later in the day I went up with Musson and extended the wire round to the road leading from Trones to Guillemont, from where we could observe well, and had quite good sport. After experiencing an hour of concentrated shelling from my battery, a lot of Huns bolted from an isolated trench N.W. of Guillemont, and took cover in a wheatfield. It was no target for us Howitzers, so I phoned down and got three 18-pdr. batteries to reap that field with shrapnel. It keeps one quite busy shooting three batteries at once down one phone.

Towards evening hostile gas-shelling increased and made observation almost impossible. None of our linesmen got hit, but there was a lot of trouble all round, and the Bantam Battalion in the front line had a bad time.

Musson was top-hole, but being up there with him straight from

FIELD GUNS IN FRANCE

England, and with some decent feelings left, made one realize what a disgusting business war is.

On going back to report on the state of the Hun wire, I found our Brigade H.Q. had been crumped out of their house in Maricourt and had retired to Colonel Stanley's suite of dug-outs at the head of Maricourt Valley. I returned to the guns shortly before midnight and we fired vigorously till 3 a.m. in support of two night attacks.

At dawn (it was now the 20th) we started the barrage before the attack on the trenches near Maltz Horn Farm, and continued incessant fire till 2 p.m. It was a gloomy day—we attacked and failed—which did not surprise me, as the attacking unit had very heavy losses in the two days' previous fighting which took place all round my O.P. Maclean was observing that day : he and his signallers did very well in keeping the line going all day, and sent back a lot of information. I heard afterwards that during the second fruitless attack, Maclean finding two platoons with all officers killed, led them over the parapet himself into the open and attached them to the leading wave under Captain Gosling, who was the life and soul of the whole show, and was then rallying his men before making a final effort.

That afternoon I managed to get two consecutive hours of sleep, a remarkable event in these times. In the evening nearly all the batteries of my division were relieved, but we, being a Howitzer battery, were switched on to the 35th Division. No rest for the weary yet, however, and I fear the pace will soon begin to tell on all the men. We've only been out for one night at wagon lines since we came into action on January 11th.

Yesterday was uneventful till midday. At dawn I went up to the front line and spent my morning registering for the group. At midday my Colonel rang up telling me to locate, and if possible destroy, four dug-outs which the R.F.C. had spotted. He said that if I could not see them, I was to fire by the map. The latter course is, however, very dull and unsatisfactory, so I made up my mind to observe those dug-outs by some means or other, but it meant getting to a point far beyond our entanglements.

Our stock of telephone wire soon gave out, and we had to piece a line together from broken bits. There was not enough insulating tape for the joints and so we were forced to use bits of clothing from the dead Huns lying around—not a pleasant business.

When at last ready, together with my telephonist, I crawled without mishap through our entanglements and found a small two-foot trench, up which we went, still on all-fours, eventually succeeding in getting a good view of the dug-outs we were after. The patched-up line held for over an hour, during which time we put in a most satisfactory shoot. When at last it broke down, I went alone up the trench with the idea of reaching Arrowhead Copse, a tiny copse which lies about 400 yards in advance of our front line. Armed with a Hun spade and a No. 14 periscope, I did some cautious crawling, and by dint of careful listening made up my mind, when I got within 25 yards of my objective, that it was unoccupied. On arrival at the far side of the copse, I found myself almost behind the Hun trenches below Maltz Farm, and could look right into one trench, where there were sixteen Huns asleep, their rifles leaning against the trench wall.

I returned to my telephonists and found the wire still broken, so shell-fire was not therefore available for our sleeping foes. I then continued back to our lines, where I got helpers in the shape of two officers and a sergeant, also two rifles and a revolver, and, thus reinforced, we re-occupied Arrowhead Copse. We got the range exact off the map, and then one officer and myself took the rifles, while the other officer spotted with my telescope, and the sergeant, as soon as the fun began, busied himself by beating us on the back with a bayonet and shouting: "Give the Blighters Hell." It was a dry day, so we could see the dust of each bullet, and as we could enfilade the trench we gave them sixty rounds rapid fire, killing one and wounding some others before they cleared out of the trench. We did some sniping at heads also, but without further success, and then some Hun machine-guns made our place rather unhealthy, added to which our ammunition was running out, so I felt strongly that I should now return to my duties as a gunner, and therefore led a masterly retreat back to our lines without loss. From the sunken road in Trones Wood I got in touch with the guns and gave the Huns, who had dislodged us, fifteen minutes of the best from my own battery plus an 18-pdr.

It was another sleepless night, as, getting back to the guns by dark I immediately had to go to Group to report, which kept me till 1 a.m. After this I reached home, but had to sit at the phone till six o'clock in the morning, as we had to support two night attacks. And then to bed three hours later, only to be awakened after half an hour by the visits in turn of an officer from each of the newly-arrived batteries, who came to inquire about their respective duties in the upkeep of the Trones Wood line.

LETTER TWENTY-TWO.

FAVIERE TRENCH. (30TH JULY, 1916.)

Observing from the French Front. A French Section in Trouble. My Birthday Feast. The Battle of the 30th July.

SUNDAY, 23rd, saw another disastrous attack at Guillemont, a really unlucky day of heavy losses and no advance.

Macdonald had gone up at dawn with no less than fourteen linesmen, but even then communication was only possible in spasms. The Hun put down a terrific barrage, and the line had to be constantly relaid for the last 500 yards.

The linesmen worked well, though the trench was choked with casualties and was being continually blown in. One of them twice ran the gauntlet of rifle fire from 400 yards by jumping over the parados, and then laying a line across the open, where it was less likely to get cut than in the trench.

It was encouraging to hear later that the information sent back by our F.O.O. had been of the utmost importance to the Division, as it was the only news they had received of the fate of our attack which was launched at 3.30 a.m. that morning.

At 11 a.m. I got orders to go up to the 35th Divisional R.A. H.Q. to see the C.R.A. on various questions about the Guillemont area. There I was also told, if it were possible, to enfilade a hidden ravine strongly held by the enemy in the French sector opposite Hardecourt. But this operation, however, would entail moving a Howitzer right forward, with its trail towards the enemy, and shooting back over the salient into the ravine.

It was not an easy task, but I thought it might be just possible. The only gun positions from which one could enfilade the ravine were a point between Trones Wood and Bernafay Wood, and a spot on the north-west corner of Bernafay. Reconnaissance in the afternoon proved that the former point was quite untenable, being under direct machine-gun fire and subject to a continual barrage. By dusk, however, I had found a position that I hoped would answer our purpose, not far from the north-west corner of Bernafay Wood.

Owing to the heavy shelling, gas and broken ground, we had

endless trouble getting the gun and ammunition up, and one wagon actually got a direct hit on the pole. This shell killed one horse besides cutting the traces of the wheelers, the team then rushed off towards the Hun front line. Although three of them were hit in the interval, they were all eventually retrieved. In spite of all our troubles, however, we got things straight by midnight, with only two casualties—not bad considering the conditions—and leaving Maclean and a detachment in charge there I returned to the Battery.

After two hours' sleep I proceeded the next morning to Hardecourt, laying a line as I went. From there, a distance of 6,000 yards from the gun, I managed to register the ravine, and the gun started its weary task of searching day by day every inch of that ill-fated target.

It proved to be an unlucky day, as we lost men and horses at both positions, and both Stevens, the O.C. of the neighbouring Howitzer battery, and myself got knocked into a dug-out by a shell which burst beside us. As a result we felt pretty rotten during the night. Next day, the 25th, was comparatively quiet in the forenoon, so I took the opportunity of visiting the French O.C.'s of the 2nd Chasseurs and the 156th Regiment, to discuss the question of the ravine we were bombarding.

This ravine had proved to be the principal stumbling block in an abortive attack they made a few days before, so they were very anxious to make sure that it was heavily shelled before their next attack. I had intended to visit the F.O.O. in Hardecourt, but being still very shaky as a result of the shell incident on the previous evening, I had to return to the battery. I think that the daily dose of gas inhaled at the Trones Wood corner tends to rot one's inside.

Walking over this country is not a very pleasant pastime, floundering continually up and down the sides of huge craters, and being tripped up at every step by strands of half-hidden barbed wire. There was one exceptionally large crater which I measured : it had a circumference of 45 yards.

On the 26th, finding that I was restored to my usual state of good health, I visited Maclean and his lonely Howitzer at dawn. He had been slightly wounded in the neck, but was carrying on ; they all looked very red and blistered about the neck, having had their gas-masks on for seven hours during the night, besides encountering tear gas the rest of the time.

The aroma round that spot is really remarkable ; I counted thirty-eight men and fifteen horses lying dead between their dug-out and the gun. Being near the main road to Longueval, the spot is continually shelled, and passing units never have enough time to clear up any resulting mess. However, I heartened them with a promise to send up a sack of lime to sweeten the place. I spent the rest of the day at my O.P. in Hardecourt. The village had been taken originally by the Zouaves after desperate hand-to-hand fighting, and, judging by the state of the dead, they are certainly rather messy fighters.

Next day, the 27th, was a victorious one, our attack being on the whole successful. We fired furiously all day, while our F.O.O. was again the only source of information as to the progress of the attack. I spent the day at the guns myself, and hence did not hear much news.

On the 28th I went forward to see the advanced gun and found conditions even worse than on my previous visit. A French 75 mm. section had come into action not far from our gun, its objective being the same ravine. I went round to call on them and found them rather unhappy. Owing to the incessant barrage on the road they had not been able to get a line back to their battery, and thus had not received any orders or food for twenty-four hours; in fact, they felt thoroughly deserted and down on their luck. They had, however, esconced themselves in some wonderful dug-outs they discovered in a deep quarry, so I promptly moved my people up to live there too, and on returning to the back areas, I located their battery after much hunting. They seemed very glad to get news of their section, and eagerly accepted my invitation to run a line to my battery and to be made honorary members of our line both to Bernafay Wood and to the O.P. at Hardecourt. They soon got this done and then shelled the ravine vigorously all day, chattering like magpies to their guns the whole night, all of which could be heard as it passed through our exchange.

Saturday, the 29th, was my birthday, and it started well, as when shaving in my hole on the firestep, to my great surprise, Peter (Capt. P. S. Fraser-Tytler, who on 3rd August, 1916, was killed near Montauban) turned up with an army of signallers. He had come into action near Montauban the night before, and was anxious to make use of our line to get his Howitzers registered at once, so we devised a great telephone stunt. His men laid a line to the French battery, thus getting in touch with our exchange. Then we went up to Trones Wood, and had a most successful shoot.

He came back to join in my birthday dinner (our light cart had previously gone to Amiens to buy food and liquor suitable for the great occasion). Unfortunately just as we were starting, orders came in that I was to go immediately to Group H.Q., and so five courses and a bottle of champagne had to be gulped down in quick time.

I returned to the battery at 10 p.m., with the orders for the big attack next day, and we started making out the barrage tables for the guns. The Hun then commenced a very heavy and prolonged gas-shell bombarament, and I found working on a map with a gas helmet on was a job very trying to the temper. At 3 a.m., after a mouthful of tea and bacon, both tasting vilely of gas, I started off with Musson and two signallers to try and get to the French line. It was a pitch-dark night with dense mist ; often the gas hanging in the hollows necessitated wearing gas-masks, so we had a difficult walk over the wilderness of shell craters, but in the end managed to find our way. At dawn the mist still hung about like a London fog, so we waited at the French brigade H.Q. in Faviere Wood, and were thus able to phone back early news of the French progress.

By 7.45 a.m. all the French forward wires were broken, so as the mist was lifting I sent Musson back to the guns and pushed on towards the front line with my signallers.

Having repaired our wire as far as Hardecourt, we found that it now lay uncomfortably near a huge store of hand grenades, which had caught fire and were exploding at intervals like giant Chinese crackers. After an exciting five minutes of "duck and dodge", we succeeded in removing it to a safer bit of ground, and then at last reached the old front line trench from which the attack had been launched in the morning.

Observation was still a little obscured by the mist, and on first arrival at the crest of the hill it was difficult to sum up the real situation from the panorama of battle suddenly unfolded below.

I was just settling down to observe, when an excited French runner gasped out the surprising news that the French had already captured Falfemont Farm.

On questioning him as to the source of this information I learnt that it was contained in a message from the attacking troops, and that the runner had given it to an officer in an O.P. a little way down the trench. I hurried off immediately to see the news in writing, but, as bad luck would have it, a shell preceded me and burst right in the O.P. Then followed a desperate but unsuccessful hunt for the piece of paper among the very broken remains of two officers and two men.

Helped by my good glass, however, I was certain it was German steel hats I saw in the trenches round Falfemont, so I telephoned to the Group and heard the rumour about the capture of Falfemont had also reached them. In spite of the mist my observation convinced me that this news was wrong, and after a little difficulty and some argument I was given three batteries with which to engage the farm. I then set to work to give it a hell of a hammering. It was anxious work, but, after half an hour, I was delighted to see about fifty Huns bolt from the ruined buildings and make off down the hill towards Combles.

Soon after this the mist cleared off, and a marvellous picture was unveiled. The country around here is simply made for battle fighting : on the left could be seen the 160th Regiment attacking Falfemont, while the 146th and 153rd were streaming up the long grassy slope towards Maurepas—the village that crowned the hill. The French did well, but their flank had lost direction in the early mist, and the fighting was now very involved. There were groups of the enemy everywhere, and we engaged many good targets, for which in several cases I secured the services of two 18-pdr. batteries.

One of such targets was a battalion of the Prussian Guard that debouched from Leuze Wood and advanced in artillery formation to reinforce the Falfemont trenches. Our shells did good execution, but they still came on in rushes across the open, and reached the trenches, into which they disappeared from view.

Meanwhile the Hun was not being idle, and was directing a very heavy fire against the old French front line from where we were now observing, causing heavy casualties all round me. Eventually, as all the officers and N.C.O.'s in the trench were killed or wounded, I had no means of getting further news, nor was there anyone left with whom to check observations as to the progress of the attack.

At 4 p.m. Musson came up and relieved me, and by evening things had quietened down. We had, indeed, gained a certain amount of ground, but the confusion in the dawn mist marred the complete success of the attack.

But it was a wonderful day all the same.

LETTER TWENTY-THREE.

BOIS DES TAILLES. (2ND AUGUST, 1916.)

A Lucky Escape. We go out of Action at last.

ON July 31st, after the inferno of Sunday, we had the usual quiet "after battle" morning, and Corps Head-Quarters sent for me rather early to give them information about various points which were visible from the front line. While there, I heard the great news that we were to be relieved immediately.

I lunched with Peter Fraser-Tytler at his battery, and then went to see Victor Walrond, who commands a battery in the same division. On my way home the Hun started airing his famous 12-inch, 8-inch and 5.9-inch barrage, a very noisy and somewhat theatrical performance, but nevertheless it made the mile walk rather exciting. Making one's way under shell-fire across a maze of craters and old trenches quite alone always makes me feel foolish, as if one was unlucky enough to stop something, there would be little chance of ever being found.

Just as I reached the road behind my position three passing teams were done in by a single big shell. I finished off as many of the horses as I could with a revolver, which I took from a very erratic-shooting subaltern in charge of the teams, and then went on to the guns to send the men down into the deep German dug-outs for safety. The position was being intermittently shelled, and the extraordinary fascination of watching a much-frequented road being shelled by big stuff, always makes the men hang about in the open until hunted into cover, but one cannot afford unnecessary casualties in these days.

One section of the battery was due to be relieved that night. An orderly bringing a message had come up with two horses and was holding them beside one of the gun-pits. I was just thinking of sending them away, when I heard a close shell coming and jumped for safety into the mess which is at the bottom of a 12-inch shell-crater: merely a square hole roofed with a piece of green canvas. As soon as the shell had burst I looked out just in time to see a red lump rising out of a red pool. It was the horse holder! I pulled him into one of the trench dug-outs and started a party to clean him and then report damages. Extraordinary as it appeared, he was practically untouched, and he told them that he lay down with the reins in his hand when he heard the shell coming. The shell must have burst on the back of one of the horses, as there was no crater in the ground.

As soon as the shelling stopped, we began to clean up the place, finding one head, three legs and one hindquarters at distances up to a hundred yards, while the remainder of the two horses was in small fragments over the whole position. It was indeed an indescribable mess, which was soon surrounded by a dark cloud of bluebottles. The horse holder seemed quite unshaken, and, having been fitted out with clean clothes, went back on foot to the wagon line.

But the rest of the afternoon did not pass with the same good luck. Captain Stevens, O.C. of the next battery, on going out to the road with his revolver to finish off some more horses, got knocked over by a big shell, and although apparently quite untouched, he died of shock an hour later. He had always been a sufferer from a wound in the head which he received in the South African War. Then a few minutes later, Gibbs, commanding the battery in front of us, was fatally wounded while trying to get his teams out of the position.

It was altogether a very unlucky spell, and the week generally was most unfortunate for officers, and I am the only B.C. left out of the five neighbouring batteries. I remember I always used to say jokingly, that crawling about with a telephone in No Man's Land was really safer than staying at the guns.

Soon after dark a section of the relieving battery turned up. It was a North-Country Territorial battery, and they appeared to be a real good lot, and I am sure will do well once they have got acclimatized ; they have come from the other end of the line where peace has reigned since last September. Their total brigade casualties in seven months' fighting were nil, and we calculated that in the month of July our battery had fired exactly eight times the number of rounds they had fired in the whole of the last ten months. They got their guns in and teams away, just in time to escape a very severe two hours' shelling.

For the sake of fresh air I usually sleep more or less in the open, in an enlarged machine-gun emplacement ; I always intend to go into the telephone dug-out (an old 20 feet deep German stronghold) when heavy shelling starts, but somehow one gets incorrigibly lazy, and after all, if one is having good luck one might as well make use of it.

Next day (August 1st) was a stifling, almost tropical day, and I spent the morning handing over to my successor. I am afraid it is a terrible legacy : there was nothing good to show him. The gun position was literally smothered with bluebottles from yesterday's incident ;

there was a forward gun in a very dangerous spot and two distant O.P.'s with lines which needed ceaseless effort to maintain. We had a long and desperately tiring walk, first to Hardecourt, then to Trones Wood and eventually back by way of the forward Howitzer.

On the eve of departure one realizes more the foulness of the spots in which we spent so many happy hours fighting. Now all the jump and life seemed to have gone out of things, and there was nothing left but the appalling stench, the torn up ground, and the eternal cloud of flies rising in front, and giving a friendly hint to prepare to meet some fresh horror.

By the afternoon, as I had only one gun to get away, my army had dwindled down to myself, Musson, the B.S.M., and three men. It was like waiting to leave school, and we were all as nervous as cats lest some disaster should happen before we escaped. Our gun team and horses came up at 10 p.m., and the relieving gun arrived soon after. Poor people! their troubles had already begun, as their cook's cart, following behind their gun, had been scuppered on the way up. Musson and the others went off at once and I merely waited to send off the final message to "Group": "Have handed over position." Having dispatched it, I wished the B.C. the best of luck and galloped up the road to Maricourt. Even as I went I saw our red S.O.S. rockets rise behind Trones Wood and heard the roar of gun-fire reopening. In the streets of Maricourt there was the usual hopeless congestion. French traffic was moving every way at once under no sort of control, but we eventually burst our way through and reached our wagon line near Billon Wood at midnight. It was wonderful to see and smell once again fresh grass and trees with leaves on them, after a month in that dusty wilderness of a modern battlefield.

On 2nd August I rode over to the Bois des Tailles and spent a cheery morning with my Colonel, who with the remainder of our Divisional Artillery had gone out to rest there on the 20th July. It was an interesting ride, as the country has changed beyond all recognition. At a spot where one had to crawl on hands and knees before the 1st July, I found a full gauge railway with four sets of shunting lines and fat guns firing from the various trucks.

I was asked to come to a big feast at the B.A.C. Head-Quarters, and so, knowing the lateness of their hours, and remembering Jorrick's good advice, "Where I eats I sleeps," I sent back word for our battery to move up to the Wood. Besides, this position would be handier for the early start next day, when the whole Division were due to march back to even more peaceful regions.

LETTER TWENTY-FOUR.

ESSARS LOCK, BETHUNE. (15TH SEPTEMBER, 1916.)

Idle Days by Quiet Waters.

ON my return from leave in August, I found the battery still at rest in the wagon lines we had taken possession of early in August. Football, re-drilling, fishing on the canal which runs through our quarters, competitions of every sort, varied with teas and dinners in the more or less untouched town of Bethune, made the days go by very quickly.

Our main work is making horse-standings, rather unselfish labour, for we are pretty certain never to reap the reward of our efforts. Already the air is full of rumours about an immediate departure for a less gentle front. It is absurdly quiet all round here ; for example, a girl cycles every morning to our second line trenches selling the *Daily Mail* of the same day.

About a week ago, however, there was one nerve-racking day. The prize-winners from five divisions, all recently up from the Somme like ourselves, were sent by motor-bus to Merville to get their prizes, or rather their ribbons pinned on by the G.O.C. of the Eleventh Corps, General Anderson.

It was a tremendous affair in the Town Place, with massed bands, a battalion in hollow square, and all of us lined up in the centre. Colonel Walsh and I seem to have snaffled the only D.S.O.'s in our Division, and, to my horror, I found that, being the only Gunner D.S.O. there, I had to be the first to march up, and so had no one to imitate as to the procedure. It was over in two hours, and we got back to Bethune in time for a great dinner at the Bethune Club.

Every day is so much alike that I really can think of no more news.

LETTER TWENTY-FIVE.

NEAR FLERS. (30TH SEPTEMBER, 1916.)

The Somme Once Again. An Advanced Position. Mud.

HERE we are back in the old Somme, and in action once more. On the 18th we left our wagon line near Bethune and marched South, trekking every day until the 24th. An uneventful march, and I am glad to say there were no casualties in the way of horses. On the 26th we marched eleven miles, reaching Dernancourt rather late in the evening.

The traffic on the roads is wonderful; for the last ten miles it was exactly like marching down an endless Piccadilly on a busy day; our road was a "route nationale", so wide that it allowed three streams of traffic to pass; one endless wave of lorries, both British and French, guns, wagons, marching troops and dust beyond all believing. On either side of the road are interminable canvas towns, dumps, workshops, Y.M.C.A. huts, headquarters of the legions of A.S.C. and Ordnance Departments, not to mention Veterinary sections and aerodromes.

At midnight I set off with two guns to go up to our future position. Owing to the dense traffic our progress was very slow, but by 5 a.m. we were passing the spot where we had that single forward Howitzer in July. We then went up the long hill to Longueval into a sunken road on the west side of the town, where we relieved a section of the outgoing battery. After breakfast I went up to their O.P. in Switch Trench, that well-known trench which had been captured three days earlier. If anyone is sceptical of Hun losses he should visit that area.

The taking over of a zone is a very simple performance nowadays; formerly one had to learn by heart endless targets in a complicated maze of trenches; now there is usually only one line of trenches in sight and the targets are mostly "fleeting opportunities" in the open. We bombarded the Hun lines heavily all day, and at 2.15 p.m. our corps attacked. It was a very pretty show to watch. Our barrage was absolutely terrific, and except at one point, where the Prussian Guard argued for a few minutes with the New Zealanders, the assault became simply a steady advance. I could see the Germans bolting from their trenches while our men dropped on one knee to fire; the Huns that escaped the Infantry ran into our barrage and ceased to exist. We made quite a big gain in ground beyond Flers, and it was altogether a very satisfactory day.

Towards the end of the barrage a premature occurred in the breech of one of the out-going section's guns, completely destroying the piece, so that they had one less to drag out.

Next day, the 28th, my other section came up. Ours was really a thoroughly bad position with no accommodation, but as we were practically out of range, it was no use making improvements. The dug-outs were merely scooped out of the bank at the side of the road, and with a squeeze one could just lie down flat. A waterproof sheet pinned with old bayonets over the open side ensured that all the drip reached the inmate at night.

The debris of the battlefield is always extraordinary, and a sunken road like the one we were in has usually been the scene of some of the hottest fighting, so the whole place becomes littered with spades, rifles, bayonets, piles of unused bombs, machine-gun belts, S.A.A. bandoliers, haversacks, waterbottles, etc., *ad infinitum*, and enveloping all, is the eternal "Somme Stench".

The outgoing batteries had more or less buried over 120 Huns, but all rather less than more, so the lane is not very pleasant on a hot night. "Blue Bottle Alley" the men call it. But all the same one always feels fit down here on these rolling hills : the autumn air is like champagne, and but little sleep is necessary.

On the 30th September, we started preparing the position we are now occupying, and it is also a sunken road, running into the south-east corner of Flers. I was allotted a position in Delville Valley, wedged in amongst a host of other batteries, but in the course of my many long walks on the previous days I had found this place, and with great difficulty got permission from Group and Division to occupy it. It is very advanced, and everyone says that we shall be blown out of it immediately. We may be some day, but not, I hope, till we have done some good execution. In any case it is an enormous advantage being close up to the enemy and well away from other batteries.

During our days of inaction in the Longueval position I was able to crawl round our whole front and so learnt a lot, as that is the only way of really getting to know the ground. We came upon some marvellous dug-outs, in one of which there was accommodation for, at least, 20 officers and 300 men. It is wonderful to reflect that the Hun should have made them here, miles behind his own front line, and that, too, in the days when he must have considered his main front impregnable. Our guns never stop now for one minute either by day or by night, and the morale of the enemy infantry is, from all accounts, at a low ebb, while, on the other hand, it is a perfect joy to be in the front line with our men, and to see how confident and full of fight they are. One day, having taken shelter in a small sap, I came upon thirty-four dead Huns, nearly all with white rags tied to their wrists or rifles, which they meant to show as a sign of surrender to our advancing infantry, but they appeared to have been all killed by the creeping barrage.

On the 2nd October we moved the guns forward to our present position; it was a peaceful dawn, and we trekked up that much barraged road from Delville Wood to Flers without loss. Advances nowadays are hardly to Drill Book pattern: each vehicle wanders off on its own and makes its lone way forward. I brought up the rear on a G.S. wagon, clinging to a red plush arm-chair strapped on top, and the other officers went each with a gun.

Luckily during the last fine week we got up a colossal amount of ammunition, otherwise we should certainly have been in a bad way. The rain started a few hours after we had reached the new position, and continued without a break for three days and nights. For twenty-four hours the road was absolutely impassable, being completely blocked with about 80 vehicles stuck in the mud, many with their teams and drivers lying dead beside them, the Hun having shelled the road practically without cessation. In fact, the state of the track after the rain necessitated putting ten horses in a limber carrying only 20 rounds, which a battery can fire off in 60 seconds. Very soon it became impossible to get limbers up at all, and all ammunition had to be carried up on horseback, four rounds on each horse. Our surroundings generally are equally bad, everywhere round the guns and ammunition dumps is knee deep, while the banks of the road are so soft that it is very difficult to make anything except scoops for cover, and they also become rapidly filled with mud.

But to all this there is one great set-off—that here we appear to be quite immune from shell-fire. We are on a forward slope, in full view of Hunland on the ridge round Bapaume, and I am sure no Hun has yet suspected that anyone can be mad enough to have put a battery in such a place. Consequently the whole of the heavy shelling goes over our heads into the crowded Delville Valley.

It would be amusing to keep a list of the many lost souls who drift into our mess by the roadside. They turn up principally at night, seeking directions to reach some village, trench, dressing-station, dump, division, or even corps. This may seem strange, but even divisions are so packed together here and so perpetually changing, that half the world appears to spend its time looking for the other half, and so our light in a hole beside the road becomes a welcome beacon promising help and guidance to the wanderer.

FIELD GUNS IN FRANCE

In one of my expeditions I called at Guillemont station (now merely a mass of craters), to see Beckwith Smith at the Guards' Brigade Head-Quarters, but I found that he had gone off on some new job. I also came across the Howitzer Battery which was beside us in the Frise show in January, but Pask, Burke and Banks had all been killed.

When I am not shooting from the front line, I use a fairly good O.P. in Switch Trench not far behind the guns. It is very handy, but really, when in a great hurry, one can observe quite well by standing on the bank above the gun-pit, for we only pretend to be in a covered position.

The area around us is littered with deserted tanks and planes, but the latter are usually minus their engines. The tanks are a great source of interest, as we have never seen them before.

I often think that the German taxpayer does not get so much for his money in the way of shell-fire results as does John Bull. During all these years of shell shortage we all became extremely careful, accurate and economical in our ranging, and secondly, all our rounds are observed by officers and generally by B.C.'s, and I am certain that especially in this form of fighting, with no safe O.P., most of the Hun observing is done by their Unteroffiziere, whose work often displays a great lack of imagination. To be a good observer a man must look at things from the enemy's point of view, and try to think out what he himself would be likely to do if he were the target. Failing these powers of imagination, rapid killing cannot be expected. Oftentimes the enemy appear to be content to plaster with shells the same spot hour after hour, with the result that the world and his wife walk delicately round the troubled spot.

I posted to you yesterday a French Croix de Guerre which I got by post from General Nourisson, G.O.C. 39th (French) Division. The "citation" is not quite correct, however; they state our forward Howitzer had to cease fire, but this was not the case, as, though twice hit, it never got quite knocked out.

LETTER TWENTY-SIX.

NEAR FLERS. (11TH OCTOBER, 1916.)

The Shoot of a Lifetime.   Good Killing.   An Overworked Phone Line.

> Long was the morn of slaughter,
> Long was the list of slain,
> Five score heads were taken
> Five score heads and twain.
> R. KIPLING.

THE weather is better again and the roads, or rather the mud-tracks, are nearly dry, so all is *couleur de rose* once more. Indeed, I do not regret losing the stalking we would have had in Scotland so long as the sport here keeps up to its present level.

On the morning of the 8th I heard that the Division was desperately anxious to get direct observation on some trenches in a little valley in front of Gueudecourt, the reason being that the machine-gun fire from this hidden valley had done much to upset our last big attack on the previous day. It meant, however, observing from the front line in Gueudecourt, and the infantry reported that it was impossible to get there by daylight, so they attempted no communication with the companies holding it except by runner at night.

Very often a locality gets a reputation like that which is handed down from one relief to another, just like giving a dog a bad name; on the other hand, I felt sure that once there I would get a grand view of the valley we wanted to pound, so accordingly in the afternoon I started off with my signallers and laid a cable as far as two blown-up tanks. The newspapers were full of one of these tanks. It knocked out a whizz-bang battery, but was itself destroyed by the last remaining Hun gun, which the gunners ran out of its pit, and from there hit the tank with direct fire at point-blank range.

Leaving one of the signallers at the tanks, we started off across the open trailing a D3 cable as we ran. We had to get through a nasty lot of Hun shells, but reached the shelter of the village safely, where we found an entire troop of cavalry horses all killed, apparently while waiting during dismounted action in the attack which captured the

village about ten days ago. We were just working our way through the
ruined village when, without the slightest provocation, the Hun
infantry had one of their frequent afternoon panics and sent up
S.O.S. rockets; within three minutes down came their 5.9-inch and
8-inch barrage. These barrages always ran on the same line—usually
close behind our front line—with the idea of preventing supports
coming up, and we happened to be in the centre of the cyclone. It
was some hot corner! Just before our cable was cut in about a thousand
places I managed to speak to Wilson, back at our O.P. on the ridge
behind the guns, and told him to give the Huns two hundred rounds
quickly, as we seemed to be in for it and might as well have a "good
send-off". He could see the turmoil from the O.P. and certainly never
expected us to win through alive; it was quite the hottest shop
I had ever been in. However, at last, with much ducking and dodging,
we worked our way back to the tank, and from there to the battery.
After that repulse it became a point of honour with us to get the score
levelled up. Therefore soon after 2 a.m. that same night off we started
again, the party being myself, Maclean and six of the best telephonists.
Eventually we reached the tank, but looking for it in that pitch dark
night in a wilderness wherein we climbed up and down what seemed
like an everlasting series of vast craters was like a mouse trying to find
a particular grain of oats in a steam-ploughed twenty-acre field.

Having at last found the tank, three signallers were left there and
made responsible for the line back to the guns and also for station
duty. From the tank we started across the open, laying two parallel
wires, as it was hardly a place where it was safe to mend the line during
the daylight, in spite of our luck in escaping yesterday. Guided by
the smell of the troop of dead horses we soon found the point of entry
into the village, where we rested for a bit. It had been a tough
walk, and dodging intermittent night shelling is trying work. The
everlasting stumbling and treading on "things" in the dark is very
unpleasant, and whenever one dived into a crater to escape a close
shell it generally resulted in the discovery that some noisome horror
had already made its home there.

By 5 a.m. we had reached the front-line trench near the desired
point, but it took us nearly an hour longer to work down the narrow
trench, as stretchers with wounded were being carried up it. They were
some of the results of the abortive attack of the 7th, and could only
be rescued from No Man's Land during darkness. When we at last
reached the spot from which I intended to observe we tacked on the
telephone and got a reply from the battery immediately. It is an
exciting moment when the earth pin, usually an old bayonet, is
driven into the ground; the next minute one will know if all is well

or whether somewhere behind the line is hopelessly broken ! The battery had been "standing to" and the first salvo went over my head within thirty seconds. In these stunts I register in salvoes at high speed as many targets as possible. If the line is then cut the officer at the guns can still shoot with confidence throughout the day ; if, however, the line continues to hold I re-commence and register each gun more accurately.

On this morning, after registering my old battery, I had my old job of doing the same for 18-pdr. batteries. Directly, however, I got busy with the latter task, a bout of Hun shelling cut our cable, and while it was being repaired we managed to boil some cocoa for breakfast. By 7 a.m. the line was once more working, and I left Maclean to carry on the registrations while I explored a new sap which had been dug that night ; while there I noticed something move amongst a big heap of dead, and found it was one of our men moving his head. An infantry sergeant beside me wanted to go over the parapet to bring in this poor fellow, but I persuaded him to wait until I could sprinkle the Hun trenches with shrapnel in order to discourage possible snipers. Back I hurried to the phone and soon wound up the clock in the shape of two 18-pdr. batteries ; after that two of the infantry went "over the top" and fetched in the wounded man without difficulty. He looked as if he might recover.

Our searchers looking for wounded in No Man's Land at night have great difficulties to contend with. The wounded men sometimes have just enough strength to cover themselves with a waterproof sheet, and by crawling into a hole get mistaken for the dead, who lie very thickly in the valley.

So far I had seen very few Huns in the front line, but when shelling further back I detected an uneasy stir of heads in a mass of trenches, or rather connected shell-holes. By careful spying I soon found that the bulk of the enemy hid there during the day. Thereupon I warned the 18-pdr. batteries to be ready, and shelled the spot hotly with my own guns. In the first five minutes alone 170 rounds were fired—not bad for four Howitzers. The Huns stood it for about five minutes, but then lost their heads and started to bolt in every direction. There was no connected trench up which they could escape, so the 18-pdrs. were then turned on and for nearly forty-five minutes we converted that torn hill-side into the best imitation of Hell that one could want to see. The Huns were now throwing away their rifles in every direction, and scattering as fast as they could move, and all the time we were only about 400 yards off, while the Division on our right was 200 yards nearer to them still. All along the parapet our Lewis gunners were sitting up and doing their share too. The wretched victims had

FIELD GUNS IN FRANCE

to run for it over 500 yards before reaching any cover, and very few escaped. The men were delighted; they do appreciate front line observation, and as they had had a rotten time in the trench during the last few days they were only too pleased to get a bit of their own back. Amidst the general panic there were, however, three really brave men, who stood up in the open, regardless of our intense shelling, trying to rescue some half-buried comrade. It cost them their lives, however. It really was the kind of shoot one meets only in dreams.

In due course came the inevitable retaliation, during which I moved the telephonists forward as close as possible to the now empty Hun trenches and boiled more cocoa in comfort, while the enemy raged against the empty village a hundred yards behind our front line: the infantry, in fact, did not suffer at all. Our cable was now, of course, cut beyond repair, so waiting till the worst of the storm was over we got home with a few close shaves. We got back earlier than I intended, but all the batteries of our Brigade were now registered, so the tap could be turned on whenever wanted.

Next day Wilson managed to relay the telephone line to a spot which could be reached comparatively easily by daylight, and from where there was a sufficiently good view of the Hun valley, now that we knew exactly where the trenches lay. Our General (Geoffrey White) and Lanyon, the Brigade Major, came to lunch, which being translated means that they sat on the sandbags outside my hole in the road and ate their own sandwiches. Having learned about the killing yesterday, they wanted to hear further details, amongst others, how I managed to raise a Croix de Guerre in such an unexpectedly direct way from the French!

Bombardment orders for a big show on the 12th came in that night, and the entertainment itself started at 7 a.m. next day (the 11th). I went up to a new O.P., which Wilson had skilfully chosen the previous day, where I had a very "temper-trying" time. Arrived there, to my horror I found that all three Brigades wished to be made honorary members of our line, so as soon as I had finished registering our own guns and those of our own Brigade on the initial bombardment line of attack, I had to start registering each battery of the other two Brigades. A subaltern had been sent up by each Brigade, but as they had not seen the country their services were not of great value, and it took a long time getting the whole lot approximately registered. If a battery was clean off the target they were told to have another attempt at working out angles and range, and meanwhile the next battery was taken in hand.

Our telephonists do enjoy these days, and bully the other batteries' telephonists down the phone if they are slow or stupid. All the batteries, of course, have different code names, and when shooting several batteries at once to save time the conversation is something like this :— "Prawn, one deg. more right, repeat," "Pilchard, drop seventy-five, one round battery fire," "Prune, what the Hades are you doing ? You have gone clean off the target !" "Sprat, shorten your corrector four points," etc., etc. It is exactly like a busy afternoon in the American market on the Stock Exchange, when New York is in a panic.

Every time that we come into a new position I say to my signalling officer, "We'll only put out two lines, one to O.P. and one to Brigade." In about three days, however, one finds a mast outside the telephone dug-out simply covered with incoming cables, and it seems quite hopeless to try and keep the number down. Yesterday, for example, four batteries and two Brigade H.Q. ran us direct lines so that they can chat straight to us when they want to be helped by our ever-moving front line O.P.'s.

It must be very unhealthy in Hunland now ; during last night, we—only one battery, a mere drop in the ocean—fired six hundred rounds up and down one road. Indeed, from what one hears from prisoners, very little food appears to reach the Hun front line at all these days.

LETTER TWENTY-SEVEN.

NEAR FLERS. (17TH OCTOBER, 1916.)

The Attack of the 12th October. Rainbow Trench after Our Bombardment. Dawn Explorations. The Gueudecourt Saps.

> They made a pile of their trophies
> High as a tall man's chin,
> Head upon head distorted,
> Set in a sightless grin.
> R. KIPLING.

WHEN I last wrote, we were in the middle of a two days' strafe, and the bombardment continued all the night of the 11th and the morning of the 12th, the attack being timed to start at 2.5 p.m. On such days I always observed from the ridge behind the guns, where all the other batteries have their O.P.'s, from there one gets a general if rather distant view; it would be useless to attempt front-line observation, as it would be impossible to keep a line going owing to the Hun counter barrages.

Just before zero hour everybody comes up to Switch trench. It makes a splendid grand-stand, and as the batteries have already all the endless lifts and alterations in range, we at the O.P. are simply spectators. I have seen many of these zero hours, and they get more stupendous each time. Often there is a lull during the last five minutes; then at the appointed second the whole world seems to explode. It is impossible to exaggerate what Hunland looks like on these occasions, erupting as it were in one vast volcano! Then the endless Hun S.O.S. rockets ascend and down comes a Hun counter barrage, followed by a period in which there is nothing to be seen except whirls of flame-stabbed smoke, incendiary shells bursting, and more rockets.

On nearly all these occasions one sees parties of Huns rushing towards our lines. They always look the same, bodies bent forward, heads low, and arms held out in front of them. Generally speaking, however, by the time they have negotiated their own counter-barrage they are somewhat diminished in number. The turmoil goes on for about an hour, then things get a little quieter, and everybody asks for the next few hours "Who's won?" At first no one ever knows anything. In our very advanced position we usually hear the news first, from the wounded and prisoners dribbling back. When it grows dark, more prisoners and walking wounded pass by, and the first of the stretcher cases begin to be carried down ; then endless long Indian files of supports going up to reinforce or to relieve, and long chains of ration parties with water in petrol tins.

Often the enemy thinks we are going to attack again and sends up lights and rockets to see what we are doing—we send up rockets to see why he is sending up rockets—the Hun starts a barrage on the right—more rockets of every colour—and finally everybody bursts into gun-fire together, merely because other people are firing. The whole of France seems to be made of gun-flashes and darkness, and everybody asks "What is it all about?" Batteries begin automatically to slow down till at last the order goes "Empty guns, cover up," and another false alarm is over ! You will notice that I never say anything about the result of all these attacks ; one's own knowledge is so limited that it is best to leave that to the newspapers.

In this attack, I heard from the infantry that Rainbow Trench and the others in the valley on which all the batteries had been registered were captured practically without a casualty. On the evening of the attack I met a German officer prisoner, complete with Iron Cross, near our guns, and on learning that he was from the valley itself I had a long talk with him. He told me that when the whistle went at 2.5 that afternoon he had exactly ten men left in his company. I can quite believe his statement, as our own infantry reported that the trenches were packed with dead, and two subalterns of mine who at dawn next day went round to discover our new front line confirmed this. It is rather gratifying, and tends to level up one's accounts with the Hun. The next few days were passed in observing with moderate success from various parts of the front line.

On the 15th, having got a telephone message from Division asking for some information about a new Hun trench, I went out before dawn to find it and had quite an amusing prowl round the front. At dawn both sides very often prance about on the lid, getting water up and looking for wounded, and in the uncertain light it is rare to find oneself the target. At one point in my walk I came across some Huns a few hundred yards off bringing in wounded, so I concluded I was pretty near the "War," and on turning back I found that I had wandered far ahead of our own forward posts. However, I at last found a spot whence a good view of the new trench was obtainable, and on my return to the battery Wilson went out with a line and registered the Brigade on it just in time for a big bombardment, which was due

FIELD GUNS IN FRANCE 117

at 1 p.m. How dull we shall find pukka trench warfare when every trench is marked down on a perfect map, and everyone knows exactly where the opposite side is instead of having to go forward and hunt for one's own prey!

On the evening of the 15th, I got a new job from Head-Quarters which proved of great interest. To the north of Gueudecourt there is a collection of Hun saps and strong points, based on an old gun position, the whole lying in a curious salient surrounded on three sides by our trenches. As a consequence, the Huns were entirely immune from our routine harassing fire, and the only spot from which one could dare engage this intricate target was our own forward saps—not a very easy place to get to. Division was very anxious to have this area severely hammered, and promised me an infantry guide who would show me the way up that night. Accordingly, soon after midnight we started off, laying our cable as we went, hampered by the pitchy dark and desperately deep going. All went well till we were half-way up the valley N.E. of Flers. I thought our guide appeared to be rather hazy, and presently, on being pressed, he admitted having lost his way. Fortunately one of the signallers recognized a deserted tank which we had been using for an O.P., so taking a bearing on that, we started off again. This time the guide followed behind, and with a certain amount of good luck we reached the company we were looking for. As our front line trench is not continuous, it is quite easy at night to walk straight into the enemy's hands. When it grew light, I was able to see the Hun steel hats in considerable numbers in various holes in the little salient, and registered our Brigade on to this point; that done, the officer in charge of the guns fixed a zero hour, and we gave them twenty minutes of concentrated shelling with all four batteries. From our trench we had a splendid view, and the infantry enjoyed it immensely.

When observing from such places, I always get on to the officer at the back O.P. behind the guns and tell him to find a "witness point". The French use the witness point (*point de témoignage*) a great deal. Roughly speaking, it means that the officer at the back O.P. picks up the stump of a tree, a lump of white chalk or any other landmark, as close as possible to the hidden target. Any day afterwards, by ranging on the "witness" point first, one can then engage the difficult target with accurate unobserved fire from the back O.P., instead of having to spend hours getting up to some forward sap. It is naturally a more accurate method than ranging and switching from an ordinary zero point.

The weather keeps fairly dry but very cold; however, living as we are, almost in the open, with a minimum of washing owing to the water shortage, one does not feel it very much. We are not having so strenuous a time as during our first innings in the "Somme Battle". The days are getting shorter, so one has not got the endless hours of observing. In battle fighting, one is either up to one's neck (and often over it) in trouble, or else there is really almost nothing to do.

We are doing a roaring trade in our wagon line canteen. On arrival at Montauban, my captain found that there was a clear field for enterprise ; action was immediately taken ; a G.S. wagon and an infantry S.A.A. cart were collected from the Flers road. The whole road, I may say, is littered with vehicles, as when a team gets scuppered many units don't seem to trouble to remove the men, let alone dead horses or vehicles.

Our new acquisitions go back each day to a big canteen near Méaulte, and during the two hours that our canteen is open for business we take between two and three thousand francs daily. There are seven sellers besides an Orderly N.C.O., who is deputed to keep the queue in order. The profits, of course, go to the battery fund for the benefit of the men.

LETTER TWENTY-EIGHT.

NEAR FLERS. (24th OCTOBER, 1916.)

Rain and Mud. More Front Line Observing.

Ubique means the crazy team not God nor man can 'old.
Ubique means that 'orse's scream which turns your innards cold !
R. KIPLING.

MY last letter carried on to the 17th. On the 18th, we attacked again at 3.45 a.m. and fired without a pause all day. The same evening it started to rain, and for thirty-six hours without a break the skies did their worst, so a description of our doings on a really wet day might amuse you.

Maclean and I sleep in the mess, and we woke up to find a vast pool at the ends of our bed bags ; also, as usual, the trench outside had had a landslide, which on this occasion thoroughly blocked the exit from the mess. After breakfast we waded about in mud over our knees, trying to repair things. The back of No. 1 gun-pit had fallen in, half-burying the gun, and No. 2 pit seemed to have bred a spring during the night and was nearly a foot deep in water. We spent the morning rescuing ammunition from the worst of the water and patching up the dug-outs and gun-pits. Hickey, my servant, and I baled out the mess with cigarette tins, and dug a sump hole under the table to collect the water. As it did not clear up in the afternoon, we did a little blind shooting at registered targets, and then I walked over into Delville Valley to see Major Stanley (A/150), and found him in an even worse plight than we, as besides the mud, they had been heavily shelled all day. At tea-time either we attacked the Hun, or the Hun attacked us somewhere close on our left flank. Universal gun-fire at once started, but dwindled to normal after about an hour.

A new subaltern came up to the guns that night, J. M. Bevan. He seems very capable and a good sort ; it was a good evening for his arrival. The rations came up in a S.A.A. limber, and although it was a light load for four horses, they managed to get finally stuck four hundred yards from the guns. Musson took some men down and unloaded it, but as bad luck would have it, soon after a close shell made the horses plunge, and the horses and empty limber capsized into a vast crater which was filled with liquid mud. After three hours' work they rescued the horses, but the vehicle had disappeared into the muddy depths of the crater. To make matters worse, while on their way back carrying the contents of the cart, one of the men got stuck in the road, sinking up to the waist in a shell hole, and it needed a passing ammunition mule and a drag rope to 'yank' him out. Incidents like this are of daily or rather nightly occurrence.

As the night was pitch dark and a big relief was taking place on our front, we had more than our usual share of inquiries from lost souls wandering hopelessly about the country. That night I left before dawn, meaning to reach our forward saps by 7 a.m., but our cable was broken in numerous places, so we had to lay it afresh for the latter half of the journey; besides that worry, a new breed of snipers seemed to have come into existence, and at a certain point, where hitherto we had always strolled across the open in peace, we were briskly fired at. The going was really bad, and one was literally waist deep in mud in the trenches for the last 600 yards, and we found two infantrymen completely overcome with exhaustion and stuck in the mud half-drowned. You can therefore understand how it sometimes takes two or three hours to do a journey of 3,000 yards.

While waiting for the line to be mended I tried to do some observing, but the Hun was disgustingly aggressive and would not permit any lengthy observation over the top of the parapet. It was a temper-trying job avoiding snipers, and by the time the line was made good, mine was worn threadbare. However, I could see clearly that the saps and trenches opposite us were very full indeed of Huns: their tall square steel helmets glistened in the sun, and it is easy to spot and count numbers, especially from here, where we are looking down upon them.

Eventually I informed Head-Quarters that I was going to fire double my daily ammunition allotment, as the target warranted it. The 18-pdr. batteries were out of the hunt after the first ten minutes. Having just been registered by a Hun 'plane they became targets for a heavy dose of 8-inch, so they naturally ceased fire to avoid unnecessary casualties. My battery therefore hammered away alone at the trenches for an hour and a half, and after ten minutes all desire to snipe at us ceased.

Early in the afternoon the Hun started his usual afternoon barrage, and the line, of course, got cut beyond repair. To keep a line going much after 11 a.m. is not usually possible, but to-day the enemy were late in starting. While waiting up at the same spot I suddenly heard an intense bombardment from about ten of our batteries; the shells fell on Stormy trench and the other trenches in front of us, but I thought that it was just a combined "hate" and though surprised at the intensity of it, I did not take much notice at the time. As our wire was hopelessly broken I determined to make my way back to the battery, a journey which took over two hours. The reason was that at 4 p.m. the Hun put down a real close barrage, including a lot of "squashed laurel leaves" (as we call his new poison gas) which forced us to put our helmets on for a good long while. Soon after our batteries started firing on S.O.S. lines, and it was not till late in the evening that I heard the history of the afternoon bombardment.

My simple statement that I had seen a good target had been magnified, as messages so frequently are, into, "All trenches near Stormy trench are massed with Huns." So the Group had turned on the tap with a vengeance at 3.30 p.m., and, as it happened, it was quite sound, as at 4.30 p.m. the Hun made a half-hearted attack. He had evidently planned quite a big show to regain the Gueudecourt trenches, but the heavy losses he must have had during our bombardment took all the ginger out of it, and our men repulsed the attack quite easily. It was fortunate in the end that the telephone line had remained broken, for if I had been asked I would certainly have contradicted any idea that the Hun was about to attack.

On the 23rd we got very urgent instructions about another combined "Strafe" on the Gueudecourt saps to be carried out at all costs before 1 p.m. Maclean went off at dawn, and owing to the dense fog was able to relay the line without getting into the communication trenches, which were still waist deep in mud. The line was through once more by 7 o'clock. The Irish were still in the front line, so it suited a wild Ulster man like Maclean.

Owing to the fog, visibility was limited to about 100 yards, but, as it was one of our "special" mornings, he went forward into No Man's Land with one signaller and the telephone, and creeping steadily forward at last saw the German saps, and from a shell-hole was able, despite the fog, to direct a successful shoot. While he was making the return journey across No Man's Land we speeded up our fire to five salvoes a minute, which discouraged any sniping activity on the part of the enemy.

By "special" mornings I mean mornings when communication must be secured at all costs. On such days I usually take out quite an army of signallers, and then drop them in pairs in various shell-holes all along the cable; they tap their telephones on and as long as they can speak to a station on either side of them they can remain where they are, more or less in safety. If the line breaks, however, it means that they must go out, often to encounter a damnable barrage (as the line does not break for nothing), and make it good. On other mornings, when one is only going out on a normal shoot, it is an understood thing that they can wait till the worst of the storm has blown over before going out to repair the line.

With our worn guns and three different sorts of powder, all of which is more or less damp, it is impossible to expect accurate shooting by paper calculation, however carefully one may work out atmospheric and all other corrections. Consequently we are now great believers in jamming our noses as close as possible to the target, loosing off a salvo, and then to business.

As our forward position enables us to haunt the front line and do all this wiping-out of nests of Huns hidden in shell-holes, we have been relieved of the ordinary routine of harassing fire by day and by night. This means that we are able to reserve the whole of our ammunition allotment for really good targets.

LETTER TWENTY-NINE.

MONTAUBAN. (28TH OCTOBER, 1916.)

Shell-hole Fighting.   The Finger of Fate.   Back to the Wagon Lines.

SINCE writing the last letter much has happened, and we are back in our wagon lines for a few days' rest. I see Beach Thomas points out in the *Daily Mail* what an important part "shell-hole" fighting plays in the autumn campaign. Round here it is impossible to pick out which is trench and which crater. The country in our hands is even more ploughed up than Hunland. This makes our front line extremely difficult to locate, and as I feel positive that the Hun rarely observes from close up, the result is that our forward saps escape shelling to a great extent because they have never really been discovered amid the wilderness of craters.

All the fine sport we have been having since September is due to the same cause. From our front line with a strong glass one can locate nearly every day some new nest of Huns esconced in shell-holes. These they enter at night probably keeping their front line relatively empty, and thus avoiding the ordinary unobserved harassing fire. There is no escape for the inmates of these nests except across the open. I told you how we always work together as a brigade and how the 18-pdrs. are invariably ready to join in any shoot. The procedure is always the same and is a simple one ; I send down the map square of the newly found nest to the officer at the guns. He lobs over a shell or two till one can get the exact registration. He then phones to "Vixen and Stoat" (18-pdr. battery code names), and gives them the exact map reference as found by the shooting of my gun.

As you will realize, in this ploughed-up land there are no landmarks, and the first map reference is, of course, only a rough and ready one. The 18-pdrs. having been registered also, the officer at the guns fixes a zero hour for a simultaneous opening of the three or four batteries. In the interval before the shoot starts, one hunts round, if the target is close, for a rifle wherewith to join the infantry in taking pot shots at winged Huns bolting out. The whole thing is over very quickly.

The only drawback to my "ever shifting" O.P.'s in forward saps is the difficulty of getting there, and sometimes one finds on reaching a place before dawn that one has jolly well got to stop there till it grows dark before any attempt to leave is possible. On one occasion I remember being very hungry, and not wishing to be pinned down in a shell-hole till dark, I phoned to the battery to sprinkle our immediate front. In this way, under our own barrage, we bolted back across the open—our objective being lunch.

We had endless work collecting sufficient wire from every possible source, legitimate or otherwise, to meet our needs, as frequently we had to lay new lines every day, the old ones being destroyed or buried in mud. The spare men in the wagon line were constantly sent out into back areas with empty drums to collect some of the miles of spare wire that is strewn all over the country.

To resume my diary, on the 25th, Major Stanley and I went up before dawn to the forward saps and had another most successful joint shoot. On returning to the Battery I saw an ominous sign— four huge new craters—and realized that we had been registered by an 8-inch howitzer battery. On the previous days hostile aeroplanes at a low altitude had circled round our position, and it looked as if our number was up. However, next day, on the 26th, I again went up to the happy hunting ground and had an extremely busy morning. I noticed a fresh collection of nests of Huns dug into the banks of a sunken road which ran up the hill away from our lines. As usual their only way of escape was to bolt across the open where the road, no longer sunken at this point, crossed the skyline. One 18-pdr. battery which covered the open space caught the Huns as they bolted out, while the remainder of the brigade searched up and down the sunken road.

Exactly at 12 noon, while this interesting shoot was still under way, a Hun 8-inch battery, evidently directed by an observation balloon, commenced to shell our positions, and, after about four rounds short and over, they got the range of the road, and then the trouble began. Trouble only for material however, because we had made every plan for evacuating the position, as we knew that sooner or later we would get knocked out. We had already fitted up an emergency telephone exchange in a dug-out, which was two hundred yards to the flank of the battery, and where there was also accommodation to shelter all the men. At an order from the officer at the guns every man left the doomed position and assembled at the flank dug-outs, the limber gunners carrying their dial sights, and everybody else their most precious belongings.

From my O.P. in the front line, I could see the fall of every shell in the position, and the exploding one by one of our many ammunition dumps. The signallers, before evacuating the telephone dug-outs, plugged me through to the 18-pdrs., so I was able to carry on the shoot with them, until the line was eventually cut. When that happened, nothing remained except to go down into the Infantry Coy. Head-Quarters dug-out and have luncheon with them, while my telephonist, watching the position through a telescope, was able to shout down the stairs and inform me when each gun-pit or ammunition dump went west. I know the infantry thought me most cold-blooded, but there was nothing else to be done, and I knew the battery would look after themselves.

After the usual two hours' struggle through the mud I got back to the battery, to find everybody busily engaged in attempting to clear up the mess. I forgot to mention that the bombardment lasted just over an hour and a half, in which time the Hun fired 120 8-inch shells. His shooting really was wonderful, but luckily he had mistaken for gun-pits two large ammunition dumps to the flank of the battery, and therefore his fire only extended over one half of the position. Every ammunition dump except one had been blown up, No. 4 gun-pit had been hit three times—the gun literally had disappeared. No. 3 gun-pit was empty, its inmate had been slightly damaged the previous day and sent back the same night. It got hit twice, and all the men's dug-outs had been completely destroyed. The officers' mess and telephone dug-out were the only ones that escaped. The sunken road itself had been hit about twenty times, and it was impossible for any vehicle to pass along it.

Our position being now known to the Hun, it was no use attempting to carry on the game from that spot any longer, so we got orders from brigade to retire into our wagon lines and hand over our two undamaged guns to another battery, which had also suffered losses in guns. We had been in that position for a month, and, with the exception of a few scratches, not a single man was wounded, so I think it will be conceded that the gambling risk taken by occupying such an exposed spot had been justified. I would have felt very foolish however, if we had been blown out of it the very first time we opened fire. One gun was certainly completely destroyed, but its loss was more than paid for by all the Hun killing we had been enabled to do.

Just before dark the gun detachments and the two guns, after much struggling, got themselves out of the morass and started back for the wagon line, while I went to Brigade Head-Quarters and had a long talk with the Colonel, trying to select a new position. Of course, we did not want one now, but we were providing for the happy day when we should get our guns replaced. Nearly every available place, however, is crammed with guns already, so it is very difficult for a late-corner to find a spare corner. By the time our search was over it was pitch dark, so I stayed the night at Head-Quarters, rather than wade through another two miles of mud back to Montauban. Head-Quarters also were in a sorry plight; their mess, office, and all dug-outs were collapsing with the incessant rain, and there was already about two feet of liquid mud on all the floors. The camp beds were just clear of the water, and, as the Colonel remarked, "if one had seen a tramp in the old days spending a night in such quarters the wonder would be how any human being could stand it," yet we've all had nearly a month of such a life, and have become absolutely accustomed to it. Orders are typed out, beautiful maps made with etching pens and coloured inks, in fact, all the old routine is gone through, even though everything and everybody are sticky with glue-like clay.

LETTER THIRTY.

MONTAUBAN. (4TH NOVEMBER, 1916.)

Rain and Mud. Mud and Rain.

HERE we are still waiting in the wagon-lines, minus guns and with no immediate prospect of getting any. It is quite a change for me to see something of the horses and wagon-line life once more. Up here the drivers certainly have a gruelling time of it; for instance, two ten-horse teams go out daily to get rations and forage—what this means will be understood when I tell you that in normal weather the cook's cart would get the rations and a four-horse team the forage—they pull out at 7 a.m., and often, owing to the intense congestion on the roads, do not reach the wagon line before 10 p.m. Had we been in action another team would then be starting so as to reach the gun position before dawn, and all this in addition to the endless journeys with ammunition.

It is quite marvellous how they find their way along the tracks in pitch darkness, missing shell craters by inches all the time. Many of the batteries have lost men and horses on the way up to the guns; both completely disappear; just as often there have been cases of single men falling into some of the deep craters and being quite unable to get out. A few are rescued in time, but of others there is absolutely no trace. The "delay-action" shells form the most dangerous craters, as they frequently explode many feet underground, forming a cavern covered by a thin crust of earth; if the weight of a horse breaks this crust, both horse and man drop into the depths of the crater, and escape unaided is impossible.

At night Caterpillar Valley is a wonderful sight. A perfect blaze of lights, extending about 14 miles, as the valley contains the wagon lines of about three Corps. I remember early in July, on a very wet afternoon, crawling out in front of our outposts to a spot quite close to where our wagon line is to-day. Then there was hardly a shell-hole in all the valley; to-day I do not think one could pick a single blade of grass.

"Watering order" under "push" conditions is very different from the orderly peace-time routine. There is no water in the valley itself, so it has to be pumped for miles into groups of troughs. No one knows when the water is going to be pumped up, so opportunities of watering vary in number from one to four times a day. Each unit has scouts out to report when the water happens to be running in to any particular group of troughs, and when it comes every unit hurries to it. The troughs can only water about 200 horses at the same time, so you can imagine the congestion there is, when I mention that the units of two army corps all water at the troughs nearest us. No one can approach them dismounted, as the mud is almost waist deep ; all the horses get mixed up together, and one simply has to trust to the drivers continuing the scramble until their horses are watered, a job which often takes two hours.

On the 2nd November I took a holiday and rode back to our old position in Vaux Valley. It was quite like getting home again, but it was sad to find our beautiful gun-pits now being used as stables for French officers' chargers. Our famous O.P. had been blown in, but the lower chamber was still intact. The view from the O.P. had changed greatly, as all the well-known little clumps had been swept away by shell-fire, and Curlu village has practically disappeared. Even the stones of the houses had gone to make the new roads round the marsh side. I rode up to the top of the old bluff, our favourite target, and doubtless, in order to impress the event more firmly on me, my horse chose to come over backwards on the top of me while climbing a very steep bank. On my way back I called at the 30th Division Artillery Head-Quarters, and got an excellent luncheon, not to mention three Romeo and Juliet cigars from General White.

Our canteen continues to do a roaring trade, and thanks to all the profits we are making, we can afford on most nights to give the whole battery hot coffee, rum, and two packets of biscuits per man. The Australians are our best clients, two or three hundred come to us every night ; their way of shopping is to slam down a 20-franc note on the counter with a "say pard, cut that out," meaning that the seller is to supply a miscellaneous mass of goods up to the value of their note.

After various changes of plans we are now taking over an empty gun position in Delville Wood, and as soon as we collect some new guns we will open shop there ; meanwhile, an officer and a few men are living in the dug-outs to keep them warm until we arrive. A necessary precaution this, as an unoccupied position disappears in about three days, lock, stock and barrel, before the horde of locusts searching for fuel and building material.

I rode up to see the men at this position to-day. One says ride, but it was really more like swimming through a sea of mud, and the road itself is always so crammed with traffic that it takes hours to get up the long hill to Delville Wood. It is no use trying to get off the road with a horse, for what with old trenches, barbed wire and craters, it is quite impossible to make any progress. Feeble efforts are constantly being made to clean up the road. It is usually, however, a foot deep in mud, if not more, and it is pitiful to see men with mess tins trying to bale it up. I'm afraid our road-making system out here leaves much to be desired.

All along the road there are "Archies" mounted on motor lorries, and these, at intervals, wake into paroxysms of gun-fire and deafen the unlucky one who happens to be under their muzzles. That afternoon the sky seemed to be absolutely lousy with our aeroplanes; nevertheless just when I was wedged in a traffic block beside two of the above-mentioned "Archies", their look-out people imagined they spotted a wolf in the fold, and uttering loud cries, proceeded to litter the sky with bursts of shrapnel from both guns.

A little higher up the road, near Longueval village, one reaches the big gun farmyard, full of vast guns seemingly dumped down anywhere near the road, with the usual piles of shells, half-buried in mud all around, and stacks of empty tin canisters and boxes which had held charges. They nearly always manage to fire just as one is passing under their noses, and so a passer-by often gets half-blown out of the saddle with their blast.

On reaching the new position I spent an hour planning dug-outs, but the wood has been the scene of SOME fighting, as you are aware, and whenever one starts a new dug-out, it always seems to be sited on the top of several buried Huns.

NOVEMBER 4TH. It is still raining.

LETTER THIRTY-ONE.

MONTAUBAN. (10TH NOVEMBER, 1916.)

Horsemastership in Mud. Idle Reflections.

Mithras, God of the Midnight, here where the great bull dies,
Look on thy children in darkness. Oh, take our sacrifice!
Many roads thou hast fashioned—all of them lead to the Light,
Mithras, also a soldier, teach us to die aright!
          R. KIPLING.

IT is still raining; in fact, it rains all day and all night. There are two things about war out here which people in England scarcely realize: the noise of a big bombardment, and secondly, the winter mud. In the wagon lines, the horses are now standing well over their knees in slush; they can never lie down except to die, and yet, marvellous to relate, look better than they did at the end of July, pulled down, as they then were, with the intense heat and water shortage.

 I believe I once read in far-off days "the curry-comb should never be used on a horse." Here the best grooming tool is an old bayonet held with both hands, and used like a squeegee to scrape off the outer coating of mud. Every time a horse goes to water he comes back almost smothered in mud from the splashing of other horses all round him. Then when the weather is somewhat drier and serious grooming is possible, a curry-comb and a clasp knife are used, and finally, if a few hairs begin to show through the mud, a brush can be brought into action. We have not had many sick horses; our chief trouble is cut pasterns and coronets, caused by treading on brass cartridge cases and the shell splinters which fly up and cut them. Men, horses, mules and dogs all constantly get stuck in the prevailing sea of mud, and quite often at night one hears frantic yells for help from the tracks which divide our wagon line from the next, and we have to send out a man and a horse to rescue some poor devil who has got stuck fast.

 We have a great game, which we always play on strangers. We get the victim to stand in the roadway for a moment, and then when his feet are nicely settled down his attention is called to something

FIELD GUNS IN FRANCE

startling behind him, e.g., an aeroplane in flames, or anything unusual. The result is that, as he nearly always tries to turn round without first pulling out his feet, he gets quite hopelessly stuck, generally requiring a drag rope to salve him. The only possible chance, when the feet are embedded in the mud, is to pull them straight out the way they went in, as if in deep snow—woe-betides the wretch who twists !

We never attempt to put hay down, but chop the whole ration, so the horses get a very full nosebag of oats and chop at least five times a day. In addition, when possible the picquet puts on the nosebag between two and three a.m., which all helps to keep the horses alive in these desperately cold nights.

We have at last managed to collect three new Howitzers from the I.O.M., but so far it has been impossible to get dial sights or carriers. However, in case we do go into action again in this neighbourhood, I have been keeping in touch with the front line by making long pilgrimages round the forward areas ; there was also the rather slender chance of finding a possible position more advanced than Delville Wood. I do not undertake these expeditions daily, I can assure you, as it is no joke to wade through mud from Montauban to Gueudecourt or to east of Flers and back. How I wish we were back in our old Flers position ! The Australian Infantry are now in the trenches which lay in front of us here. With their help we would have killed faster than ever, as they are wonderful people for finding out such things as hidden nests of Huns, or the precise hour when their ration parties come up, and moreover thoroughly enjoy front line observation and are always game for any wild stunt.

During the last three months I have seen a good deal of the Anzac Corps. The Infantry are certainly top-hole and the Artillery keen and hard-working, though inclined to use somewhat quaint orders. I was sitting one day in an Australian B.C.'s dug-out and when an urgent target came through, his orders to the guns were : "From the broken tree, side angle 90, and shoot like Hell, boys !"

One needs good infantry on this front now, as the German morale is far better than it was a month ago. They are evidently bringing their best divisions down, and in a little show a few days ago near the Butte, a certain crack Prussian Battalion, although completely surrounded, fought, chiefly with bayonet, for two hours, and only seventeen prisoners were taken out of the very large number rounded up.

This kind of fighting is somehow very like stalking. When stalking one may be held up with the wind wrong watching "the head of heads just feeding out of range," and in this game one spends hours in the early morning crouching in a shell-hole with a glorious target only a few hundred yards away, listening for the faintest telephone buzz which signifies that one is in communication with the battery. Fortunately, having trustworthy linesmen, one knows that if a line can be kept going by any means they will do it.

In July, however (at Trones Wood), the task was more difficult. There the line was too long, and laid through such an impossible zone that trying to maintain it single-handed would have cost the lives of all my men. Indeed, the price was high enough as it was, and it was far from easy to drive a mixed team of telephonists, which at one time were drawn from 11 batteries of two Divisions.

To return to the dawn sport. When one gets through on the phone, the world is *couleur de rose* once more. The guns have been laid on some point close to where we have decided to hunt that day, and a quick round of "battery fire" is ripped off in order to see if the old things are feeling as strong as usual that morning, because often the charges are more than ordinarily wet. A quick correction follows, and then "gun-fire" on to the machine-gun point or whatever the target may be, as fast as they can shovel it in. In one of my recent shoots "A" Sub-section gun fired twenty-one rounds in two minutes, really an indecently rapid rate of fire for the type of cannon we affect.

I am quite convinced that sudden intense whirlwinds of fire are by far the most deadly, and rattles the enemy much more than twice the number of shells fired in slow time.

As soon as the target has ceased to be "interesting," and while I am waiting for the light to improve, I usually boil coffee in a cooker in the shell-hole we are using, or if there is a Company Head-Quarters near, there is a chance to grub with them. With a cheery battalion in the line which enjoys a shoot of this kind the telephonists have a very good time and finish the day looking like "poisoned pups" with overeating.

After breakfast—the morning mist having usually cleared by then—one can look round for fresh game, though it may not necessarily be found close at hand. Then follows a certain amount of careful registration of other points for future use, a few shoots with other people's batteries, and perhaps the luck to find a new Hun-filled shell-hole post requiring attention.

It is really wonderful how, by endless patience, and equally endless spying with a strong telescope, one can often spot some slight movement which gives away the position of a group of machine-gunners or snipers.

By the afternoon the line is not of much reliability, as the Hun usually indulges in fifteen minutes of his full-steam barrage, which wipes it out beyond repair (the forward half of the cable has to be newly laid each day), so one makes for home, on the way back picking up the children out of their respective holes beside the cable.

I seem to have drifted away from our doings at the wagon line, but after all one cannot fill a whole letter with the sole topic of mud, which is the main feature of our lives here.

LETTER THIRTY-TWO.

DOULLENS. (19TH NOVEMBER, 1916.)

Shutting up Shop on the Somme.   A Comic Relief.   A Wandering Sausage.

ON or about the 12th November further rumours about our departure became rife, and on the strength of them we commenced preparations for our departure to more peaceful regions. Thanks to all the money we had made from our Canteen, we had been able to supply every sort of luxury for keeping the harness in top-hole order, and in spite of the quagmire we lived in, all the appointments and Battery Staff gear have their steel-work burnished, leather-work polished, and head ropes clean and white. The team harness also is in quite fair order. Again, thanks to the Canteen profits, we have been able to buy gum-boots and oil-skins for the use of the stable picquets and line orderlies which, to a great extent, has saved them from the epidemic of trench feet prevailing among the drivers.

The weather after a fortnight of rain has now turned Arctic, quite a clever idea of Nature's to kill everyone first by wet and then freeze them all ready for winter storage. It is quaint, but somehow I feel quite sad at leaving this part of the world, which I have got to know so well. It was winter when we first saw it ten months ago, and later on, during the spring and early summer, we watched with delight the opening of masses of flowers and blossom. Later still we helped to batter it beyond all recognition, till it reached its present state of hopeless wilderness. To-day we are leaving it once more for winter to clean up and repair, and, however one much one may like the country, it must be admitted that now it is badly in need of "tidying-up."

The air is full of victories at present. There are rumours of prisoners by the thousand, and dozens of captured guns. From the wagon line we could hear every other day the roar of a great bombardment, but I am pretty certain that if a boy were to come along with the "extra special edition, all about it," as in London, not a soul would trouble to wade across the road and buy a copy. Complete indifference is the rule. If the battle had taken place somewhere on the immediate front the news would probably come in sooner or later, and if it didn't, what does it matter ? We have either won or lost, or else it is a draw ; some have gained their objectives and some haven't, and that is the end of the matter.

The difference between peace soldiering and push-fighting is really vast ! By peace soldiering I mean the days when we used to sit looking at each other from nice tidy trenches, and shooting from well-kept gun-pits. The happy-go-lucky muddle that we live in here would horrify anyone well versed in the science of the latter sort of fighting, but if we didn't treat things in that spirit the ordinary individual would pretty soon become insane. There is, however, a wealth of comedy and tragedy in every moment here. Take for example the day before we marched out (the 15th). An officer of the Divisional Ammunition Column who was on the point of marching out, looked into our mess to say that he had been ordered to hand over to us two G.S. wagons and teams to help our move, as they themselves were moving empty. Profuse thanks and the request that the wagons should be sent at once to nestle in our horse lines for the night. The first wagon successfully negotiated the 250 yards stretch of mud to our lines. But the second, also empty, despite all the efforts of its team of twelve mules, managed to stick after the first thirty yards, and when once anything halts, it begins to sink at once. Much advice from onlookers was wafted across to our lines. At that moment a Hun 'plane loafed up, and having approached from our back areas, none of our " Archies " had spotted it. The area round is littered with observation balloons, and when they are sitting on the ground the Hun loves throwing things at them. The third bomb came near us by mistake and killed the D.A.C. cook and three of the above-mentioned team of mules, or rather two were actually killed and the third lay down and died out of sheer cussedness. The poor cook we laid to rest not far from the scene of his labours, and the mules were decently interred by the simple process of standing on them until they had sunk out of sight in the roadway. Exit the Hun 'plane and the D.A.C., leaving the wagon to struggle for the next hour till it got half-way across, when it was finally brought into the fold by our water cart team of eight horses which came to its rescue.

On the 16th the Battery marched at 8 a.m., but I had to go up to our nominal gun position to hand it over to the relieving Australian Battery, and so did not see the actual departure. The main road, Fricourt to Montauban, is only 300 yards from the wagon lines, yet it took from 8 a.m. till 11 a.m. before every vehicle had reached it. Day and night it is one seething mass of traffic ; there being no hard ground on which to form up the vehicles near it, and once on the road of course no chance of halting, the only thing to do is to throw in the vehicles a few at a time, and let them disappear down the stream of traffic. In this way, by the time the whole of the Battery was on the move it was scattered over seven miles of road. However, as everybody knew their destination, by 3 p.m. they had all drifted into camp, which proved to be in an area with permanent tents and horse lines. The hinterland of the battlefields is full of these areas, and very useful they are are too, for night travellers. In the meantime I had joined Maclean at the gun position, where, with a few men, he had been living for the last four days, though not shooting, of course, because, although we had managed to collect at least four Howitzers, we were still short of dial sights and carriers.

Presently some Australians blew in and said they belonged to the incoming Battery. There were no officers, but I managed to persuade them to take over the telephone exchange and thus was able to send off the rearguard of my army. As there is an excellent motor lorry service running at quarter-second intervals to every point, it is never necessary to provide transport for rear parties; they can always get food somewhere, and will turn up sooner or later. Do you remember all the fuss in the old days in England about handing in "Marching-out States"?

The relief was a comic affair altogether. As no officers appeared to be coming to the position I set out to search the country for the Australian Colonel who owned the missing Major of the relieving Battery. After a long hunt I ran him to ground in a dug-out in a Battery behind Flers, and by painting a vivid picture of my sad plight, I was able at last to persuade him to sign the wire acknowledging the taking over of the guns and ammunition. Maclean had to be left behind to hold their hands during the first night and show them the country, so he did not join us till the next day.

It was fortunately a lovely sunny day, and lots of fun was going on in the air. I saw five planes brought down, mostly Boche I think: two of them landed quite close to me. One was in flames, but the other made a wonderful landing among the shell-holes, and both men strolled out lighting cigarettes and holding up one hand.

I rode off at 2 p.m., and as usual, met a lot of friends on the main road, Merton Beckwith Smith, Tip Bennett, and many others in the Guards and other Divisions, and also passed the Prince of Wales, looking, as he generally does, fit and hard as nails. He goes about everywhere. I met him one day right forward in Switch Trench, just behind our guns.

It is an extraordinary feeling to find oneself walking on grass once more, free from knee-deep mud. The feet feel so light that one does the "heather step" with a vengeance. Our transport seems to grow bigger every march, but one might as well be comfortable. We now carry tables and chairs, also a lot of portable oil-can stoves with chimneys made of 18-pdr. cartridge cases joined together. We had a great four-course dinner, and during the night fed the Head-Quarters Staff and many others. One Battery got in about midnight, but "A" Battery stuck on their way out and only joined us as we were marching next day. Our Colonel also came in late, as he had some trouble in finding anyone to take over his Head-Quarters. However, he arrived and went to bed. He had just got to sleep when a lost and wandering "Sausage" bumped up against his tent and enveloped it completely. In the darkness nobody could find the vent to let the gas out until a small army of panting French balloonists turned up and gralloched the beast. It had broken loose from its moorings, and they had been chasing it for miles as it trundled across country.

I had a dim recollection of a crisis outside my tent, but each night has its crisis. I certainly heard someone crying for help, but did not realize it was the Colonel, and, being half-asleep, paid no attention to the frantic yells of the strugglers in the dark.

Next day we marched 20 kilometres to Bussy Les Daours, and the day after I rode into Amiens with Musson—a ride of about three-quarters of an hour. The Colonel was coming with us, but a comfortable bed and the blizzards of snow outside made him change his mind.

The Head-Quarters Staff are billeted in a chateau with a fine ball-room, so the Colonel gave a great dinner there to the Brigade the night before we marched away. We are now resting in a rather dirty village (Grouches), about five miles from Doullens, so we pass the time cleaning up and straightening things generally, ending up with Poker every night.

LETTER THIRTY-THREE.

NEAR RIVIERE. (20TH DECEMBER, 1916.)

A Pale Pink War. Nursing a Quiet Parish.

> Lord God of Hosts, be with us yet,
> Lest we forget—lest we forget !
>
> R. KIPLING.

WE were still "resting" during the first week in December, and on the 9th a reconnaissance party from each Battery was sent up in motor buses to look at our present positions, with a view to our taking them over in the near future. My bus detachment was a very cheery party, but owing to some of the roads being blocked we did not arrive till the afternoon, so there was not much time to look at the War before returning to the wagon lines.

Rather to our surprise, orders arrived at midnight that we were to relieve one section of the outgoing Batteries by noon next day. However, the move was boiled down eventually to the simple procedure of Maclean and I riding off after breakfast, followed by a small selected party of gunners and telephonists on bicycles. There was also two G.S. wagons, which were presented with a map each and left to find their own way up. As we were exchanging guns as well, the main body were left in peace in the wagon lines, and they followed next day. We have taken over a top-hole position with every modern convenience ; it is the first time we have fired from covered pits since the 4th July. The outgoing Battery had been there since last March.

I mentioned in a previous letter that there was a bigger gap between push-fighting and trench warfare than between soldiering in England and that in France taken as a whole, and here again one sees how true it is. The scientific orderliness, the notice boards, the cleanliness, the returns and paper strafes, the Generals and inspections, also the complete damnability and peacefulness of this place, simply takes one's breath away. And the curious part is that to many Divisions this still represents War. War I suppose it is, but a very pale pink variety as compared with the crimson red of the old Somme. Here there are endless observing stations, loathsome little cement boxes with tiny slits, or frequently only periscope holes. There we spent happy months observing in the open and crawling about in the maze of connected shell-holes officially called the "British front line trench." The contrast is too great, and we all feel rather fed up.

I nearly split with laughter as I watched Gunner Ryding's face while he was being shown round the perfect and intricate system of cable trenches, every wire neatly labelled and stapled up. Figure to yourself Ryding, our D.C.M. telephonist, as I met him once on our old front an hour before dawn, resembling an animated lump of mud and explaining to me (I was going out with a telephonist for the day): "We have laid the wire all right to Smell Sap, sir, you can't miss it, it is a new D.3, and I tied the end round the foot of one of them Huns in that heap, the big chap and all blown out."

Of course, the present sort of place is essential for smartening up things generally, particularly Gunnery. For example, in our map-room here we work out temperatures, barometer, and muzzle velocities, etc., with the utmost solemnity, and use a vast 3-foot protractor on the map-boards, which latter are a novel luxury for us. It is all very good for a change, no doubt, but one can't help longing for the old order of things, when one really did kill Huns.

I have not written for a long time ; somehow we are always desperately busy in a position of this sort. In battle-fighting, except for spasms of intense activity, there is usually plenty of time on one's hands. Firstly, sleep is reduced to a minimum, and when at the guns there is nothing to do except sit in the shell-hole where the telephone exchange is, and wait hours for some line to be made good. There is little to inspect ; one is in the happy position of knowing that everything is filthy and stinking and utterly loathsome. Then as it is only possible to get through to anywhere on the phone for short periods, the rest of the time is employed in waiting for something to happen, perhaps idly watching the next Battery being shelled, or, better still, a wagon ricochetting down a road as it dodges salvoes of 5.9's. There are but few returns to send in, and no infantry to fuss over. By the latter I mean that divisions come and go with such rapidity that one rarely knows who is in front calling for assistance, the result being that we simply fire on S.O.S. lines on a narrow front. Each battery had a tiny zone and little switching to do ; just as well, perhaps, as the guns were often axle deep in mud. At our present position, however, and in our perfect pits, one has to engage every sort of target in a big arc at thirty seconds' notice; there are dozens of secret codes all referring to fire to be brought for mutual assistance on to sectors far right and left of our own, and there are other codes to bring concentrated fire on every imaginable spot in our zone. All this entails sheaves of gun registers.

Here, again, there is an allotment of shells for a week only about equal to what I often used to wipe out a single nest of Huns at dawn. With that allotment all the needs of one's infantry must be satisfied. The personal element comes in very much. There may be frantic appeals down the phone from, say, the right Company complaining that they are being entirely destroyed by a heavy Minnie. The memory is immediately taxed to recall who is O.C. of that Company, whether he usually exaggerates or not, and whether he will take nobody's opinion but his own as to the Minnie's position. That decided, about four rounds gun-fire are fired on the pet position. Every infantry officer in a section believes he knows the exact position of any particular Trench Mortar. Usually they all differ, so one selects the spot to fire on according to whoever asked for retaliation. Besides all that, there are the infantry colonels and company commanders to visit, as I always like myself and my subalterns to know personally every officer of the battalion in front. In short, it is exactly like having a large fretful parish to look after, and anything one does to establish a really close relationship between infantry and artillery is worth while.

In some divisions there is unfortunately a very slack liaison between the two arms, and it makes all the difference if the infantry know that one is always ready to help them. The snipers love to get off their chests some weird and improbable yarn to our observing officers about how a Hun whizz-bang gun fired at him out of "yon wee hole", perhaps only 100 yards away, or some other equally fantastic tale. Hence, if there are a few rounds to spare, one can generally demolish some perfectly harmless chalk heap which they swear harbours all sorts of villainy.

We have had various visitors to our comfortable position. General Ross Johnson, the C.R.A. of the Corps, came one day to talk about Peter, who used to be his A.D.C., and I motored back with him to lunch at Corps Head-Quarters. The Corps Commander (Snow) was there, and General Lyon. Lord Farnham, who commands a squadron of the North Irish Horse, came up from the back regions to stay a couple of nights, and I am glad to say the War played up in honour of his visit. We were quite briskly shelled one day while observing, and also had a false gas alarm late one night, which entailed a few rounds being fired.

Soon after we got into action here, I caused great excitement. I always like to have a practice alarm on the first night at a new position, in order to settle things down and to see that everybody can find their gun-pits quickly in the dark. The practice alarm was duly given, and the guns reported ready on the lines ordered. Meanwhile, unfortunately, a new and very keen signaller obeyed the rule of passing on any alarm to the flank battery. Consequently, Major Gregory's howitzers, a few hundred yards off, started firing. To pacify the angry B.C., I had to send over next day a wagon with twenty rounds of my surplus ammunition to replace his night's expenditure. We have now got our own Divisional Infantry in front of us once again, but in the two battalions (2nd Royal Scots and 18th Manchesters), which I am covering at present, the Colonels are the only originals left.

NOTES BY THE AUTHOR.

Between December, 1916, and March, 1917, I do not think I wrote any letters. Early in this period I got fourteen days' leave and also received two severe blows; later, while we were employed in preparing forward positions for the great Spring offensive (Arras) it was difficult to write anything at all without hinting at future operations. The first blow fell at the end of December. My Colonel, F. A. Dixon, was ordered to leave the Division, taking "A", "B", and "C" batteries to form an army brigade, while a new howitzer battery just out from England was to constitute his "D" battery. The second tragedy was that the howitzer battery of the last brigade of each division was to be broken up and used to bring the other two howitzer batteries in the division up to the six-gun basis.

This meant splitting up my battery, and appeals to the powers that be to split up the new one instead availed nothing. It had been ordered by G.H.Q., and that was the end of it. After a final visit to Divarty, I left for England on New Year's Eve, getting a lift in the General's car as far as St. Pol, where I caught the midnight express with one minute to spare.

I felt very bitter, and determined I would try and get a job in Mespot or Palestine; in fact, on any other front except France. The sequel will show, however, that after exchanging various telegrams I returned happily to the old division to command temporarily "C" Battery, 148th Brigade, while its O.C. was on a six weeks' course.

I had an interesting time, too, as Colonel Wedd Jelf had just taken over the command of the Brigade, and it was a lesson to see how he tightened up every link in the unit without once interfering with a Battery Commander's powers. We were in action in a southern suburb of Arras and chiefly employed in making many forward positions in preparation for the coming battle.

Towards the end of February Major Stanley, O.C. of "A" Battery of my old brigade, went sick, and I took over his battery. It was very pleasant, indeed, to return to one's own colonel and brigade, though I regretted leaving so top-hole a C.O. as Colonel Wedd Jelf. My new battery proved to be in a very cushy position on the Doullens-Arras road not far from Beaumetz.

LETTER THIRTY-FOUR.

BOISLEUX AU MONT. (20TH MARCH, 1917.)

The Hun Retires. Comedies of the Advance.

NOW that we are on the move at last I can write about the doings of the last month.

While I was with the 30th Division near Arras, our chief occupation was making forward gun positions, but on moving down here we were spared that job, as the attack was not supposed to extend so far south. However, we were not idle, as there were many raids to test the Hun line.

For three weeks we had the 49th Division in front of us, a most sporting crowd, who fairly entered into the spirit of a night raid, and it was quite a joy to work with them. Just before they went out to rest we had a most successful raid on a point called "The Block-house", not far from Blaireville. As our Brigade was the only Artillery covering the raid, we felt it was quite a personal show, and were very anxious to help in making it a real success. The party as usual was in fancy dress with blackened faces. They were armed with clubs and all sorts of other quaint weapons. There were ten minutes of pandemonium and then out and home. Our casualties were practically nil, and a good many of the enemy in the dug-outs and trenches were killed, in addition to 14 prisoners brought back. There should have been another one, but he seems to have bitten the sergeant who was taking him back, so was slain and left in a crump hole in No Man's Land.

We also busied ourselves in cutting wide lanes through the Hun wire, no light task, as in some places the belts extend to a depth of nearly 100 yards, so that when the expected withdrawal took place we would be able to get quickly across the wire. As the Fifth Army were following up the Huns to the south of us, the withdrawal was expected to commence any moment.

My dug-out is under the route nationale leading to Arras, and at night it is like being in a hotel over a London tube. There is no traffic in daylight, but all night long the ceaseless roar of motors persists as caterpillars pulling big guns and thousands of ammunition lorries rumble along.

From the 6th March to the 15th the Hun splashed a good deal of

H.E. and gas shell into Basseux, Beaumetz, and Bretencourt, which hitherto, although close to the front line, had been very little shelled. As we always used to retaliate with double the amount into his villages, it was a sure sign he was going back and no longer troubled about our retaliation.

From the 12th to the 15th we saw an unusual number of the enemy walking outside their communication trenches, and on the 16th, on my return from the wagon line, I heard that not a single hostile gun had fired all day, and that very few Huns had been seen. Also after dusk, the glare of many fires could be seen in the east. While playing Poker that night, the news came in that the enemy had evacuated Monchy, a front line village about five miles to the south. I felt convinced that he had gone from our front, and just before dawn went down to our front line, having first extended my wire from the O.P. further back. A sergeant told me that his Company had gone across No Man's Land some time before, so, leaving a signaller with the telephone at our front line, I started off, meaning to establish visual signalling across the 500 yards which separated us from the old German strong point called "The Block-house".

I got through our barbed wire without difficulty, in fact in that section it would not keep a healthy chicken in, but while crossing No Man's Land the company on the right opened a brisk but inaccurate rifle fire on me. They were evidently in blissful ignorance of the morning's happenings. Being unarmed I was unable to reply to their fire, but fortunately the light was very dim, and we were not seriously inconvenienced.

I reached "The Block-house" at last and found that our people had only just occupied it. They were a new Third Line Division just out, and seemed to be chiefly employed in collecting souvenirs in the intervals of taking cover from the intermittent fire from our lines. A message was signalled back visually to request the company to stop firing at us, and then some young officers turned up and asked me to point out their positions on the map, as even in that short distance they seemed to have lost their bearings. As they all had revolvers at full cock there was a short interval for necessary precautions before I felt inclined to start my map-reading class.

At this stage of the proceedings two resolute Hun bombers could easily have cleared us all out, as dispositions for defence of the position of the new front appeared to be nil. Their major, however, turned up at 6 o'clock and got a move on things generally, and a little later the Brigadier, a real good sort, appeared, and detailed the barrage lines he wanted in case of attack, as the enemy were still to be seen on the ridge behind.

On being relieved by a subaltern at 8 o'clock I returned to Brigade Head-Quarters for breakfast. Orders and counter-orders all day. Some of the other B.C.'s and my F.O.O. explored far into Hunland, often a thousand yards in front of the infantry, and yet no signs of the Hun could be seen. Our teams came up that night at 9 p.m., and we dumped the guns down in a position about a thousand yards behind the old British line. I spent the night in a comfortable cottage belonging to Major Sarson's Howitzer battery, which had not moved.

Next morning, the 19th, Major Sarson, myself, and my reconnoitring officer, Wilshin, went mounted to try and get in touch with the enemy, and to find if it was possible to get the guns along to a certain valley. The roads and bridges across the trenches were being repaired with great energy, but in every road, and especially at cross-roads, there were 20-foot deep mine-craters, so it was not easy to scheme out a way to advance. The Hun had, besides, left every sort of booby trap. There were helmets with bombs underneath them, bunches of bombs behind half-closed dug-out doors, detonators under dug-out steps, enticing iron boxes which exploded when the lid was opened, and many roads ready to blow up as soon as traversed by a vehicle. The R.E., however, did wonderful work in spotting quickly and removing all these toys, and I did not hear of a single casualty.

We had a topping gallop across clean grass country till we reached a point $4\frac{1}{2}$ miles from our old front line, and then rifle and machine-gun fire from the village in front warned us that it was time we ceased to be cavalry. Leaving our horses to be watered and fed in a deep donga, we walked to the village of St. Boiry Marc. The main street was rather unhealthy with enfilade machine-gun fire, so we worked our way through the ruined houses till we reached our advance posts, which were facing the enemy in Boiry Becquerelle.

After some crawling and spying to locate the machine-guns we returned to give the news of contact at last with the enemy to "C" Battery of our Brigade, which was the only battery which had moved up that day.

The hinterland is certainly a wonderful sight. Only the grass is left, that had proved too much for the Hun to destroy or to remove, but every village is razed to the ground, every tree cut down and the roads blown up. I noticed a few willow trees still standing, but nearly all the hedges are levelled, and the rails and sleepers are gone from the railway tracks. The crucifixes have not been touched, and the French and British cemeteries are in good order, our men have been given as good a cross as the Huns supplied for their own. I noticed in one cemetery that the hedge around the Allied portion had been carefully cut down. Verily the blonde beast is a curious foe.

On the 20th there was still no order to advance, which was rather fortunate, as it was a pouring wet day, so we were able to collect and dump in a barn all our goods and chattels, including my red arm-chair and green plush settee. Next day, the 21st, we were due to advance at 5.30 p.m. It was snowing hard, a regular blizzard in fact, and very dark. It is something of a wrench tearing a Battery away from the tentacles of siege warfare and galvanizing the unit into mobile life, but we managed to get off only ten minutes late, and marching due east were in action by nine o'clock near the village of Boisleux-le-Mont.

There are a succession of villages running down the valley of the Cojeul River, and across this valley lies the great Hindenburg Line, which also crowns the high commanding ridges on either side. At this time the enemy were still holding with rearguards two demolished villages, Henin and St. Martin, in front of the Hindeburg Line, doubtless to prevent us from interfering unduly with his final preparations on the line itself.

Behind the hostile line one can see the untouched villages of Heninel, Wancourt and Guemappe, and in the far distance the high summit of Monchy Hill is just visible.

"B" Battery turned up later in the day, and took up a position in prolongation of my line of guns. This had the advantage that by using the same zero line any registrations carried out could be utilized for either battery. In order to screen the guns, we have planted a long hedge covering the whole twelve of them. This was a simple performance, as a blackthorn hedge on the opposite side of the road had been carefully cut down by the enemy, and so it simply looks as if a hedge had walked across the road. During the afternoon we had a lot of good targets at large working-parties on the Hindenburg Line; in fact it was one of the best day's sniping we have had so far.

On my return to the guns in the evening I found them very comfortably settled in. We carry five tents and fourteen large tarpaulins, so as there was plenty of timber in the ruined villages it was easy to rig up excellent shelters, and with plenty of small stoves we all were kept fairly warm despite the Arctic weather. On the 22nd the country was quite white in the morning, as there had been a heavy fall of snow during the night. Major Jack, O.C. "B" Battery, and myself did a long mounted reconnaissance looking for forward gun positions. Our front line now is represented only by posts dotted about, so there is an exhilarating uncertainty each day as to the whereabouts of the enemy. It is a choice of evils, whether one rides or walks. A mounted man is fired upon more by the Hun and less by one's own side, as the latter seem to be accustomed to the Bengal Lancers and others cantering about in No Man's Land. On the other hand, for some reason they appear to think that anyone dismounted must be a Boche.

In the afternoon we had a curious target outside Henin and quite close to us a 77 mm. gun, which fired from a cave in a grass bank. Although in full view in the open it proved to be a most tricky target to hit, and it needed over a hundred rounds before we were assured of its destruction. The valley is literally dotted with Hun working-parties, so there are moving targets the whole day long, though often at long range. However, we had one close chance as we discovered that the enemy were using a cemetery on the hill above Henin as a rearguard post. Unluckily for them there was no escape from the place except across the smooth open country, and when Jack and I got twelve guns on to it we immediately cleared them all out. I think we killed about twenty, as their only cover was the headstones.

We have to do all our observing from the Nepal Trench, which is a long communication trench and the only one in the valley : it runs from our post through Henin and then on to the Hindenburg Line. Our infantry post had made a block in this trench and did not seem inclined to push further down. About 200 yards down the trench towards the enemy there was a most attractive mound, from which it appeared likely that a much better view of the whole village of Henin could be obtained. A very sharp snow squall from the west suddenly began, which suggested to us the possibility of attacking the place with the bayonet under cover of the storm. Accordingly Jack, two subalterns and myself made an artillery charge across the open and succeeded in taking possession of the crater on the side of the mound. We then emptied our magazine at some dim figures we thought we saw further down the trench, and satisfied ourselves that it would make an excellent O.P. Apparently we had chosen a lucky moment, as the Hun since then has held it with a few snipers, which we have to shell out each morning before occupying it.

On the 23rd Jack and I were ordered to map out all possible battery positions in three map squares, which entailed another mounted reconnaissance. As only two of the map squares were in our hands at the moment the reconnaissance of the third was of necessity a somewhat hasty one. Rather a curious incident happened after we had returned to our front line and were dismounted in a sunken road talking to the infantry. Someone spotted two men walking towards the Hun village of Henin. With my telescope I could see that one was wearing an airman's cap, the other a Balaclava helmet. By firing in front of them with a Lewis gun the wanderers were guided back to the sunken road. They turned out to be two airmen who had come down with engine trouble some miles away, and got completely lost. They brought us news of the Fifth Army, who are pushing forward to the south of us.

Talking of airmen, the papers now say that we are about to re-establish our air supremacy. This is very good news indeed. During the month of March I have myself seen thirteen of our planes down, but not one Hun. One day, while in our Arras road position, two came down in flames quite close to the guns, and it was reported that the great Richthofen was himself the attacker.

I imagine we bagged a favourite Hun officer yesterday. We had been sniping all day with all guns loaded and laid on various active points, and one of our shells knocked him over. Two guns were then laid on the spot, and on two occasions during the afternoon parties ran out to try and bring him in. We were ready, however, and had an observer with his eye glued to the spot, so each time three rounds "gun-fire" closed the episode for all concerned.

LETTER THIRTY-FIVE.

BOIRY-BECQUERELLE. (8TH APRIL, 1917.)

The R.A. Attack Henin.

> The earth is full of anger,
> The seas are dark with wrath,
> The Nations in their harness
> Go up against our path.
>
> R. KIPLING.

THE same snowy weather continued until the 29th of March, but we experienced a very pleasant time away here on our own. We were but little worried with papers and returns, as Divisional Artillery and Brigade Head-Quarters are miles behind in Arras. During the day the Hun very rarely shelled us, but at night his long guns worried us a good deal. Splinters have fairly riddled the top of my tent, so after two bad goes at night we have sunk our beds to below floor level and put two rows of sandbags round the tent-walls as well. Now our tents are beautifully warm, with a big stove burning wood in each.

"B" Battery has settled down in a cemetery, and all their furniture, beds, tables, etc., are made out of empty Hun coffins, a pile of which were found lying near.

We had an amusing day on the 27th. The dawn observer reported a new camouflaged detached trench about 50 yards long, quite close to our O.P., which is itself in front of our forward posts. He was told to watch it carefully, and on no account to disturb the occupants till we came up. After another reconnaissance to determine our exact bombardment positions for the coming battle, Jack and I, having first sent our horses back, went on to the O.P. We found that in order to get a good view of the new trench it was necessary to push forward about another 100 yards down Nepal Trench, and there we placed a blocking post of two telephonists with rifles while we dealt with the trench itself. It was quite like an old "Somme" morning, and with the help of a section of Howitzers borrowed from "D" Battery we very effectually settled the occupants of the new post. As it lay only sixty yards from us and to a flank of the Nepal Trench, there was that "sinking feeling" in the back of one's neck while waiting for the first round of each battery to fall. Our blocking post soon after fell back and recounted some rather tall yarns about Huns creeping up the trench, so we stiffened them with another telephonist armed with a rifle and my subaltern with some bombs, while we, the main body, had lunch in a mine crater.

After lunch, some misguided Hun started firing at us from the bottom of the trench near Henin, which gave us the idea of advancing on Henin to discover the approximate strength with which it was held. It meant advancing 1,200 yards in front of our most forward posts, but the scheme was not quite so mad as it might seem. It must be remembered that Nepal Trench was the only one running down the side of the green valley. We had already dealt with the post on the upper flank, and its occupants were no longer taking any interest in things. As our flanks were visible from the mine-crater, we could not get pinched from behind while we had an alert observer in the crater. and besides, there were our four batteries at the end of two well-laid telephone lines. I wanted to be the leading bomber of the party, but Jack objected, and although firmly convinced that my *métier* in life was bomb-throwing, I could not convince him, so an officer went back and cajoled a professional bomber, also his carrier with a supply of bombs in a sandbag, and a bayonet man, into joining our party, a 5-franc note being the attraction.

Jack then started two guns at the village end of the trench, and searched up it till the shells were dropping a hundred yards in front of us, while my battery stood by to put down a standing barrage at the junction of the trench and the village. A subaltern who was selected to remain in the crater then took over the guns, his duty being to reverse the programme and search down the trench, lifting fifty yards every minute and to turn on my battery when we were approaching the village.

The main body consisted of five telephonists, four officers, and the two hired gladiators from the infantry, every one armed with rifles. We started down the trench behind the barrage and found traces of very recent occupation and various bits of booty. All went well till we reached the entrance of the village, where the trench bifurcated, when cautiously pulling with a strap a suspicious-looking wire, we let off a packet of stick bombs which were evidently placed there to warn the Hun of any attack coming down the trench.

As soon as the explosion occurred a succession of Very lights and rockets were sent up, and a moderate barrage dropped across the trench behind us. We saw a good many Huns manning the trenches in the village, and we had a good deal of rifle shooting at them. After that, having proved that the village was strongly held, we beat a successful retreat back through the barrage to the guns. We heard afterwards that the bomber was recommended for the Military Medal, while I got into trouble with the powers that be, who regarded me as ringleader and responsible for the picnic.

On the 21st, ours and "B" Battery were the only guns in that corner. Since then, every night we have heard caterpillars advancing, and the everlasting R.G.A. night refrain, "All together 'eave, 'eave," and when Hickey comes in with early morning tea and bunch of weather chits from the signal-pit, he generally reports "Another 8-inch or 6-inch Battery just beside us."

We started work on our bombardment position on the 29th. There were a lot of working-parties about, and the Hun was shelling the whole area. Major Nunn was fatally wounded. He was one of the original Battery Commanders in the old Division (30th), who happened to be once more beside us.

From the 31st March till the 8th April we were desperately busy every night getting up ammunition. It meant that practically every horse and man had to be out each night working over very congested and bad roads, and fighting through continual blizzards of snow and hail.

Owing to the lack of water the wagon lines are away back at Bellicourt, and the shells can only come by wagon to our Boisleux-le-Mont position. From there they have to be carried to the bombardment position, a mile further on, by pack with eight to ten rounds on each horse. We have often shifted 2,000 rounds in a night, so what with shooting all day and ammunition fatigues at night, all ranks are pretty beat. Besides that, for our own sake we have to do repair work such as filling up craters in roads, etc., as if we waited for the R.E. things would never be done in time. We built quite a substantial bridge for our wagons across the Cojeul River, and we had a pretty hot time at it, too, while doing it, as the Hun now continually shells all important points like bridges and roads.

On the 31st March the infantry attacked Henin without artillery preparation : they reached the village, but were eventually repulsed. The next day, however, under a strong barrage the village was again attacked and finally captured. The prisoners reported that they had been ordered to hold it at all costs until the 18th April, to allow time for the final work on the Hindenburg Line. These rearguards are all picked men and fight desperately, so we got out of it cheaply when we waltzed into Henin that afternoon under our private barrage.

On the evening of the 3rd April we attended a conference at Brigade Head-Quarters, and were informed that all dates had been put forward and that we were to move up four guns that night in preparation for the first day of the bombardment on the 4th. Blinding snowstorms as usual all night, with the whole British Army apparently on the road at once, and all along the route a hopeless tangle of guns moving forward, mixed with long streams of pack-horses. I rode my two horses nearly cold with fatigue during the night, and it was a real "coarse" night, with a lot of very accurate shelling on every bridge and road, pitch dark, and horribly cold. Our teams were lucky, but there were heavy casualties all around, and one began to believe in the truth of the old statement that "War is Hell".

In order not to disclose our positions, no gun-pits had been dug until the guns got in, but by 5 a.m. we were more or less ready and started the bombardment of the Hindenburg Line, which had been hitherto out of range. The bombardment had continued right up to to-day, the eve of the battle. It is a very unsatisfactory job trying to cut wire with H.E. at this long range, in fact an impossible one for us 18-pdrs., and only the heavy Howitzers are doing the job successfully.

The 6th of April was one of my unlucky days. I went up early to the O.P. to observe a Chinese bombardment (a very intense but short bombardment, not followed by any infantry attack). I had also to report to Group the line on which the Hun counter-barrage fell. This I was well able to do, because I found, as I had expected, that the path of the barrage lay directly over our own O.P.

Both sides stopped firing after fifteen minutes, but during that time the narrow trench was twice blown in on top of me. Then, on my return to the Battery, I saw a sight I had only once previously seen, a shell in the last hundred yards of its flight coming right at me. Although it burst four yards off and a sergeant and I were both knocked down, we were not touched by any splinters. After that experience I decided to retire to the safety of No Man's Land, so Jack and I crawled through Henin and found an excellent O.P. in a pig-sty on the far side of the village. My troubles were not yet over, however. In the evening, while standing in the trench beside our battery watching Sarson's battery being shelled by 5.9's, a safe 400 yards off, a disgracefully inaccurate short shell suddenly landed on the traverse three feet above my head and blew me headlong into the telephone dug-out.

Yesterday, the 7th, I again observed from our pig-sty O.P., which is getting quite well furnished, as we have found and annexed some chairs and tables. It was a good flying day, and I saw a lot of planes come down in flames, but when there are a large number of planes, all tied up in fighting knots in the sky, it is difficult for an amateur to distinguish which is which.

LETTER THIRTY-SIX.

HENIN. (14TH APRIL, 1917.)

The Battle of Arras. The Capture of the Hindenburg Line. A Good Kill at Dawn.

> E'en now their vanguard gathers,
> E'en now we face the fray—
> As Thou didst help our fathers,
> Help Thou our host to-day.
> R. KIPLING.

SOON after I last wrote, the guns moved up to their bombardment position, while the bulk of the men remained for a few more days back at our former position. As usual, we have been desperately busy getting up ammunition, and every day there are new traffic problems. The A.P.M. controls the roads, and we have to find out which are open and when we can use them. Then there is the question of which roads are available for getting forward, one dependent on how the R.E. repair work has progressed during the day and where the Hun is shelling during the night.

On the afternoon of the 8th, which for a change was very fine, orders came in for the great attack on the 9th. This meant a very complicated barrage, needing sheets of different angles for each gun. The reason was that the division to the north of us were to open the attack, which would then gradually extend south, eventually reaching our position on the extreme right, and consequently our set task would begin at zero—plus 6 hours 9 minutes, lasting to plus 12 hours and 49 minutes. We put up rather a fitful bombardment that day, but as usual up north there was a devil of a din. Jack and I had decided to observe the show from a spot in the forward slope in front of our lines overlooking the whole valley, but at midnight, on the eve of the battle, the working party at the O.P. reported that it had been blown in completely by a big shell.

On the previous night the same thing had happened, and two of our men had been buried, and were only rescued with great difficulty after three hours' hard digging. After a hurried phone conversation with Jack, it was decided that the O.P. must be abandoned, and instead we arranged to have two small slits like graves dug in No Man's Land, with telephone communication on the "treble laddered" line system, which reduced the chance of a "break" to a minimum. In spite of all this, however, our prospects looked decidedly unhealthy, but the only alternative was crowding in among the observers of about fifty other batteries on the popular Railway Embankment, a long way back.

Z day, which was the 9th, began with heavy rain and hail. For the Northern Divisions zero hour was 5.30 a.m. Our own band, however, did not start playing till after 11 a.m. There was Hell let loose all the morning up North ; by 10 a.m. we heard that Telegraph Hill was captured and that our tanks were careering onwards like rabbits. Just before eleven I went forward with my telephonist, and advancing across the open in full view of the enemy dropped quickly into our slit, the Huns being luckily too busy to worry about us. Jack also reached his hole in safety, and thus we waited for the first act of the drama.

About noon the 56th Division streamed across the ridge on our left, the left half of the attack getting through the wire, but the right eventually had to come back and line a sunken road some four hundred yards from the Hindenburg wire. Our counter-battery work was most vigorous, and the enemy only put up a very slight barrage, although our infantry must have presented a perfect target during their long advance across the open. About 2 p.m. the Brigades of the 30th Division commenced their attack, advancing down the slope and passing right over the holes in which we were standing. They were naturally surprised to see us there, and much chaff was in the air about our having secured front seats for the show. They had a long advance in full view the whole time, and did not launch the actual attack on the Hindenburg line till 3.30 p.m. Previous to their final attack they had had very few casualties, which shows how non-plussed the Hun was for the moment.

While the 30th Division were advancing along the bottom of the valley the 21st Division attacked all along the high ridge of Henin Hill on our right flank. During the last few days we had all reported time after time that the wire across the bottom of the valley was quite untouched, and sure enough the infantry found this was the case and had to dig themselves in along a stretch of dead ground about 400 yards from the wire. However, in spite of this attack failing, our losses were not heavy, and I really think that the wire was so dense and strong that the Hun could neither see nor shoot through it from his front line.

The 21st Division did better and got through by two gaps on the extreme summit of the hill, and disappeared from view. But while we, the right-hand pivot of the attack, were being held up to some extent, the Divisions which had attacked earlier in the morning to the north of us began to press down almost in the rear of the enemy on our immediate front; from our perfect O.P. we could see great confusion on the roads behind Heninel, and our set programme being over at 5 p.m., we were able to engage some glorious targets—roads congested with gun limbers, retreating Huns and vehicles of every sort, all went into the hash together. The Hun asked for war, and now at last he is getting it in good measure, heaped up and overflowing.

Next day, the 10th, we experienced blinding snowstorms till darkness fell. As usual, there was great uncertainty about the position of our infantry. Observation being practically impossible, I rode up to Henin Hill to find out how the 21st Division had got on, and then went back to Brigade Head-Quarters, but the only news they had was that our Cavalry were in Monchy.

The evening was not so peaceful, however. At 6 p.m. I was at the O.P., when a terrific barrage against the 21st Division opened. In the bad light it was difficult to see what was happening, but one could make out our men coming back through the wire, and it was clear that the Hun had counter-attacked and regained his old front line. I stayed on at the O.P. until quite late that evening, but owing to a heavy snowstorm, darkness, and general turmoil, one could not do much good.

Wilshin made a tour during the night of all our front line, and came back with a report which was very valuable indeed, as no one knew exactly where our infantry was.

Soon after midnight orders were received for a fresh attack down the centre and left side of the valley. The attack was launched at 4.45 a.m., but again our infantry were completely held up by the uncut wire. Four tanks, however, suddenly appeared on the scene, and were asked by the infantry to come along and lend a hand. One tank stuck in a sunken road, but the others surged through the wire and for over an hour moved up and down the Hun trenches, one of them spending its entire time roaming about in Heninel, which was infested with machine-guns. On hearing of the tanks I thought it time to leave the bed from which I had been conducting the war so far, and cantered up to the O.P. The light being fairly good, we had excellent targets at Huns bolting away from the tanks, but in spite of the wire being levelled in two or three places our infantry did not immediately reach the front line, and the attack was reported to have failed.

The rest of the morning passed quietly with no movement on either side, but at 2 p.m., while observing with my good telescope, I was surprised to see a succession of heads and shoulders filing down the front line trenches. Each came in view for about a second, at a point where the parapet was blown in. The unmistakable outline of the British box respirator convinced me that they were our men, and the news when passed on was received with great surprise by Head-Quarters. It appears that our infantry had worked their way through the wire, following the exit tracks of one of the tanks, and thus regained possession of the front line, and were beginning to work their way steadily downhill into Heninel.

The next thrill was provided by the enemy. After a fierce barrage against Wancourt, dense masses of the Boche could be seen attacking across the open, but they were well in range of our guns to the north, and melted away under a whirlwind of shrapnel; for us, of course, they were out of range. By dusk our Infantry had bombed their way down the front line as far as the River Cojeul.

There was good sniping all the afternoon, and at least one ideal kill. The Hun was bolting back across the open, abandoning both front and support lines. Several single men made tracks for a sunken road which we enfiladed, so during a lull I registered all six guns on it. Within ten minutes I saw to my joy a more or less formed party of about forty Huns making for that exact spot. There was sufficient time for each gun to get eight rounds ready, and at the moment they reached the fatal spot, one long buzz on the phone let loose the forty-eight rounds, and it was all over in 20 seconds. Thus ended the 11th, with our Division at last just in the Hindenburg Line, though two days late.

At dawn next morning the 21st Division attacked to regain the lost crest of Henin Hill. They reached the front line without opposition, as a very curious thing had happened during the night. The 30th Division, encountering but slight resistance when they reached the bottom of the valley, had continued their triumphant progress up the trench on the southern side of the valley, and received the 21st Division as they stormed through the wire. Thanks to the perfect dug-outs, they had suffered no casualties from our preliminary bombardment.

After breakfast my captain and I rode forward to look for new positions, and then went on to inspect the far-famed Hindenburg Line. It is rather disappointing in some ways, being merely a very wide traversed trench, only half-completed and with very few fire steps. The wire in front of it is of course marvellous. The machine-guns are either in between the front and support trenches, or in the support trench, with just a few right forward in front of the wire. Here and there were marvellous concrete machine-gun forts. The dug-outs were all in the support line; in fact the entire support line has a passage below it 30 to 40 feet deep at this spot, running from Heninel over the hill to Fontaine, a distance of about 3,500 yards. No wonder the Hun was annoyed at losing all this so quickly.

We were ready to move forward at 5 p.m., but what with nasty rumours of counter-attacks and other disturbing factors, the position was so obscure that we were not allowed to advance. A little later, however, the word "GO" was received, so off we scuttled and went to ground in a nice corner in Henin, on the river bank.

Our line had been laid out as we went and just as we were unlimbering I was rung up by H.Q. with the news that counter-attacks seemed imminent and that the Division advised me to return, so I had to tell them that our teams had long gone back and that I had no intention of moving. The decision was perhaps influenced by the fact that we had taken possession of the only house left standing in the village and that our cooks had already got the dinner under way. The house had been a machine-gun post, and we had to remove about six of its dead tenants before we could settle down comfortably. The other batteries, however, not having started, were unable to escape from their old positions, and so we were left all on our own.

Early in the morning I started off to lay a telephone line up to the newly captured support trench on the top of Henin Hill. It was pitchy dark and through unknown country, involving many detours and much searching for gaps in the impenetrable wire entanglements, so it was daylight by the time I had reached our front line. Quite like old times in the Somme—a newly captured front and Huns digging like fury in new and shallow trenches quite close, and, as formerly, neither side knew exactly where their men were: all unobserved fire was thus rendered impossible, and the chance of a lifetime fell to him who could observe.

Feeling full of hope and glory and forgetting the Hun might still be aggressive, I climbed out of the trench into the open with my compass and map in order to try and locate my whereabouts. I was just settling down to work when two Hun M.G.'s opened fire on me from an unpleasantly close range, so there I was pinned down in a shell-hole with bullets harrowing its top, but luckily within shouting distance of my telephonist, who had wisely remained in the trench. I gave the Battery a rough range and a very short corrector, and then told them to fire a salvo, which I heard far away on my left flank. A few very bold corrections brought the bursts right over my head and high up, then some rather more precise ones brought them down close in front of me, whereupon I ordered some rounds of "Gun-fire" under cover of which I regained the trench, but not my temper. Anyway, the morning's prey was located.

We prolonged the wire down the trench until I found an M.G. sergeant with his gun in working order, and then we settled down side by side to slay. The enemy were to be seen in great numbers digging hard, many in trenches only knee deep within 200 yards of where we were. Our infantry, having come up in the night to relieve the troops that had attacked, were far too busy cleaning their rifles and putting their new home in order to pay any attention to the Boche, so not a gun or rifle on either side was firing.

We got the guns going, and in twenty minutes one could stand upright and observe over the parapet, and my temper began to recover!

Soon after we started, a very keen Lewis gunner brought his weapon along to join our group, so between the three of us hardly a Hun escaped. We fired all the 1,200 rounds we had with us at the guns, besides another 800 that were hurried up from the wagon line. It was indeed a grand chance, and one which we would have lost had we not advanced immediately, as in another twenty-four hours the old Hun would have got really well dug in.

Thank Heavens our Brigade H.Q. leaves its Battery Commanders to kill Huns by their own devices as best they can, and to report AFTERWARDS. All this because on my way home in the afternoon, I met observers from another Brigade, all complete with telephones and in touch with their guns, but not firing a round. They said they had got orders not to hurt the enemy until they had found the Senior Infantry Officer of that section, and had learned exactly which were our men and which were the enemy and their locations. Truly a quaint way of waging war.

Returning down the hill to Henin 1 met an old friend in the shape of a polo pony that had been in my joint stud for two years, and on searching round I soon found his master (Gordon Dickson, killed soon afterwards), O.C. of one of the many batteries which were coming into action on the slope of the hill. Finding that my line, laid in the darkness, crossed the spot where his battery were coming into action, he gladly made use of it to register his guns. The remainder of our brigade also advanced before dark and used the same line, which had certainly earned its upkeep that day.

Next day I took a holiday and rode back to the wagon lines to see if we had any horses still alive, and found quite a number, which was remarkable considering their recent hard work and the intense cold. It is not the mileage which tells, but the hours spent on the road viz., 17 hours to fetch forage from a dump five miles back. An extreme case, perhaps, but suggestive of the congestion and hopeless state of the roads. I called at the Brigade, of course, for a meal and to see the Colonel. He always accuses me of eating like a half-famished pike, but they do keep such an excellent cook.

As usual, there was little news of how the War was going, but I heard that the Corps Commander had sent his congratulations to the Brigade for certain incidents in the previous day's fighting, and for our having been the only battery which had done any effective firing on the 13th. The following day proved to be a peaceful one all through, omitting the usual dawn scuffle, when the Hun barraged us and we barraged the Hun for thirty chilly minutes, chilly because one always arises from bed too lightly clad to conduct in comfort an early morning war.

CHAPTER THIRTY-SEVEN.

HENIN HILL. (25TH APRIL, 1917.)

Another Advance. Splendid Sniping. The Battle of April 23rd.

FROM the 13th until the 20th the War has been stationary and dull. It is only on an occasional Red Letter Day that one really gets a chance of effective fire, for the rest of the time it is merely endless shell slinging into the allotted map squares. The weather, too, has been vile, with samples of all sorts—hail, hot sun, high wind and snow.

On off-days it is very interesting to ride away back to the rear, for what one sees there is much more thrilling than anything on view at the front of the stage. After a week's absence, the old battery positions are hardly recognizable, the whole country looks like a vast fair, with dumps of everything under the sun—thousands of motor lorries, tents, marquees, huge sheds, and light railways running everywhere.

The pace at which railway reconstruction on the broad gauge line goes on is marvellous. Within five hours of the time that the attack on the 9th started, there was a gang of about 2,000 Canadian railwaymen relaying sleepers and rails on the embankment behind our guns, and before night a light engine was running. The only thing one never discovers is the home of the Tanks. They come and go mysteriously from nowhere into nowhere. A big convoy of them must have flitted past our guns in the night, as traces of their fairy footsteps were plainly visible disturbing the morning dew.

One wet day, observation being impossible, I spent a happy afternoon laying our wire all along the support line, or rather 40 feet below it, through the dug-out tunnel. We laid it for 500 yards underground with the help of siege lamps, staples and hammers. It was a curious pilgrimage. We passed through several Company and one Battalion H.Q., and made our way past ammunition dumps and bomb stores, and even carrier pigeons sitting disconsolately in their wicker baskets. We seemed to step over half the British Army sleeping in the passages, and in other disused corners one blundered over forgotten unburied remnants of the German Army. As usual, however after all our work, orders came in next day, altering our zone of fire into the next valley round Fontaine, which meant a mounted reconnaissance for a new O.P. two miles further south, and the selection of the position we are now occupying on the high ridge above Henin.

From information obtained from prisoners and captured reports, the Hun must be having a very desperate time. After the old days of shell shortage, it is difficult to realize that we now fire thirty shells to his one. His recent counter-attacks must have cost him dearly, and he has made many more than he used to on the Somme, as it is now of far greater importance to him to keep us back.

I suppose if all telephones were suddenly to cease work, the War would have to stop till both sides had recovered from the shock. Even in a simple push position like the one in Henin village we used one in the Mess, one in my dug-out, one at the O.P., one at the new position on Henin Hill, one at the wagon line, two at the Battery exchange switchboard, one at the guns for firing orders, and one at a linesman station on the O.P. line.

On the 20th, the guns moved up at dawn to the new position, and later in the morning, on riding up, I found everyone comfortably installed. Disgustedly close to the Hun, in fact, only 300 yards behind our forward infantry posts, but owing to the nature of the ground it is not quite so dangerous as it sounds. All the same, I must put up a few strands of wire in front of the guns to keep the enemy in his proper place.

A new subaltern, Taylor, joined us that day. He is an Old Etonian, and has seen service in Gallipoli and Salonika, and looks a good tough nut, the sort which is badly wanted, for lately the pace has been pretty fast and more than one of my new officers has cracked up.

From the 21st, until the morning after the battle of the 23rd, the bombardment continued night and day, the 18-pdrs. wire-cutting and sniping all day. The wire-cutting, however, is more in the nature of sweeping up after the heavy Howitzers have made the gap with 106 fuses, as shrapnel is quite useless against uncut Hindenburg wire.

An order having come in that every battery was to have a forward gun for wire-cutting, we complied, though it meant putting the gun practically in the front line. I remember that a gun team and limber, not being available at the moment, this gun made a masterly advance tied behind our water cart ; all hands followed carrying ammunition, and afterwards each night a forlorn-looking object, covered with brushwood and minus sights, breech or any fittings, was left to its lonely vigil, while the detachment put more space between themselves and the Huns on our left flank.

The sniping possibilities are wonderful, as the enemy has no proper communication trenches leading into his two lines of defence, and from the hill-top, which is delightfully close to the battery (about 300 yards) we have a marvellous view. The enemy had made an attempt at a communication trench leading down into some dead ground behind their support line, and there was constant movement up and down it. We enfiladed the whole of the visible portion of the trench, and kept one or two guns laid on it from dawn till dusk, while an observer with a fixed telescope in a shell-hole only 200 yards from the guns watched it unceasingly. One or two buzzes on the phone meant "Stand by", one long buzz, "Three rounds gun-fire". A simple and automatic form of death, as the range was short and the gun, being re-registered every hour, perfect bursts in the trench was assured. As fresh troops who did not know the evil habits of that trench doubtless arrived frequently, this game continued for nearly ten days.

The big attack was due to start at 4.45 a.m. on the 23rd. It was a perfect simultaneous opening on the whole Army front, followed by the usual rocket display in Hunland. One of the first shells must have hit a big rocket store, for at least 500 coloured rockets went off in every direction, an extraordinary sight. We had moved our O.P. to a shell-hole on the crest, because on the previous evening the Hun had spotted the sunken road from which many other batteries besides mine were observing. They made things pretty hot, and poor Cairns, formerly in my battery, who was in the next hole to us, was done in.

For the first two hours, what with smoke and dense mist, one could see nothing in the valley beyond the general turmoil caused by the Hun barrage, and occasionally a few Tanks rampaging in the distance. We thus had plenty of time to dig out our shell-hole, and soon secured considerable protection from the British prematures, which constituted our chief danger, as there were no Hun shells anywhere near us.

The light improved as the morning went on, and at least 1,500 prisoners came past us. Until 6 p.m. the fighting was most involved, attacks and counter-attacks followed each other in rapid succession, and detached parties of both sides were struggling everywhere. The light, however, remained perfect for spying, and so we were able to sling it in ceaselessly—and got through a heavy day of tricky shooting, making a good bag.

Of course, if the guns can be trusted and one's own knowledge of the country is sound, fire can safely be opened on the best targets, which are nearly always those closest to our own men.

On several occasions I could even see the Huns climbing on to their parapet, shooting at point-blank range, and even their officers

FIELD GUNS IN FRANCE

were visible directing the fire, so, as our men were attacking from a direction safe from our line of fire, we were able to get in some potent doses of well-burst shrapnel, which, at a range of 2,000 yards, sweeps away the occupants of an enfiladed trench like autumn leaves in a gale. After such a burst of shelling, it is glorious to see our men surge forward without casualties.

Early in the afternoon the enemy brought reinforcements into the trenches south of Fontaine, and presently things began to get more hectic than ever. Huns bombed their way up to the front line and cut off a lot of our men who had reached the enemy support line at different points. There was a "Regrettable Incident" in the centre, which brought back with it the right hand company, which, up till then, had been making good progress. It was sad to see a big mob of our men pouring back through the wire and retiring down the road towards Croissilles.

With a telescope one could almost see the badges on their uniform. In spite of the good light, various Zeiss binocular enthusiasts described this minor debacle as follows : That the Huns were advancing down the road—that Hun prisoners were being escorted back—and even that it was only walking wounded returning—all rather confusing for their H.Q. getting such reports. At 6 p.m. we started a fresh barrage along the front, and the people on our left attacked at 7.46 p.m., making some progress, but on our immediate front there was no move.

During that night the Huns withdrew from about 600 yards of the Hindenburg Line, thus removing the danger of a flank attack on our guns. Wilshin made an early reconnaissance to try and discover something definite, as the location of our infantry was still very uncertain. In one of the concrete M.G. forts he found 12 Huns waiting with kits all packed ready for their journey to England. They had evidently been overlooked by our men, and he relieved them of various bits of booty before handing them over to the infantry. All the dug-outs were crammed with wounded of both sides who had been captured and recaptured so frequently on the previous day that they were now somewhat muddled as to who really owned them.

The day after the battle afforded, as usual, extra good "sniping" targets, as there was much movement behind the Hun lines. For the first few days that we were here there was no competition to engage these quick targets, but lately a large number of batteries have been detailed for sniping only, and now, when a small party appears, it is often engaged by two or three batteries at once.

One knows from personal experience the demoralizing effect of being perpetually sniped at by guns of all calibre whenever one shows one's nose above the parapet, and being chased by shells across the open. And what hair-raising accounts the outgoing troops must give to the incoming unit, all helping to weaken "morale"!

It soon became noticeable how constant practice at picking off parties in the open improved the daily kill. The most important thing is to judge the time of flight accurately; by this I do not mean the range table time of flight, but the time it takes from the moment "Fire" is ordered at the O.P.—down the telephone to the exchange, by megaphone to the gun-layers, right hand to jerk the trigger—and finally the flight of the shell itself.

Just after dawn and the hour after sunset are my happy hunting hours, which usually yield the best sport. One morning Wilshin just at daybreak saw a party of fifty men advancing to a previously registered spot and scored twenty-one. Certainly twenty-one bodies lay there till evening, but I fear some wounded got away, although he industriously sprayed the spot with shrapnel after his initial opening with high explosive. The latter was used first because the corrector for the day had not yet been found.

For small parties one gun is sufficient, and all the guns are kept loaded and laid on the popular points of the landscape with two men sitting beside them from dawn to dusk. It is difficult to understand why the Hun does not snipe us in return, as here, just as it was on the Somme, the whole British Army walks about collecting firewood, etc., in full view of the enemy. Yesterday, however, he did deign to turn a machine-gun on to me. I was out shooting partridges with the new Irish pointer which I have annexed, and must have come a little nearer to the precious Hindenburg Line than he quite approved of. Probably also he considered pursuing partridges in No Man's Land during April contrary to the laws of the Hague Convention! So he plashed some bullets about in an aimless fashion till I removed myself to a quieter spot.

LETTER THIRTY-EIGHT.

HENIN HILL. (8TH MAY, 1917.)

The Attack of May 3rd. Rifle Paralysis. A Scientific Kill.

SUMMER has fairly set in, and we have been having day after day of glorious hot weather, and our present position, which looked so cold and draughty when we chose it in rain a fortnight ago, is now becoming most comfortable. The Hun has left us in peace so far, and, being on the top of the ridge, there is no need to fear shell gas. When he was driven off Henin Hill, the Hun certainly lost a magnificent view point.

Even the long ridge, on which runs the Arras-Doullens road miles away to the west, is clearly visible to us from here, and luckily also the wagon lines two and a half miles away in Boiry can be seen from the guns. By day we keep up a constant stream of messages by helio or flag—at night by lamp ; not that there is really much of importance to talk about, in fact, the messages sent are all about the canteens (one of which is at the guns and the other at the wagon line), ordering up long lists of stores required, etc.

Our Mess is a tarpaulin erection on the road itself, with a high canvas screen which forms an open-air dining-room, and we have gradually managed to collect our furniture from the dumps left behind during the advance. Just outside the mess is a sandbag wall jump with brushwood wings, and each horse coming up with a message from the wagon line is made to jump it. The only drawback is that just behind us are twelve 60-pdr. guns, which as you know make more noise and vibration than anything else in the world, and as they are usually shooting with a big angle of depression, and their shells only just clear our roof, they put out every candle with unfailing regularity. However, we have found that by putting the candles on cigarette tin lids suspended from the roof with a soda-water bottle wire we can put a stop to the trouble. Though they fire all night they never wake me up, yet my private call K.K. (long short long) in the microphone on my pillow, rarely fails to waken me immediately.

We have been wire-cutting again with two very forward guns, but we pull them back each night, as the infantry have put up a lot of wire behind them, and it feels a bit chilly for guns to be left out in front of the wire. We have also wired in our own battery position, but as I walked absent-mindedly straight through it one day on my way to the O.P., I believe I hurt the feelings of the sergeant who was in charge of its erection.

Our new triplanes are splendid ; they have fairly got the command of the air for the time being, and the Hun planes seem only to fly for short periods, and that behind their own lines.

From the 29th April till the night of the 2nd May was one long bombardment, and Hunland looked like a vast smoking inferno day after day. On the night of the 2nd the rate of fire was speeded up, and an incessant stream of gas shells and incendiary stuff was sent over. For once I found sleep rather difficult, as the whole earth shook like an animated jellyfish. The show kicked off at 3.45 a.m. on the 3rd, but for us it was rather a dull fight, firing without a stop until 4.30 p.m., and without any chance targets.

Again we were the pivot of a big move, and in our sector we did not advance far. Practically the only incident in the day occurred during breakfast, when No. 4 Gun—a cross-eyed brute at the best of times—decided to retire from the conflict with a premature right in her bore ; the detachment were having breakfast behind the gun, and the layer, who was working her single-handed, was luckily untouched, though the piece itself was blown to atoms. In fact, beyond that and prematures from other batteries behind us, it was a thoroughly dull day, with a total absence of hostile shelling. I think we fired about 1,800 rounds that day—probably more—about 800 rounds over our normal daily expenditure.

From that day until the 8th there has been very little change in the situation. Every day has been cloudless and hot, and the grass all round is burnt yellow with the early summer heat. The valley behind us looks more like a country fair than ever, with tier after tier of batteries of ever-increasing calibre, reaching a climax in the shape of a 15-inch Howitzer in Boiry-Becquerelle.

It is curious that both sides seem to have almost entirely forgotten that a rifle can be used in war for some other purpose than the propping up of a waterproof sheet over a hole in a trench. It seems that after all the lectures in England on modern artillery work, on tanks, and on bombing, our infantry have got the idea that their sole offensive action should consist in occasionally advancing behind the barrage and occupying a new trench, and that their best means of defence is to signal back to the artillery, or to begin throwing bombs long before the enemy are anywhere near them. I have been in the front line during a Hun counter-attack, and have seen both sides commence bomb-throwing at absurd distances—100 yards or thereabouts—while glorious chances of sniping at close range were entirely neglected.

FIELD GUNS IN FRANCE 167

The enemy, too, with the exception of their professional snipers, are equally harmless with their rifles. The other night, when I was pursuing a wounded partridge on a grassy slope within 700 yards of the Hun main line and in full view of them, not a single shot was fired at me, except a few rounds of Hun whizz-bang shrapnel, which burst as usual harmlessly high in the air. Curious when one thinks of the South African War, with accurate rifle shooting up to 1,500 yards.

As things are quiet at Head-Quarters, the Colonel has been spending several afternoons with us sniping from our O.P., and his home being in the midst of the best partridge country I have frequently been over there for joint drives, utilizing the orderlies and spare signallers as beaters, so neither partridge killing (forget the month) nor Hun killing (always in season) has been neglected.

We are now getting familiar with the angle of sight and range to every popular point in the landscape, and above all learning by constant practice the right moment to let them have it, so that we have been making more than our usual good bags. Only too often good targets are squandered by a premature opening of fire. How true the French maxim is : *"En guerre l'art ne consiste pas a frapper fort ni à frapper souvent, mais à frapper juste."* Here is an actual example. We had three guns accurately registered on a road. A party of fourteen Huns were seen moving parallel to the road and 200 yards to a flank of it. One way would have been to have guessed their location and then switched these three guns on to them, a 5-to-1 chance against our getting them before they scattered in every direction. The way which did score, however, was as follows : A fourth gun fired a few rounds of percussion shrapnel on to a spot 400 yards in front of the party with the object of making them incline on to the road at a point short of the one we had registered so accurately, and taking care not to fire close enough to make them break their close formation. It worked beautifully, as they edged off little by little, and eventually got on to the road and advanced down it. No. 4 gun then stopped firing, and Nos. 1, 2 and 3 stood by for an intense burst. "Fire !" The taxpayer did indeed get his money's worth that time. Again by careful watching one often gets other chances at the same spot, when sightseers come investigating the trouble and examining the mess lying about.

It is difficult to follow the working of the Hun brain. Having decided that on the sea it would suit him better to disregard the Red Cross, he has frequently had the sublime impertinence on land to march across our front in large parties carrying such flags, and doubtless hoped that he would not be wiped off the face of the earth. Alas, how illusive are human hopes !

LETTER THIRTY-NINE.

HENIN HILL. (15TH MAY, 1917.)

The Hun Artillery Wakes Up. Two Days at Rest. Army Brigades and C.R.A.'s.

Who recalls the noontide and the funerals through the market
(Blanket-hidden bodies, flagless, followed by the flies),
And the footsore firing-party, and the dust and stench and staleness,
And faces of the Sisters and the glory in their eyes?
R. KIPLING.

WE are beginning to outstay our welcome in these parts, and the enemy has become very much more aggressive and seems to have realized at last that the whole valley behind us is packed with guns. He started shelling our area on the 10th, and has kept at it night and day intermittently ever since.

The 11th was a particularly unlucky day; casualties had been mounting up all the morning, and as we had not much firing to do in the afternoon, I sent the bulk of the men back to the baths behind us near Boiry, to keep them out of harm's way, but our bad luck pursued us, and a long-range shell landed in the bath-house and did much damage among the many men there, our share being one man killed and one man wounded.

During the afternoon the shelling increased in violence, and we had a busy time extinguishing fires in the many ammunition dumps and the camouflage covers over the guns, as owing to the intense heat everything was as dry as paper.

Unhappily, as always seems to be the case, it is the best who get "done in" on these sorts of jobs, and our Q.M.S. Wheeler (Edwards) was killed in one of the pits. He had 28 years' service, had been in France since August, 1914, and was beyond doubt the best all-round soldier I have ever met, as brave as a lion and a perfect genius with that most tricky partner—the buffer of an 18-pdr. gun.

Meanwhile, as Nos. 1 and 6 pits both caught fire and some more men got wounded, things were in a bad way until we got them carried into safety and the fires put out. The death of Wheeler Edwards was a great loss to the Battery and to the whole Brigade, as he was always "a very present help in time of trouble" to any limber gunner, and was really an extraordinary skilful mechanic. When his body was going back at dusk in the mess cart we gave him a "Nunc Dimittis" in the style he would have liked best, all six guns with full detachments at battery fire for 100 rounds plastering the Hun back areas, and at his funeral the whole Battery turned up, my captain having been able to catch a padre, which one was rarely able to do during the Somme fighting.

At midnight orders came in that each battery could go out to rest at the wagon line for two days in turn, so the guns pushed off at dawn. I lazily stayed on for breakfast in the empty position, and got caught in another Hun area shoot, and had to leave in a hurry, abandoning our mess kit, to be rescued in a lull later.

Next day, battery sports, mounted and dismounted, were held, a well-run show, stage-managed by two of the wagon line officers and the battery sergeant-major. Owing to the canteen having done so well, we were able to spend 1,100 francs on prizes, free drinks and so on. One of the comic events was an obstacle race in P.H. gas helmets.

A hot and dusty ride into Arras for lunch, and a partridge drive with the Colonel, completed the programme of our two days' rest, and then we went up to take over "B" Battery's guns and position during their turn of rest. This scheme kept my guns safe in the wagon line, but it is somewhat uncomfortable being the caretaker of another fellow's position.

Rumours of an early departure are in the air, and we shall all be glad to be off for some new push, because, as I said before, we have certainly over-stayed our welcome here. It is without doubt a great advantage to belong to a "hired Gladiator" unit, i.e., an Army Brigade, rather than to be with Divisional Artillery. There is all the fun of each push, and by moving we escape the aftermath.

The enemy seems to take far longer than we do to settle down and shoot well from a new line, and I always maintain that his direct observation powers in push-fighting are contemptible. It is only when he has got quite dug in that he commences his accurate shooting guided by map, balloon or aeroplane. Of course, in his concrete O.P.'s in the old front line he observed well enough, better, in fact, than we did, because he employed professional observers who, for the duration of the war, lived in the same O.P., and literally knew every sandbag in their zone. Our observers, on the other hand, were continually changed, and never got the chance to learn a given area as the Huns did.

It is, of course, a little trying for us to be perpetually under different C.R.A.'s, as they all have their pet mania. During the beginning of the push one is not worried much by them, but later on they begin to come round the batteries, and one has to remember their various ideas as to how to win the war. Some require two men perpetually sitting at each gun, and some like to see all hands washing clothes, while others prefer digging or resting. I may add that we can, when required, give an exceptionally realistic performance of the latter!

On the 16th we re-occupied our old position, the same old shelling was going on, costing us some good horses. As luck would have it, a salvo of high velocity 5.9 shells landed close beside the mess-cart, killing the horse, puncturing my bed-bag, and slightly wounding one of the servants. Apart from this episode, however, all was peaceful, and as the light for observing was hopeless, the Colonel and I had another partridge drive, yielding the heavy bag of three brace.

Most of our dug-outs had been blown in or the roofs stolen during our absence, so I brought up as few officers and men as possible, besides it was also a good chance to give everyone a rest at the wagon line before our next move.

LETTER FORTY.

HENIN HILL. (24TH MAY, 1917.)

*The Loss of Mehal-Shahal-Hash-Baz.   Our Last Fight at Arras.
Telescope Reflections.   Northward Bound.*

If He play, being young and unskilful, for shekels of silver and gold,
Take His money, my son, praising Allah.   The kid was ordained to be sold.
R. KIPLING.

SOON after we were back in action Fate dealt us a cruel blow. My Irish pointer, which had joined us a month previously, was reclaimed by one who declared himself to be the rightful owner, so off went Mehal-Shahal-Hash-Baz, which was his name for short, meaning in Hebrew "rending and destruction", and right well did he earn his name if ever he was left in a dug-out alone !

A rumour which I did not contradict got round the Battery that I was prepared to give a large sum for the dog if returned to me on our march away from here, at a safe distance from Henin Hill, so the many professional and unprofessional dog-stealers in the Battery set to work to effect his recovery from his home about half a mile to our flank. By day, however, the dog was carefully guarded, and at night kept securely tied up in a dug-out in a trench. The plans tried were many and various. Individuals carrying telephones and pretending they were signallers looking for an imaginary battery at night, asked the guard of the dog for directions, while another gang came up from the wagon line and with Red Indian stealth tried to stalk the sentry and get into the dug-out unobserved. Others again started sapping up a disused trench hoping to tunnel into the trench, and it was only our move out of the locality that brought to an end these pious efforts.

5.15 a.m. on the 19th was the zero hour for the last battle we were to have before we moved away, which was to be preceded by the customary all-night bombardment. As usual, the dense morning mist veiled the whole valley until late in the morning.

I often move my O.P., in order to teach the observer to pick up the same targets from different points of view, and having moved that morning had the satisfaction of seeing a 21 cm. (8-inch) shell land fair on my old post.

I met Lord Farnham hereabouts with his captain (North Irish Horse), styling themselves "Corps Observers," which they found distinctly more interesting than escorting prisoners from cage to cage. They came back to breakfast with me in the road just in front of the 60-pdr. Brigade, and the blast of all the massed batteries behind us nearly drove our guests distracted, accustomed to the relative quietness of a forward O.P., or a billet behind the line. There was my telephone on the breakfast table, too, and as usual, I was engaged in conversation with O.P., Exchange or Brigade almost incessantly, which helped to prejudice them against the profession of a gunner.

Right up till 6 p.m. we fired steadily according to programme, and also took on many chance targets. The enemy made a number of weak counter-attacks, but in the perfect light of the afternoon every move could be seen, and they had no earthly chance of success. By 6 p.m. we had captured all the front line south of Fontaine, and a fresh Brigade came up to finish off the support line 400 yards beyond. To cover this final attack a terrific barrage was put down between 7.30 and 8.30 and by nine o'clock the fight was won and we stopped firing.

What with the intense heat of the day and constant work unloading shell, and getting away empty shell cases in preparation for our move, to say nothing of firing of 2,400 rounds in the twenty-four hours with only three men per gun, everyone was rather beat. I was in the cook-house superintending the doping of all ranks with a fearsome beverage of black coffee, rum, and a bottle of liqueur whisky, all boiled together, when a very hungry wounded man escorting two low type Huns drifted in ; while their guard was being fed I got some interesting information out of the prisoners about the effect of our 15-inch Howitzer shells (with No. 106 fuses) on their front line. Before the attack, in a forward trench without dug-outs, they lost over a hundred killed in one short length of trench. This was also confirmed by others who saw the place.

The night passed quietly until 2 a.m., when Taylor at the O.P. began to foresee trouble owing to heavy machine-gun fire, so the sentry at one of the guns and I at another gun opened a slow rate of fire. To manage a gun single-handed is an excellent way to keep warm when one is prowling round the guns before dawn lightly clad. Our last day in action, being the day after a battle, yielded as usual excellent sniping chances, and at intervals the enemy made some feeble efforts across the open, which hardly deserved the name of counter-attacks.

Word came along from Head-Quarters that we could pull out any time after 8 p.m. (21st), handing over our ammunition to a neighbouring battery. Our kits having been sent off earlier, the gun teams came up at 8.1 p.m. and we were clear of the position by 8.4 p.m., quite in the old Salisbury Plain style, communication with Brigade Head-Quarters being cut off as quickly as possible to avoid any chance of the receipt of further orders. It was a perfectly gorgeous sunset, and two Martini cocktails, followed by dinner with champagne and the absence of the ever-busy telephone, completed a good evening. There was a Poker party, of course, with a neighbouring unit. We rarely play Poker among ourselves, as I always prefer being able to take the gloves off with another unit rather than one's own officers.

So ended for us the Battle of Arras, a pleasant war, all things considered, as for two months we had not worn our gas helmets. Our area was on the whole quite a peaceful one, although in the centre of the battle front, at Bullecourt, south of us, life was full of turmoil, and to the north the evil spots, Monchy, Oppy, and Gavrelle seemed to be wreathed in a perpetual barrage.

In this push, even more than in the Somme, one realizes what a difference it would have made if every Brigade, or still better every Battery, could have a Highland stalker among its observers.

You know the difference there is between first class amateur billiards and first class professional billiards : well, there is just as much between an amateur spyer and a professional who is born to the use of the telescope, and yet I suppose only about one man in 10,000 could ever earn the name of a good amateur.

On the 22nd we marched away, leaving behind us in the deserted wagon line a forlorn heap of beds, chairs, sofas, tables, and about ten stoves. They will be a good find for someone, I hope, and with the prospect of long marches ending with a train journey, it was impossible to carry much surplus gear.

Two months before, we had made a bridge over the Cojeul in order to get our own guns into action. It was only meant for private use and not for the motor lorries of the whole British Army during April and May, so its condition was by now naturally the worse for wear, with the result that while crossing it for the last time the Officers' G.S. Wagon managed to fall off the bridge and caused a good deal of hard swearing. I took a different route from the battery in order to lunch with the North Irish Horse (Farnham's Squadron), and also to pick up a horse hidden there for certain reasons during the last two days. The battery had quite a successful march, picking up a horse and two mules and having only one horse reclaimed, also a nice-looking young setter joined them on the road, which will be useful for partridge shooting further north. Owing to all batteries grazing their horses in large herds in the open clover fields, a good many had changed hands, so every outgoing battery is carefully examined by those who are anxious to reclaim their horses.

After two very hot days' marching we reached Luchieux on the 24th. In order to escape the heat we had adopted for our battery Indian hours, marching at dawn and sending on in front of us the mess wagon and cooks to prepare breakfast. We thus reached our destinations by 10 a.m. Luchieux is a delightful little town. In its centre is a very old chateau belonging to the Duchesse d'Uzé, who used to have a well-known pack of hounds in the neighbourhood.

Next day a short march brought us to the entraining point at Doullens, whence we and Brigade H.Q. left by the first train at noon. It was a terrific day of heat, so the canteen fund was brought into action to provide drinks for all ranks on the journey, and as the train crawled slowly northwards the drivers were able to keep jumping out to cut and collect green fodder for the horses all along the embankments. Wonderful to relate, no one got lost except at Hazebruck, where the battery dog "Jack" got mixed up in a street fight with most of the other canine inhabitants of the town, and a batman had to be left behind to disentangle the combatants. No one yet knew our destination, but the pair came on by a later train and rejoined us at our new wagon lines at night.

We detrained at dusk, and after a march of eleven kilometres reached our future home outside Westoutre by midnight. Our lines are in a young wheat field, as pasture land is usually reserved by the farmers in preference to wheat when they are forced to give up more ground.

So here we are in a new land awaiting a new Push.

LETTER FORTY-ONE.

DICKEBUSCH LAKE. (6TH JUNE, 1917.)

A Stormy Reception on the New Front. Casualties and Explosions.

THEN I last wrote, I described our arrival at Westoutre, where we stayed for three days preparing our present position. Down South, we had always been hearing of the comfort and peace in which the Northern Armies, particularly the Second, lived since 1915, and we had found it to be even more luxurious than we expected. In the back areas, there were perfect wagon lines, harness rooms, hutments, laundries, ablution places, clean kitchens, millions of notice boards, white paint, red tape, and warfare of the most virulent and rigid type. What with Camp Commandants, Area Commanders, and all the rest of them, everywhere behind the line, elaborating each detail, and ordering everyone about, it was just like going to school again. In fact, during the three days of rest at our wagon lines, the worry of coping with all the regulations was a most severe ordeal, but now these cares are left to my captain, and we are up in action in a notoriously hot place, where we get strafed to Hell all day, and gassed most nights. On the other hand, as some compensation, we enjoy perfect immunity from that far greater affliction, the lower ranks of the British Staff.

The wide open hills of the Somme and Arras country, being ideal for battle fighting and observation, have spoilt one for this cramped country, which is a maze of hedges, trees, and houses, with Messines Ridge the only feature in view; it is rather like shooting partridges in Essex after grouse driving in Scotland.

On the 27th, the Colonel and all the Battery Commanders went up to see the positions that had been partially dug for us by various residenter batteries, and good work they had done, too, much better than the shallow scratches in the ground which one usually finds when a position has been dug to order for an incoming battery. We are just in front of Dickebusch Lake, and our H.Q. is near by in Gordon's Farm.

The guns went up to the position on the night of the 28th, and

I followed next day. On our way up we all inspected the famous "Bull Ring," which is really a big scale (1/200) model in clay and sand of Messines Ridge and the neighbouring country. On one side of it there is a long stand from which the whole can be clearly viewed. Every house, trench, and mine-crater are shown on it, even to the wire entanglements.

In the afternoon we got the guns registered from an O.P in a ruined house. We only succeeded, however, after a desperate struggle with many other observers who were all waiting to use the one line. This business over, Major Jack and I made a long tour of the front line. Before our position there are a number of new and very obvious light railway tracks, which always draw fire, and we saw at once that we had got into a pretty poisonous locality, which is the usual fate of a battery new to an area, and events soon proved that our misgivings were well founded. All the first night and the following day we were continually shelled, and on the second night, after three hours of very heavy shelling, which caused explosions and fires in the ammunition dumps all round, the Hun suddenly began to pour in a hail of gas shells. It was the first gas attack we had had for many months, and after a long period of immunity men are apt to get careless. Besides, it was not easy to warn them all quickly, as they were scattered about in pairs in two-foot-deep shelters, under curved sheets of iron. Owing to the swamp it is impossible to dig deeper than this, and it is safer to have many small dug-outs, thereby avoiding heavy losses from any one shell. However, Clark, the officer on night duty, and I managed to blunder on to them, after some difficulty, what with our gas masks and the pitchy darkness.

This gas shelling lasted for about an hour and a half, after which they continued to send over 5.9's, one of which caused the most terrific explosion that I have ever heard. Just in front of our guns the light railway trains had dumped a stock of several thousand trench-mortar bombs ; this dump caught fire, or rather the boxes caught fire, and sufficient heat having been generated the whole dump suddenly detonated. To give you some idea of the force of the explosion, the solid wooden door of our mess, 300 yards from the dump was shattered into small splinters about a foot long. The resulting crater was about 30 feet deep and about half the size of a tennis court, while all round lay huge lumps of solid blue clay, many 6 feet high, ejected from the depth of the earth. Luckily none of them fell on our flimsy dug-outs.

We got through the night without casualties, although "B" Battery, including Jack himself, who was slightly gassed, was not so lucky. Next day, which was the first of June, the band started again at dawn, and "C" Battery had heavy losses amongst officers and men. For me, however, the day was peaceful, as I spent it wire-cutting from the comparatively tranquil front line. On my way up there I called at Gordon's Farm to see the Colonel, and found that the greater part of the building had fallen in as the result of the night's explosion. All the morning heavy shells were falling round the farm, and at noon another large ammunition dump near by blew up and the remainder of the building collapsed in flames. The Colonel and his Staff, having just managed to escape from their cellar with the greater part of their gear, came over to shelter in our position, where, finding things little better, they moved further back to another ruined farm behind us. Although we had been firing all day, we got off pretty cheaply—two gun-pits blown in, but the guns not much damaged, and eight men slightly wounded. But the other batteries of our brigade were unlucky, the "Hows." in particular going on fire all along their position and every gun, of course, being put temporarily out of action; "B" battery had about 12,000 rounds blown up, and "C" several officers and men killed. Things became quiet towards evening, and we were able to get the position ship-shape once more, but I was the only Major left in the Brigade. Shell-shock, gas and sickness accounted for the others. All night long heavy shelling continued; I had been able, however, to get a complete relief up from the wagon line, and with fresh men around one the world looked brighter. Head-Quarters seemed to be clean out of luck, as an 8-inch shell completely wrecked their new home, and they were reduced to camping in a wheat field far from hedges, roads, houses and other abominations which the Hun always shells.

Our counter-battery work started to-day, and I heard that we had engaged 62 batteries and had completely knocked out 22, and had chewed up a good many others, so things should soon improve. On the 3rd of June the Hun left us alone all day, and in the afternoon I rode up to the famous Kemmel Hill, about three miles on our right flank, in order to observe a "Chinese Bombardment" on the whole Second Army front. Kemmel Hill, rising up from the plain to a height of nearly 500 feet, is a marvellous spot. Outside, the hill is covered with dense masses of flowering bushes and shrubs, but the whole of its inside is tunnelled through, and is a labyrinth of timber-lined passages, from which open out square O.P. rooms, each with its numbered door, exactly like rows of opera boxes. Just before 3.15 the road below the hill looked like the outside of the paddock of a race meeting, cars tearing up and unloading their cargoes of glittering Staff. As we had not right of entry into one of these O.P.'s de luxe, Wilshin and I and a Major of a Tank Company sat under the cover of a large bush of flowering currant, just below the Greek Temple which crowns the hill, and from there we had a most perfect view.

At 3.15 the whole front, from Ypres in the North, to below Plug Street in the South, was simultaneously outlined by a sheet of flame and smoke, a sheet which for ten minutes crept forward steadily into Hun Land, and then for the last five minutes dropped back on to their front line. While Hun Land was paved with bursting shells, our own country appeared to be studied with tiny pin-pricks of fire—so packed were our guns. Every hedge, bush or earth hummock emitted its quota of flame and the narrow, quick flashes of the 18-pdrs., the long broad flashes of the high velocity guns, and further back the broad belch from the mouth of some heavy Howitzer made up a striking picture of modern war. But the enemy evidently realized that we were only amusing ourselves, and made no reply to all this demonstration.

On my way back I called at Brigade Head-Quarters for tea and found them up to their necks in paper connected with the most ambitious and complicated Artillery Barrage that has ever been evolved by the British Army. On being bribed by the Colonel with a well-polished Dunhill pipe, I weakly promised to lend them for a few days my private Corona Typewriter to enable them to cope with this flood-tide of paper.

We were gassed all that night, and as usual the light railway line was blown up, necessitating the customary struggle to get the ammunition train away before dawn and the Hun aeroplanes arrived. I spent the 4th of June wire-cutting from the front line, so for me it was a peaceful day, but at the guns it was as stormy as ever. Alas! I had to refuse all Old Etonian dinners that night, and in fact spent most of it wearing a gas helmet.

The 5th of June was a very unlucky day. Early in the morning about fifty men came up from the wagon line for ammunition fatigues until the morning mist lifted, as the daily expenditure and the requirements for zero day are perfectly colossal. Unfortunately, before we could get this big party away, the Hun opened a very heavy fire on us and the neighbouring batteries, using both 5.9's and 4.2's. We got most of the men safely into the marsh behind the guns where there is less risk from splinters, but as bad luck would have it, just as several officers from "B" battery, who had been blown out of their position, were coming down to shelter with us, a 5.9 landed near the door of our Mess, wounding three of them and two of ours, as well as other ranks. Wilshin, Taylor, and our mess waiter, all wounded and blown into the cook-house, performed a very gallant act. Although wounded and in some sort of a shelter, they nevertheless, led by Taylor, rushed out and carried into the Mess, Hill, who was lying desperately wounded in the open. All this time 5.9's were coming in at the rate of four a minute and a dump was exploding violently just beside them, and the mess waiter got hit twice more. Wilshin who was only slightly hurt, and I had a busy time for the next hour. Six wounded men were already in the Mess, and seven others had to be dragged into safety, but with the help of two sergeants we got them all in without further casualties. By a series of rushes I got to my dug-out and back with some morphia for Hill, and he remained conscious and happy till in about an hour the end came. A very stout fellow, he, in April, on the eve of the battle of Arras, got the M.C. for an excellent piece of work. After about an hour our doctor got through the barrage, and a little later we were able to get away all the wounded on trucks down the light railway.

In the afternoon, under another Chinese bombardment on the whole front, several companies followed the barrage up to the second line on our sector, and took 80 prisoners, finally getting back without any casualties. Our infantry, of course, were greatly bucked over the affair. After the seven days of shelling the Huns that still remained in the trenches were mostly off their heads and not very warlike.

Our heavy bombardment (I mean 6-inch to 15-inch) is wonderful to listen to, especially at night, for in the day time the bark of the 18-pdrs. drowns all else. After dark, however, while we slow down to 400 rounds per night per battery, the siege guns never stop firing, and when lying in a dug-out with one curved sheet of iron, it sounds like a series of electric trains rushing by overhead.

LETTER FORTY-TWO.

WESTOUTRE. (10TH JUNE, 1917.)

A Well-Staged One-Act Show.

> Mithras, God of the Morning, our trumpets waken the Wall!
> "Rome is above the Nations, but Thou art over all!"
> Now as the names are answered, and the guards are marched away,
> Mithras, also a soldier, keep us true to our vows!
>
> R. KIPLING.

WE hardly seemed to have got into action on this front before we were back in the wagon lines again. The battle was over, and, as usual, we were awaiting orders to push off elsewhere.

It was a short "one chapter" battle distinguished by an ambitious and intensely complicated barrage. Almost every breed of gun and Howitzer were included in the moving barrage, with an objective seven lines deep. The first line was, of course, the Hun front-line trench, then came the red line, the blue, the green, the black, the mauve, and then another green, the whole series of attacks lasting over a period of 16 hours. For every period the most minute tasks were given to each gun; in fact, there was a change of target every two or four minutes.

Many entirely new features were introduced into the barrage. For example, during periods of consolidation, the barrage, instead of remaining a stationary wall of smoke just in front of our digging infantry, giving away their location to hostile M.G.'s, now danced wildly about the country, only 50 per cent. being left for the immediate protection of the infantry.

The whole battle, or rather series of operations concentrated into one short day, went through to scheduled time without a single flaw from start to finish—each line was consolidated, fresh divisions went through each other like clock-work, brigades of Artillery moved up for the attack on the two final lines, and light railways were running to our old firing line before dark. Of course, we know only what was happening on our own narrow divisional front (a very narrow one at that), but I have never met before an attack such confident infantry. Our battery was covering a Lancashire Battalion, and the men in my Battery knew many of them, in fact the gun-pits when we were not being shelled were always full of visitors. As their company commanders put it, it was indeed fortunate that a few days before the show the Kaiser had published his speech about not taking prisoners, as none of them felt they could have expressed that excellent idea so well. They were fairly out for blood, and after seeing the practice barrages, which were only at quarter or half-pressure, there was some confidence flying about.

The severe shelling of the 5th was the last effort on the part of the Hun Artillery, and by the day of battle our counter-battery work had smothered every hostile gun.

At 8 a.m. on the 6th I went with the Colonel to a pow-wow held by General Monkhouse. In the middle of his harangue we had to take ground to a flank rather swiftly, as the Hun suddenly developed a hate against the corner of the field where we were sitting. Among other things, we were told that Z day was to be on the 7th. The rest of the day we spent in putting finishing touches to the barrage tasks for each gun; the bulk of this work had been done in peace at the wagon line, any delicate work while at the guns being quite impossible. Our preparations were completed by a final registration of the guns, full dress rehearsals of the most complicated parts of the barrage, arrangements about water, oil, gas helmets, etc., and finally a long explanation of the barrage tables to the double detachments.

In order to keep the time from Zero, we had a sort of cricket scoring board erected behind the guns at a point easily visible from each pit. The battery clerk with a stop-watch lay in a pit beside it, and as each minute passed he put it up on the board by means of large 12-inch numbers made by cutting ammunition box lids in half, and burning the numbers on them with cordite. These were then illuminated till dawn came by means of lamps.

When the 390th minute was hoisted, our set task was done. As one never knows until the last moment the actual hour of Zero it is difficult and inadvisable to convert to actual day time every gun table. Garnett Clarke, a new officer, also hailing from the Argentine, had eagerly accepted the chance of being F.O.O. with the Head-Quarters of one of the assaulting battalions, so he went off to join his H.Q. at 7 p.m. along with a combined party of signallers from each battery of our brigade. The two nightly ammunition trains turned up before midnight without mishap; usually they got gassed, blown up or else ran off the line, so punctuality was not their strong point.

All night long the usual bombardment continued, the Howitzers, however, firing lethal gas shells. What a bombardment it has been! One can hardly wonder at the gibbering lunatics captured next day that were formerly human beings.

Pongo, the Brigade H.Q. dog, turned up at 1 a.m. with an orderly bringing the synchronized watch and the news that Zero was at 3.10 a.m. I remember noting down that 3.10 a.m. plus 13 seconds by our Battery watch was the moment the flag should fall. After that I slept till the guard woke me at 2.30 a.m. Having made final corrections from the thermometer for the range, which was somewhat anxious work, as we were one of the creeping batteries and had to shoot just over our Infantry's heads the whole time, I got my army dressed in their gas masks at the "alert", though, once they saw the Hun's number was up, they rapidly reverted to their usual state of undress while working the guns.

It was difficult not to get the fidgets during the last ten minutes. The Hun was gas-shelling a little on our right, and one knew if by some miracle of spy work he had learnt the Zero hour, he might open a barrage on our packed assembly trenches. It was a reeking night, hot, damp and dark, with a clouded moon. Mist rose from the marsh, and a poisonous smell of gas permeated everything.

At 30 seconds before Zero the whole earth shook with a sideways vibration, as the whole line of mines went off together. The sappers had been working at them for nearly a year and even longer in some places, and they extended for a great distance under the Hun lines. I forgot how many hundred tons of explosives were in each. The stupendous roar as they went up was followed 15 seconds afterwards with one rippling crash as the whole world broke into gun flashes. What an intoxicating and exhilarating noise is a "full steam" barrage. It reminds one somehow of the glorious thunder of hoofs down a hard polo ground. Once it had started all cares and troubles vanished, and beyond strolling round to visit each gun there was nothing to do. But the concussion of the myriad guns stirred up all the latent gas lying in the shell-holes, and that, mixed with the N.C.T. and cordite fumes and the dense clouds of dust made the atmosphere like nothing on earth.

The pace of our fire varied according to what was going on, e.g., during the periods of consolidation of each captured line it would drop to a round per gun per minute, and which gave us the chance of resting the guns and doing small repairs. Then as soon as the Infantry were ready to move on the barrage re-formed in front of them, and having gradually worked up to "intense" crept forward once more. Very soon it grew light, but the mist persisted as usual before a hot day till late in the morning.

The main track to the dressing-station for walking wounded and to the prisoners' cage ran just behind our guns. No one could possibly lose their way, as along every track were big white notice boards. Remembering how thirsty wounded men always are, we had placed forty ammunition boxes in a circle beside the track just behind the guns to serve as seats, and two of the batmen were on duty as waiters. The water they handed out was a God-send to the many that came, and soon the ammunition boxes were seating a cheery crowd yarning with our relief detachments. The bulk of the wounded had been hit by our own shells, as they admitted having followed the barrage too closely, making no allowance for the inevitable back-flying splinters.

All the wounded officers I talked to were very bucked with the barrage. Up till the capture of the Black Line, which meant an advance of 3 kilometres, I only heard of one M.G. firing, and no one had seen a Hun using his bayonet or rifle. After the Black Line there was a little more fighting, but practically all the cement M.G. forts had been blown in or half-buried with thrown-up earth, so the few remaining M.G.'s were compelled to fire from the open, and their shooting was most inaccurate. Clarke, our F.O.O., who went over with the third wave, saw a Tank trying to squash a small M.G. fort by sitting on the roof and rocking to and fro, but the reinforced cement was too strong, so it waddled back a few yards and spat its 6-pdr. H.E. shells through the slits for the necessary few minutes. On our immediate front our losses in killed were very small indeed. Clarke penetrated to a distance of 4 kms., and told us he did not see more than eight British dead all day. In the first part of the attack the Huns were mostly all killed, but later, as the day grew hot, the men tired of that amusement and prisoners came in faster.

Early in the morning a very quaint pair turned up at the Battery en route for the dressing-station, consisting of a young subaltern and his Irish sergeant. I sent off the former to our mess and was chatting to the sergeant, who was very amused on seeing his charge going off for a drink. "An' him going for more drink, indade, and how'll I be getting him past the prisoners' cage at all, whin he's fair fighting mad already." Then he described how the pair of them had reached one of the cement M.G. forts. The sergeant had evidently mounted on the roof from a flank—"an' there was meself poking bombs down the slits just as quick as you like, and the varmints coming out at the back door to surrender, all so sweet and aisy, and thin whin I got to the back I found himself had been waiting on them as they came out and had them all kilt in a row."

To return to the guns. They stood the strain pretty well on the whole, but by 5 a.m. they were almost red-hot. The scenes in the gun-pits were rather like the battle pictures of Nelson's day, a bunch of gunners stripped to the waist, covered with oil, a mountain of empty shell cases, clouds of steam rising from pools of water raised to boiling point even though poured only once through the bore ; mops, rammers, more oil, dust, and debris of sandbags made up the picture, the whole being veiled by the green mist made by the bower of verdant spotted netting which encircles the gun-pit—netting which never loses an opportunity of catching fire.

At about 7 a.m. I went up to our nearest O.P., but there was nothing to be seen, as our men had by that time crossed the top of Messines Ridge. The enemy were not putting up a genuine barrage, merely scattering shells at random all over the country.

I talked to a lot of Hun officers during the day, and the rage they showed against their own Artillery was most marked. Throughout our bombardment they had always been told "that it really did not hurt them, that they must remember that they were supported by an enormous force of Artillery, and that at the critical moment such a blast of shells would open that the British would never get beyond the support lines." A Hun Brigade-Commander captured by our Division said that he never believed it possible that such a mass of guns could be manœuvred as one in all that complicated barrage. He was fairly lost in admiration, and said one could neither advance nor retire, as our barrages were moving both in front and behind them.

All round the O.P. the country had changed greatly since the day before. The communication trenches were hardly used at all during the last night, as all the hedges previously cut low at the roots now showed wide gaps every few yards, allowing a free passage to the front line, and the whole landscape seemed to be smothered in flags of every colour. Each Brigade of Artillery due to advance had its own route marked out with its particular coloured flag at every 25 yards, its route through hedges and over trenches having been prepared overnight by the Sappers. The whole show moved with a wonderful "click." By 10 a.m. there was a flagged-out track running 3 kilometres into Hunland, a fully-equipped dressing station near the top of Messines Ridge, and stores of every description were pouring up by convoys of pack mules. Several brigades advanced at 8.30 a.m., and during their move our Brigade and the others remaining behind carried on the battle for the next two lines, which were successfully captured by 9.40 a.m., after which there was a lull for all except the heavy guns, which still fired incessantly.

On my way back to the battery I overtook eleven German officers, followed by a curious-looking object covered with blood from head to foot, brandishing a bayonet, rather drunk, and so busy telling everyone he met that HE was the Black Line casualty that at intervals he had to run after his charges, who walked steadily and sulkily up the hot dusty road through Ridge Wood. The whole attack had been explained and practised in such detail by all ranks that every man knew the name of each trench and the whereabouts of each imaginary coloured line.

We had stopped our set programme of fire at 9.40 a.m., but soon after that somebody's aerial mast received an L.L. call from one of our 'planes, so off we all went again, barraging in front of the last line we had captured. One always imagines vast counter-attacks, so our Battery alone ripped off 760 rounds. A little later an indignant message came through from the front line asking us if we would kindly stop firing, as the counter-attack reported by aeroplane was only a battalion of Huns advancing with their hands up, and as they had been mostly wiped out, our men were anxious to go forward and rake in the survivors, who were now hiding in shell-holes about 300 yards in front of our outposts.

The new battle covered by the brigades which had advanced, and in which we took no part, started about noon and was equally successful, but as I had not averaged much sleep during the last nine nights I retired to bed for a couple of hours, and then spent the remainder of the afternoon photographing Hun prisoners as they passed, varying this amusement by tinkering with the guns, which by this time had been reduced to a rather delicate state of health.

At 8 p.m. orders came for us to move back to the wagon lines. Luckily Wilshin, who was living at the wagon lines recovering from wounds received on the 5th, had come up to dinner with us on a fast horse, so he raced back the 7 kilometres to Westoute, and the gun limbers and horses arrived before 10 p.m. To save our men some hard pulling one of the subalterns caught a big bunch of prisoners and made them man-handle the guns out of the deep pits, and in the meantime I galloped back to spend a great evening at the hospitable B.A.C. Mess, with the Colonel and the H.Q. which had also got down.

The newspapers say that Lloyd George heard the mines go off in England—he must have sharp ears! Roberts, my captain, came up to the guns the night before, as a holiday from the cares of the wagon line, and to see the battle, but having crept into an empty officer's dug-out (a hole covered by two sheets of tin), and not having been called, he slept soundly through the whole thing and never woke up till late in the morning.

The absolute quietness of the back areas feels very strange at first, and it is curious being able to get into one's bed bag without all the preparations necessary in a "quick-jump" position, when steel helmet, gum boots, pencil, electric torch, matches, map of angles, gas box, and the phone receiver on the pillow have to be arranged, and the line to exchange O.K.'ed. When all this has been done there is the correct time to get from the battery watch, and the blanket which forms the dug-out door has to be treated with anti-gas mixture. Then, and only then, can we try to sleep, although possessed by the firm conviction that awakenings during the night will be many.

Reinforcements in the shape of officers, men and horses soon arrived, and in two days the Brigade was up to strength again.

About a week ago a Hun aeroplane came over very low, and dropping one bomb, killed thirty-six horses and wounded many more in B Battery lines next to us.

To-morrow, the 11th, we pull out from here and move on to our next scene of activity, so life will not be dull in the near future. Battle-fighting may be an acquired taste, but once acquired it is a very lasting one.

LETTER FORTY-THREE.

NEAR THE DEAD END, YPRES. (28TH JULY, 1917.)

The Curtain Rises on the Ypres Tragedy. A Fiendish Ten Days.

> If blood be the price of Admiralty,
> Lord God, we ha' bought it fair!
> R. KIPLING.

AFTER our short visit to the Messines front we had a pleasant rest back at Wattou, where battery sports, gymkhanas, general spit and polish, glittering harness, and dinners in the little restaurant in Wattou Square were the order of the day. From there we had our first introduction to the plague spot where we are now in action.

We all went up in motor buses—a huge army—three officers and 25 men from each of the eight batteries that were out at rest in that neighbourhood. The idea was to inspect the positions we had to prepare and to commence work on them, but out of that army of about 250 of all ranks, I do not think more than five ever reached the positions that day.

Having alighted from our buses, we were taken in hand by guides and made our way forward in small groups. All went well until we were within a mile of Ypres; then down came a really first-class barrage on the whole area. Very soon the guides got lost and parties began to separate, dodging from shell-hole to shell-hole, until finally the bulk went to ground in the deep dug-outs by the canal. Only a few of us managed to make our way forward by map, and at last reached the positions, marked out by white pegs on the ground, but beyond voting them all equally pestilential we did nothing, and after a long delay the army eventually found its way to the waiting buses and so home.

Soon after this the wagon lines were moved forward to near Vlamertinghe, and work on the new positions began in earnest. Besides that, there were the usual nightly ammunition fatigues, getting up shells to the various positions, and carting them on to forward dumps.

During the days in the beginning of July there was intense aerial activity on both sides, and the Hun 'planes were especially offensive against the chain of sausages which haunt the sky near our wagon line, looking like a row of aerial sentry boxes. Five of these were brought down in three days. On one occasion three Hun 'planes attacked the balloons nearest us. As soon as the 'planes began to swoop down, the six occupants of the balloons jumped out and came floating down below their white parachutes, but none of the balloons caught fire, and the Huns cleared off suddenly and made for home. A moment later a squadron of our new fighting 'planes dropped out of the blue on to them, and after a real good scrimmage two of the Huns whirled down in flames, and the remaining fellow was forced to within 50 feet of the ground and then headed back over our heads. His speed was at least 120 m.p.h., and in close pursuit, about a hundred yards higher up, were two of our 'planes with their machine-guns going like blue murder. It was a real tally-ho chase. Though the dust was being flicked up in every direction around us, none of our horses were hit with the bullets from our 'planes. The Hun made a marvellous landing at full speed on a parade ground behind us among the mass of infantry camps. Jack and I and most of the battery tore after him to be in at the death, which proved to be very nearly true, as when we reached the spot there was a raging crowd of several thousand men round the tent in which the prisoner had been placed. Feeling was running pretty high, for everyone thought he had machine-gunned the camp on landing, though probably our own machines had done it! As we could not get anywhere near we returned home. We heard later that soon after we had left someone cried "Remember London," and the tent ropes were cut. In the ugly rush that followed the two British officers with the prisoner had a very thin time of it. From our wagon lines a mile away we could hear the mob howling for blood. The Hun was eventually rescued by a small body of Colonels armed with thick sticks! I fear this is not a very creditable incident, but it is indicative of the trend of feeling out there. In a few years we shall doubtless have got down to cannibalism.

On the 13th July mustard gas made its début with great effect, but although we had a lot of working parties out in it we got through the night fairly cheaply; but there was a hideous total of casualties elsewhere. This gas is very difficult to detect, and when one is floundering about in pitchy darkness with a lot of teams, hopelessly entangled, and horses down in shell-holes, it is often impossible to make the drivers keep their respirators on.

We had great difficulty in getting the work finished on the various positions we were detailed to make. On some of them it was impossible to move in daylight unless there was enough wind to keep the Hun balloons down, while on hot still nights work became almost impossible owing to the gas. Besides all this we were continually shelled; in fact, this July has seen a real revival of all the old horrors of the Salient.

At last, however, all was ready, and on the 19th, at the fashionable hour of 2 a.m., the first four guns went up into action, and I followed when the dawn was slightly aired. During the last few days before moving up into action I had been very busy with endless details, rather like reefing and battening down for a sou'-wester off Barra, for in a position like this one has to consider every possible scheme which may help to economize the lives and energy of all ranks.

Here we have to change the detachments every two days, and I only keep at the guns with me one subaltern by night, and two officers by day, which gives them thirty-six hours in action and three days at the wagon line. This relief is absolutely necessary, because all-night doses of gas leave them very feeble. So far it has not affected me much, beyond making me more unpleasant than usual at breakfast. Certainly the days and nights we have experienced of late are the worst I have ever known in France.

Our position has every possible drawback. It is surrounded by much-used tracks, a large ammunition dump is alongside, and behind is the canal with its perpetually shelled bridges. On the top of this the position is already known to the Hun, a battery having been shelled out of it earlier in the month. However, being visible from the Hun lines we are chiefly employed in doing harassing fire by night—our only blessing!

I touch but lightly on our life during the ten days' bombardment: it proved to be a monotonous foretaste of hell. On the 20th we got the guns registered on a corner of a hedge, about the only suitable point for a Zero point within range. All that night and the next day there was an incessant bombardment with gas shell and 5.9.'s, and we had many casualties again, including four Nos. 1. It was quite impossible to get any communication with the O.P., and two linesmen were wounded. The following night, unfortunately, was ideal for gas, damp and muggy, with a dense mist, and the Hun shelled the roads and bridges very heavily, at the same time drowning the whole countryside with gas shell. We managed to get the last two guns up and into action, but failed over the ammunition supply for our future position at Potijze Chateau, and had some gas casualties to horses and men.

On the 22nd we relieved the gun detachments, or rather what remained of them, but the Hun made up for letting us have a comparatively peaceful day by deluging the tracks with shell all night, costing us five drivers and a lot of horses killed or wounded. The same story holds good for the 23rd, 8-inch and 5.9.'s all day, and every dug-out missed by a few feet, and gas all night. To fire 900 rounds nightly is no easy matter, but we have now got our dug-outs very gas-proof, and we had luckily no further casualties.

The bad luck that has followed D Battery of our Brigade still persists. Already they have had nearly 50 casualties, and last night a 5.9 came through the roof of the Officers' Mess, killing or wounding all inside except Major Sarson who was badly shell-shocked.

The 24th was another roastingly hot day. I went up to the O.P. early to register the guns for a daylight raid due at noon that day. I had just done two of them when the Hun started shelling our position and the neighbourhood generally with heavy shells, and kept it up for two hours. However, as we were only registering, Clarke wisely cleared the gunners away, there being already two hits on the pits.

Disasters on the telephone always seem worse than they really are. I picked up the receiver and heard that an 8-inch had landed at the door of the telephone pit, and that the operator was alone with his companion wounded; the next moment a distant voice told me that another shell had hit the pit, and that the roof was coming in, then silence—then Clarke's voice for a moment—then silence again.

Enough registration for my purpose being accomplished, I left Prest at the O.P. to watch the raid, and hurried back to see if anything was left of the battery. I found Clark and two N.C.O.'s sitting serenely on the position, and as the shelling was slackening we collected the men out of the holes in the canal bank where they had been sent for safety, and set them to dig the half-buried guns out of the wreckage, so eventually we were ready for the raid barrage at 1 p.m.

The barrage was due to last for 60 minutes, and it seemed an eternity expecting that the Hun would re-open on us at any moment, as once the Infantry are over the top one cannot stop the 'bus to wait for calmer moments, as we do when casually firing on our own. Ten minutes after the barrage opened, the Hun started his counter-battery work, but chiefly on the batteries behind us, and we fortunately only got the benefit of a few short rounds. D Battery had a hopeless time of it; during the morning their new mess was again blown in, and an officer buried, but luckily dug out unhurt, and later during the raid they lost so heavily that they had to cease fire. That afternoon it was our turn again, but we had blocked every doorway with sand-bag screens to escape casualties from splinters, and we had no direct hits on dug-outs, though many shells came far too close to be pleasant.

Prest returned from the O.P. in the evening with the news that Jack (O.C., B Battery), while watching the raid, had been badly wounded in seven places. He will be a great loss to the Brigade, for he is a born fighter and equally brave in hot or cold blood. At the beginning of the War he held a very high post in the Indian Civil Service and joined the Regiment as a 2nd Lieutenant for sheer love of fighting—rather a good effort ! He also realizes that the way to win the war is to kill the enemy, and not merely bombard his country.

As sleep at night is almost impossible, I had turned in at five p.m. with the hope of snatching an hour's rest, but soon after an officer of D Battery came round with the message from the Colonel that I was to try and find them a new position, as theirs was untenable. This was not an easy matter, as every available corner is studded either with guns or ammunition dumps. Gas as usual all that night. As I am up at the guns all the time, the senior N.C.O. and I sleep in a dug-out on a slight rise in the ground, 200 yards from the guns, where there is some relief from the gas ; the officer who is on duty for the night only, conducts the night firing from the Mess beside the guns.

Although we have excellent gas curtains, a lot of gas always comes in when wounded or gassed men blunder in during the night, and as my dug-out is beside a much-used Infantry track I keep a large supply of shell dressings and ammonia capsules for our many visitors. To clear the air during any lull in the gas-shelling we light bonfires of newspapers and use flapper fans. I may add that the telephone line from my dug-out to the guns is always cut early in the night, and as it is useless risking men to mend it until dawn, we have to do without.

On the 25th there was a break in the hot weather and it rained most of the day, but as there was no wind the gas hung about the guns until late in the morning. I rode down to the wagon line, had a bath, and turned in for a few hours. Having brought with me the barrage orders for the great attack, the officers down there were able to start working them out, as it is quite impossible to do any consecutive work at the guns. Our Mess up there is about 8ft. by 5ft., and when we are not being heavily shelled ourselves it is usually crowded with other people who have been temporarily shelled out of their own messes, besides which there is nearly always a medley of people eating and sleeping, wounded being dressed, gassed being given ammonia, somebody trying to phone or fugitives from some other temporarily impossible mess dug-out sitting in corners endeavouring to work out their angles for the next practice barrage, while maps, orders, instruments, dust or mud, crumbling sandbags and candle grease complete the picture.

I got back in time for a pow-pow at our Brigade H.Q. in the ramparts. Once those dug-outs are reached, one is in perfect safety, but the trouble is getting in and out. When things are stormy it is like a game of baseball, with short dashes from one hole to the next at top speed, but by carefully noting the interval between the salvoes or single rounds, 15 or 30 seconds or 1 minute, one can progress with comparative safety. It is a quaint existence, and one can usually tell the haunts of the people by their appearance. If an individual has had to live in one of the deep mine dug-outs—often 50 feet under ground—he looks pale and washed-out and has the "Rampart Face". The Hun always shells the neighbourhood of such dug-outs, so the inmates are forced to live in the poisonous atmosphere down below, except for hectic dashes out to breathe. If he lives in the suburbs like us, his face carries a healthier but hunted look, and if he has been long in the district he will have the "Wipers Slink", a furtive way of moving across all open places, eternally listening for the hum of an approaching shell! The main trouble is of course due to the salient, as shells come from every direction, and from the extreme accuracy with which the enemy has registered every bridge, track and road. On bad days one has to move about the position in a series of dashes from mess to phone pit, or from one gun-pit to the next.

For us the night was quiet, but the bridges 200 yards behind had a very poor time of it. Early in the night we had twelve wagons up, but luckily all except one had returned across the bridges before the trouble started. I went to the bridge next morning to see if it was possible to rescue our wagon, but the whole of the long earth ramp was a solid block of vehicles, dead horses and men, while a light railway engine which used to run on a ramp raised above the vehicle route lay overturned on top of them all!

On the 26th I went again to the wagon line to complete the last of our preparations for the battle. These details were many, as we are due to move forward twice on the day of the attack, and there is a most intricate time-table fixing the starting points, assembly points, and routes to be followed. This methodical procedure will, I hope, ease slightly the usual hopeless state of congestion on the roads.

During the last few days a huge dump of 18-pdr. shrapnel intended for general use during the advance has been gradually collected on the hill between my dug-out and the guns. Unfortunately a stray shell hit it, and gradually the fire spread from one line of shells to the next, and about 20,000 rounds went west in half an hour. As it was shrapnel shell we were fairly smothered with boxes and fuses flying in every direction. Luckily, being a cloudy day, the Hun did not detect and shell the dense clouds of smoke.

That evening the lull in the hostile shelling still continued, and several people from batteries a hundred yards off ventured to cross the open and visit us, and before dinner we were actually entertained by hearing a succession of 17-inch shells coming over. During the last

FIELD GUNS IN FRANCE

month this gun has only fired on two days, and on this occasion five rounds came over, four of which were duds, fired at intervals of nearly twenty minutes. They make a noise like an elevated electric car passing overhead, and usually land near the canal 200 yards behind us. The concussion from the duds is even greater than that of a shell exploding.

Some hint of the impending attack on the 28th has leaked out, I am afraid, and the Hun barraged the whole of the back areas on the evening of the 27th with the idea of catching troops moving up. The result was heavy casualties, and this should be taken to heart by those at home who talk too much.

Another successful daylight raid, together with practice barrages on the whole army front, took place on the 27th and 28th. There was but little hostile fire during those days, but the night of the 28th was certainly the worst I have ever had in France. From midnight to 3 a.m., we had about 2,000 rounds of gas and heavy shell right on top of us, three of the gun-pits were hit, though fortunately the guns were not damaged, and every dug-out had shell-holes within a few feet. I counted in the morning eight 5.9 craters within fifteen yards of mine, though in the dark the mass of earth they throw on the roof makes one imagine they are much closer. After such a night one always expects to find ammunition dumps on our forward positions blown up, but in the morning I was surprised to find only a few small dumps had gone west. The night of the 29th-30th was a red letter one: nothing at all came near us, though the day as usual was stormy, and two pits were again knocked in, but without damage to the guns, and with only some slight casualties to personnel.

The morning of the 30th was spent in describing, for the benefit of the N.C.O.'s, the routes leading from the wagon line to the forward positions, and in the afternoon I called at H.Q., which I reached after the usual fashion—dodging from hole to hole.

It is the eve of the longed-for Z day! What a relief it is when one has reached the last night, all anxieties and preparations over, six guns in action, and a prospect of a real good slam on the morrow. This time, however, I feel somehow that I have never faced a big show with less confidence in the result.

The eternal ammunition problem is ever the chief worry. Each night the Hun is certain to render impassable some road or other, and it is a pure gamble whether one hits on the right route, and the right hour, to get the ammunition up. There is no telephone to the wagon line, so orders or counter-orders take a long time. On a busy night twelve battery wagons, 6 B.A.C. wagons, and a few lorries are generally due to arrive bound for three different spots, our present position, our future position, and a still more advanced dump. Guides have to be posted to meet them on the road up, and it is not an easy job for them in the pitchy darkness to pick their own wagons out of the seething mass of traffic. Unloading parties have also to be posted in safe places to wait for the convoys, who are often many hours late.

Then, all these arrangements made, a gas shell deluge, or a barrage, makes certain areas unapproachable, and everything has to be changed at the last moment ; more guides sent out to look for the first ones, and to recall unloading parties who have probably gone to ground in some dug-out with their gas masks on and cannot be found, and so on *ad infinitum*. But it is wonderful how everything and everybody muddles through somehow, and on the whole we have been lucky during the last two days, having had no drivers killed and only 25 horse casualties.

Lying in a dug-out alone at night, the slow lumbering shells are heard continuously coming over. If they are destined to burst close but short, they suddenly gather speed and the muscles at the back of the neck tighten involuntarily, then the sickening downward swoop of the big shell and the earsplitting explosion, followed a second later by the rattle of earth on the roof and the whine of flying fragments. If they are due for "over", the downward swoop is not heard and one knows there is no cause for worry.

It is always a good test of nerves to see if one can finish a sentence without a change of voice and only the shortest of pauses for the explosion itself.

LETTER FOURTY-FOUR.

IN THE GARDEN OF POTIJZE CHATEAU.

(15TH AUGUST, 1917.)

*The Battle of the 31st July.   Checkmated by Rain.   More Stormy
Times.*

HERE beginneth the story of our fourth big Zero day. Taken in order they are as follows :—

1916, 1st July. This year, 9th April, 7th June and now (31st July). But besides these four days we have been in about thirty other shows in which at least one Corps attacked.

During the first portion of the night before the battle, we got it pretty "hot", the front of the mess was blown in by a direct hit, and much "valuable" crockery broken. What was worse, however, was that a number of fresh craters appeared in the track that we had carefully prepared behind the guns to allow the gun limbers a faint chance of getting up to the guns in the morning without falling into 8-inch holes at every step. Eventually at midnight all our Howitzers began to drench the hostile batteries with gas-shell at 3.30 a.m., and from midnight on the night was for us blissfully quiet.

The curtain rose at 3.50 a.m., accompanied by the usual racket, reek of H.E., and rocket display by the Hun. On the whole our area was fairly peaceful, and Wilshin arrived with gun limbers at 5.45, having made an easy advance. We were due to cease firing and advance at 6.10 a.m., so at that hour, the backs of the gun-pits having been previously pulled down, we started the heavy labour of man-handling the guns out of their sunk pits. Luckily at that very moment a Highlander came down the track escorting 25 prisoners. I called to him to go into the cookhouse and have some tea, and to hand over his rifle and the prisoners to my tender mercies. The Hun was sending over some 8-inch shell, and when I ordered the prisoners to man the drag-ropes they started to argue that they ought not to be made to do it, but the arguments only lasted 30 seconds ; the well-known sound (almost "Esperanto") of a rifle bolt going to full cock and a few well-chosen words of abuse learnt on a Pomeranian barrack square, quickly got them to work, and meanwhile our gunners were safely under cover and able to have breakfast.

We then limbered up to make our next jump of about 2,000 yards forward, moving chiefly along tracks deep in mud, and covered with new craters. A trestle bridge on our route gave way at one side, letting the leading gun fall half into the stream, which caused delay and much "heaving". We were the last battery to advance, and all the previous batteries had to pass over our future position to reach theirs, so when we reached Potijze Chateau we found the narrow strip of ground (our position) a solid block of vehicles, with horses down everywhere, and a good deal of hostile shelling all around. It was useless waiting until they cleared off our position, so we managed to get the guns up one by one across the shell-holes.

It was like a puzzle, and in the jamb of vehicles even a limber with wheelers only, reversed with difficulty. However, by sending them back the way we had come, we managed to get clear fairly quickly; it was not the proper route, but being the last battery and having no vehicles behind us, it was no use keeping the teams waiting on that dangerous spot.

We had been ordered to bring up twelve wagons of ammunition, but it had been easy to foresee just such a block, and by dumping a larger quantity of ammunition than authorized, I had been able to arrange that our twelve wagons only moved up to our vacated position, and unhooking there the horses returned to an advanced wagon line. As we expected to advance twice on that day, every yard saved for the horses was of value.

We commenced firing again at 8.15 a.m., joining in the barrage at the point it had then reached. I think it was the noisiest corner I had ever been in, for trees, water and buildings double the noise of gun-fire, and we were now in the gardens of the Chateau with an ornamental moat just behind our trails, so there was such a din that one hardly heard the salvoes of 5.9's bursting only 150 yards in front. Luckily no shell hit the road, as the knot of vehicles beside us did not untie itself for over an hour. From 8 a.m. to 10 a.m. we were putting up a slow protective barrage in front of the Black Line (the second line captured). At 10.12 a.m., the barrage rattled up to "intense" and crept forward till 11.30 a.m., when the Green Line was captured. After that, until 12.30., we put up another protective barrage to allow the battle posts to get settled down in front of the Green Line.

Things were pretty warm everywhere, but we had only one detachment completely knocked out, everything else being just over or short. Of course, the many cloudy days recently had hindered our counter-battery work, and it is hard to say which were the greatest

FIELD GUNS IN FRANCE

failures, tanks, 'planes, or the counter-battery work. The Hun 'planes seemed to be able to do what they liked, and flew about everywhere quite low.

At about 11 a.m. Wilshin and I, with two signallers and a similar party from D Battery, who are beside us, went forward to join the Colonel at his new H.Q. for a brigade reconnaissance of our next positions. With a good deal of difficulty and much dodging we all reached the mine dug-outs called the Cart dug-outs, in Oxford Row, not far behind our former support trenches. I will describe later what a mine dug-out is like, briefly it is a wet hell 40 feet underground, its chief constituents being water, filth and stench. Having forced our way down the dripping staircase, which was lined with wounded, we found the Colonel, and as soon as all the B.C.'s had arrived, we started off to try and discover new positions near Wine House, south-west of St. Julien.

Being a hot, muggy day, with low clouds, the atmosphere was like a Turkish bath, and it was desperately heavy going, ploughing one's way through the sea of smashed-in trenches and endless shell-holes, while broken strands of wire lay in wait to trip one at every step. To cross a battlefield when one has a job on hand that brooks no delay is always a trying experience, because then there is no time to help the many wounded lying about. It was difficult to find positions for batteries, and still more so to find a way to get the guns there, as nothing had been done in the way of preparing a road across the trenches.

By 2 p.m., we realized that something had gone wrong with the works ; there was far too intense a barrage, which gradually advanced towards us, and machine-gun bullets were coming in from unexpected places. Then rumours that the Green Line had been heavily attacked reached us, and soon little groups of retiring Infantry came in sight. We chose our positions, though we knew full well that we could never occupy them that day, and hurried back through infernal shelling to H.Q., where we heard that our men had been driven back almost to the Black Line.

On reaching the guns at 4 p.m., I found that they had been firing S.O.S.'s since 2 p.m., and I began at once to make arrangements for a long stay in our present positions instead of the eight hours we had expected, and for a commencement I annexed some excellent empty dug-outs in the Mound at Potijze Chateau. Having galloped back to our former position where the teams were waiting, expecting a fresh advance, I sent the gun limbers back to the wagon line and then dispatched to the guns fresh detachments and eleven wagons. I retained one for Hickey and my kit, as by that time I was in a lather of heat and dirt, and wanted to have a bath and change, so as to be ready for a thick night.

Then came down the rain, heavy rain which continued for the next three days. Through it I floundered up to the guns again along roads so congested that one was often stuck even when riding. All the siege guns in creation seemed to be heaving themselves forward, tied on respectively to caterpillars, tractors, or heavy draught horses, and thousands of men were laying light railways in every direction. I relieved the subalterns and then carried on till 10 p.m. at that very necessary but unpleasant task of digging-in guns against time, with weary men and under an intermittent shell-fire all the time.

All that night and next day (the 1st of August) we were firing S.O.S. or protective barrages, and hostile fire was increasing against the position. It was obviously a bad place for a long stay, as it was on a track, next a main road (Ypres-Zonnebeke) and in front of a well-known mass of dug-outs, which gave us the benefit of every stray shell, so I decided to move even though it meant a new position and shifting thousands of rounds of ammunition. It meant, indeed, trebling the work of all ranks for the next few days, and the men were already pretty beat. Nevertheless all were as keen as mustard for the move; we dug a very neat little position with guns at four yards interval, all connected by a trench with dug-outs for two men beside each gun, the site selected being in a field of thistles near the Chateau. The whole position was covered by a continuous piece of fish netting camouflage, so that the guns were quite invisible when looked at from a point 100 yards in front or behind the position.

We moved out without further casualties on the afternoon of the 3rd. Rain was falling heavily, and the guns were sunk nearly to their axles in mud, but we got them into our new position, which of course was not completed for many days.

During this four days of rain it felt like being back again on the Somme of November, 1916. The same tattered tree-trunks, without a leaf on them, the same wilderness of mud-filled shell-holes, the same muddy traffic-filled roads, with wagons, dead horses, equipment and material of every sort lying about on them. The roads here are indeed literally paved with ammunition boxes and loose rounds fallen from wagons or from pack horses.

From the 1st until the 10th August practically nothing of interest occurred, though we fired endless S.O.S.'s. The battle seems to be at a complete standstill, though nevertheless our ammunition expenditure is enormous. For instance, except for our short advance, we were firing without a single pause from 10 p.m. the night of the 30th till 4 p.m. on the 2nd August. Not having had so far very heavy casualties, our systems of reliefs every two or three days can still be carried out, the officer on duty and two men per gun sleeping on the position, the rest of us living in considerable comfort and safety at the Chateau dug-outs.

On the 8th I went down to the wagon line for a couple of days, my Captain (Roberts) having relieved me at the guns. During luncheons and dinners in Poperinghe at Skindles' Restaurant or at the Club I met many old friends, chiefly from the Guards Division, also Farnham, of the North Irish Horse, who seems fated to follow us about. Pop was looking rather the worse for wear, for during the last ten days the Hun has been fairly pumping the stuff in. I also found that the neighbourhood of our wagon line was flowing with milk and honey in the shape of game, and I got three brace of partridges one morning with the assistance of four men dragging a long piece of rope. This plan was necessary, as the birds were sitting very close. On the next day I had a drive with twelve beaters, and got several partridges, a hare, and two pheasants.

The Hun 'planes have been very active lately bombing the back areas, and on the 9th they brought down the sausage just behind our horse lines. Both the occupants landed safely in their parachutes, though they were swaying very violently from side to side in the high wind.

On returning to the guns on the 10th, I found them still pounding away night and day at unseen targets, to prevent the enemy repairing his wire in a hidden valley. This is not a very interesting type of gunnery, for having found the correction for the day on some visible point there is nothing to observe. I spent the afternoon at H.Q. enjoying the usual war arguments with the Colonel, and actually sitting outside in the sun among the millions of sandbags filled with the very evil-smelling grey mud taken from the shaft. However, pretty soon the Hun began to be tiresome with shrapnel, and we were driven down the shaft into the reeking warren below. The water under the floor was less deep than usual, but the atmosphere was worse. Men have to work continually at the air pumps or water pumps, and one or other of these pumps is always going out of action.

The H.Q. Room is about 10 ft. by 6 ft., in which all four of the occupants have to sleep, eat and work ; a tiny table, four bunks and three stools comprise the whole of its furniture. I tried to persuade the Colonel to come back and join us in the luxurious quarters in the Mound, but as he was always expecting an advance he did not dare risk losing his present home. I hope he will not go sick, as temporary command of the brigade would be an unpleasant legacy for me in these times.

Each night there is usually an S.O.S. call. No one ever knows who starts them, and no one cares what happens in them. There is a sudden burst of gun-fire somewhere, somebody sees or imagines he sees an S.O.S. rocket, and like a plague it spreads all down the line, and for ten minutes there is a hell of a racket gradually dying down to the usual rumbling thunder.

The 12th was an unlucky day. It started with two casualties at the guns, then at night a big joint convoy from two brigades (one of them ours) going forward to form a very advanced ammunition dump, got into serious trouble on the Zonnebeke road. We got off cheaper, however, than most, with only two drivers wounded and 10 horses killed. The same night Wilshin, who was doing brigade F.O.O. with the infantry, had a bad go during an S.O.S. barrage, a 5.9 killing his signaller and slightly wounding him. This was, in fact, his second lucky escape that day, as in the morning, while standing outside our mess in a momentary calm, he and I were both blown over by a stray shell.

The next night I took up a large party to dig a new position on the Frezenberg Ridge, about 100 yards behind our front line. What with looking after their work, and nursing a string of eighty pack horses bringing up shells to that position and trying to extricate five of our wagons, I was kept busy and interested till 8 a.m. These wagons were upset and mixed up in a solid wedge of dead horses and other people's wagons, as the result of last night's work, and to sort them out proved to be a regular Chinese puzzle. The night closed, however, fortunately without casualties.

Next night more work was done in the new position, and another big convoy got up in safety, and they managed to pick up en route two clinking good horses which were wandering about the country, the driver being doubtless a casualty.

I went down to the wagon line on the 14th meaning to stay two nights, but orders coming in about the next big attack on the 16th, caused me to hurry back after twenty-four hours. But in my short visit I managed to get in a lunch at Vlamertinghe Chateau with Corps H.A. Head-Quarters, a visit to Pop for haircutting, a good partridge drive, and the inevitable Poker party at night.

The air fighting is now almost continuous. One often sees pitched battles between fifty 'planes, seemingly an aimless nose-diving and somersaulting scramble, but I suppose the fighting is not really so aimless and disconnected as it appears. I must stop now—it is the eve of another big battle.

LETTER FORTY-FIVE.

POTIJZE CHATEAU. (30TH AUGUST, 1917.)

The Failure of the 16th August. A Hopeless and Endless Push.

> Old Days! The wild geese are flighting,
> Head to the storm as they faced it before!
> For where there are Irish there's bound to be fighting,
> And when there's no fighting, it's Ireland no more!
>   R. KIPLING.

THE battle of the 16th is now over and done with. It was one of the worst days I can remember, and only equalled by those fiascos at the end of July, 1916, when we were attacking Guillemont. By the end of the day we had not advanced a yard on our front, though on the left we captured Langemarck, and the French did fairly well. With us it was the same old story, a multitude of hidden machine-guns, and the Hun Infantry practically withdrawn from the front system. By this arrangement they were ready for an immediate counter-attack on our forces, which as they advanced were greatly reduced by M.G. fire.

In a country which is simply a tangle of fallen trees, broken planks, and timber of every sort scattered over a brown wilderness of craters one could easily hide a 15-inch Howitzer, to say nothing of a hundred machine-guns, which remain silent and undiscovered until the attack is launched. When this combination is coupled with an intense barrage, a disaster can be easily understood.

At the battery, as is often the case on such days, we did not have a shell near us, but unfortunately Duerden, my senior subaltern, while doing F.O.O. for the Group, was badly wounded, and died on the 17th. He was one of the last eight of the band who left England in 1915 with the 30th Divisional Artillery. We shall miss him—a good comrade and a fine soldier.

If the attack had been successful the battery was to have advanced to where we had dumped ammunition, on the Frezenberg Ridge, not far from Rupprecht Farm. In fact, we were supposed to be the leading battery of the twelve due to move up there. Not having had heavy officer casualties, we were asked to supply a Liaison Office

(Prest) and an F.O.O. (Duerden), who went off with a joint army of signallers and runners to join the infantry at Plum Farm.

All night long there was an intense bombardment, a succession of orderlies from Group, or heated couriers from the wagon line arrived with fresh orders issued very often at the last moment.

Zero hour was 4.45 a.m.; there is a deadly sameness about them all. By 6 a.m., hundreds of walking wounded, but no prisoners. At 7.15 a.m., the gun teams and transport, the latter with iron sheeting and sandbags, arrived, halting at a nominally safe spot behind the guns. Soon after I stopped the men from demolishing the back walls of the gun-pits, and by 9 a.m., orders came in to send back the gun teams and to get all the ammunition we could to our present position.

The set barrage came to its useless end at 7.30 a.m. Useless, because after the first fifteen minutes, owing to deep going and much opposition, the infantry were unable to keep up with it, and as means of rapid communication in battle has yet to be devised, it moved implacably forward, finally leaving a 2,000 yard belt of perfect security in which the Hun could appear from his dug-outs loaded with machine-guns, and counter-attack to his heart's content.

When the barrage ended, an interval followed when there was nothing doing, except the eternal strafing by the Heavies. After that came the order : "Rebombardment of the 30 minutes line", meaning a shortening of range of 1,500 yards, and later still, "Fire on the five minutes line." Then we had another long period of waiting, during which we rebuilt the pits, previously taken down for the advance, with the despondent feeling that the whole weary show would have to be done again. As the day wore on we got the signal, "S.O.S. on old S.O.S. Line," meaning that the Hun was counter-attacking and must be stopped, but the whole of these barrages, of course, fell on the top of our wounded, who had fallen during the advance.

We got no definite news till at 11 a.m., when one of our signallers, very beat, drifted back from Plum Farm, where he had been with my two officers, an infantry colonel and six men. He said that at 8 a.m. things were as bad as they could be, and as he could not find a spare rifle Duerden told him to clear out and try and get the news back.

Prest returned at 1 p.m., having first reported at Main Group H.Q. It was the same old story. All five armoured cables to the front line farm were cut to pieces, and wireless masts smashed in the first five minutes; the carrier pigeons were stunned and useless owing to the concussion, and nearly ever runner knocked out while trying to get back. There was again the same maddening feeling of seeing the barrage march away and being unable to do anything to stop it. When he left, the C.O. had just been wounded, and the Adjutant (who was also wounded before the evening) was the only officer left. They were a really good lot, an Irish Regiment of the 36th Division, and we knew them all very well, because while they were in reserve for four days before the attack they had been allotted a very poisonous deep dug-out for their H.Q. close to the Mound, so we had invited the whole H.Q. to come and eat and sleep with us. By evening we heard that Duerden had been wounded, but not knowing where he was, Roberts and two men rode round inquiring at all the C.C.S. hospitals, and at last traced him.

That night the Irish Brigade in front of us were relieved. Each battalion in turn having lived with us for a few days during last week, they all knew our mess and came back to us, our cooks serving a continuous dinner from 7 p.m. to 4 a.m. That night we were able to feed and shelter practically the whole brigade at once, and till late next morning they were sleeping in clumps on the floor quite oblivious to all noise around. It was a bad show.

The 17th was a gloriously sunny day, peaceful with the usual day-after-battle feeling in the air. That night more operation orders came in, which necessitated us getting up in a hurry from the wagon line 800 rounds of smoke-shell. They only arrived just before Zero (4.45 a.m.), and were used to cover an operation slightly to the north of us. Judging by the way the Hun retaliated on our neighbourhood, it must have been successful on the whole. It was not a bad day, as, in spite of a perfect deluge of shell, we did not have a man touched, or a round blown up.

After breakfast, Wilshin and I had just turned in to sleep for two hours, when a 5.9 landed on the roof of the dug-out over the foot of my bed, bursting in the huge tree trunks which formed the walls and smothering me with earth and rubbish. The din of the Hun shells all around, coupled with the usual ceaseless roar of our bombardment, prevented Wilshin from hearing it, and he never woke up, but thinking that the whole roof was coming in I yanked him out of bed by the hair, and we retired to the outer room, which was our mess, while the army wrestled with the debris and propped the timbers up again. About half an hour later another shell landed, this time on the top of the mess, lowering the iron roof about 9 ins., chiefly on the top of Roberts's steel-hat covered head, as he had just arrived from the wagon line, and was standing up with his hat on at the time.

After these two incidents I thought it safer to make for another haven of safety in the shape of our forward O.P. in St. Julien's Farm. To be precise, it was really in a cement M.G. fort built on the site of that farm, and when I got there I proceeded to fire 400 rounds to cut wire in front of Somme Farm. On my way back I thought things were blowing up for a storm, and only just reached the dug-out before a super-concentrated hate opened on our wood and the area all round. We had been having these area strafes every two or three days but this one was the worst of its kind so far, as about 15 batteries of every calibre were fairly pelting it into us. On these occasions everybody goes to ground exactly where he is, and it seldom pays to make a dash across the open, even to secure more complete protection. After an hour and a half of this diversion we all emerged from our respective hiding-places, and found everything and everybody, even to the ammunition, O.K.; we were rather lucky, too, as the whole neighbourhood around was dotted with blazing ammunition dumps.

The newspapers reporting the battle of the 16th having arrived, we learned that the people further north of us had done fairly well, but the Ulster Division in front of us had as bad a day as on the 1st July last year, when they got left in the air at Thiepval. One Battalion of that Division has literally disappeared. We heard it had gone right through to the final objective, and then silence; so far no stragglers from it have returned.

Every day is much the same: we bombard the Huns and the Huns bombard us. I wonder what life in Hunland can be like! On normal days our 15-inch Howitzers fire 50 rounds per gun, the 9.2 Howitzers 80 rounds, and so on down the list in proportion, the 18-pdrs. firing 600 to 900 rounds per battery. There is hardly a green spot to be seen from the old German front line right back for many thousands of yards. The old-time No Man's Land is a delightful spot to walk over after the dust and stench of the newly captured country, as it is now a broad belt of rushes, green grass, and a few clean bones scattered about, relics of the past. The dense wood and ornamental shrubbery round Potijze Chateau has now been stripped of all its foliage, thanks to the incessant shell-fire it has been subjected to, and one can hardly realize that we have lived in the middle of it for three weeks with scarcely any casualties.

Our mess at the guns is dwindling fast. Wilshin has gone on leave, and we have had no more Infantry guests—even the "Body Snatcher" or "Cold Meat Specialist" (Corps Burial Officer) has left us to rejoin his battalion. The latter was a very cheery Irish boy who had messed with us for ten days; we never learnt his real name, since he always answered to the above sobriquets. He was in charge of our area and was most useful in removing our pet aversions, which otherwise might have remained unburied for months.

Our next big Zero hour was 4.45 a.m., on the 22nd. It was preceded by a rather strenuous night, as by the time we had finished working out barrage orders which did not reach us until late, a severe gas shell spasm came down upon us. Our gas curtains always gave us excellent protection, but on this night I found dense choking fumes coming through the floor under my bed. A hasty investigation of this phenomenon showed that it came from the group signal office situated in a dungeon beneath. Below my bed there is a trap-door forming an emergency exit for both parties, which is reached by fifteen steep steps. The signallers below had lighted a bonfire to drive the gas out, and the whole of its smoke ascended to us, causing much language and hard work with the invaluable flapper fans.

It was a perfect morning, for Zero hour was dead calm, no mist, and the barrage opened almost like one gun, a great contrast to some very ragged and ill-timed openings I have heard. It started about two miles to the south of us, and ran up north in one vast ripple of flash and thunder, then two minutes later the whole eastern horizon was marked out with countless rockets of every colour.

An incident which occurred that morning made one realize how stupendous is the noise on such occasions. A young gunner straight from England had reached us late the previous evening, and as he was not wanted at the guns, his four companions in the dug-out had not disturbed him when they filed out a few minutes before Zero. Crash went the barrage, and he woke up certain that the end of the world had come. Finding himself alone in the dug-out he dashed out into the darkness, where he saw on all sides myriads of gun flashes, apparently all firing straight at him; that finished him, and he fell into a deep shell-hole where he lay until daylight, when one of the batmen, on his way from the mess to the guns with a mug of tea for the officer on duty, found him lying there, and had commenced first-aid before he discovered the joke. I may add that afterwards the boy turned out a first-rate gunner.

We fired without pause from zero till 8.50 p.m. that night. As may be imagined, this meant a pretty heavy expenditure of ammunition, and included two "S.O.S." and three concentrations on "Enemy reported at . . . ."

On our front the advance was only two hundred yards, Gallipoli Farm, and the four old gun-pits in front of it, again proving impregnable, and a further attack on the Farm, launched at midnight on the night 22nd—23rd, was also unsuccessful.

Sometimes our night firing is varied by the news of a Hun relief, in which case every battery, each working up and down a narrow lane, pours shells into the suspected area.

On the 24th there was a heavy gale of wind, which is always a handicap. Of course it renders us immune from gas shelling, but at the same time it prevents us from hearing shells coming, very important in a spot like ours, and on my way to H.Q. after lunch one caught me napping. However, on disentangling myself I found that it was only a chunk of mud on my thigh which had knocked me over, so visions of a Blighty were dispersed. The same evening, having been relieved at the guns by my captain, I went down to the wagon line for a couple of nights ; the high wind coupled with a stiff leg rendering partridge shooting impossible, I was reduced eventually to killing time by digging for field mice round my tent for the benefit of "Pongo" (the H.Q. dog). Taylor rejoined us that evening, though still rather lame from the wound received at Messines.

I spent the next day motoring round with Tiger Dennistoun visiting friends, and in the afternoon on our way to tea at the Guards Division Head-Quarters we met on the road outside Pop the 4th Battalion Grenadiers (Gort's), all in a frenzy of boot-cleaning and button-polishing. On inquiring from Gort the reason for all this glitter, we discovered that the French Army Commander, General Antoine, was going to present Croix de Guerres to the 3rd Brigade, so we turned back and went to the aeroplane landing ground, where the review was to be held. The Brigade then marched in, complete with bands, etc., 1st and 4th Grenadiers, 2nd Scots Guards and Welsh Guards. Soon after numbers of French Generals arrived, and the inspection and show commenced. It was a treat to see again perfect brigade drill after the sloppiness entailed so often by this war.

Then about 20 N.C.O.'s and men, together with 30 officers, the latter being nearly all staff, were marched up to near the Tricolour Saluting Base. The Prince of Wales, who was watching them, said that they represented the "Very Brave" and the "Very, Very Brave," the latter being the staff. What a cheery soul he is, and always looks as fit and hard as nails ! A dog fight enlivened the pinning-on of the medals, but to the intense disappointment of all spectators, there was no kissing. A march past, first in column of companies, and then with the whole brigade in line, completed the show. Before leaving I found that the landing ground belonged to a squadron of Spads commanded by Sandys, and while talking to him, General Longcroft, who commands the Fifth Army Planes, turned up. I had not seen him since 1911, when I flew with him at Montrose, in the days when he was a Captain in No. 2 Squadron. Bagging six partridges before dinner, and a real good sitting at Poker finished the day.

In view of possible moves in the future, we have been quietly accumulating various small items of late. These include five extra horses, three G.S. wagons, and 2 S.A.A. limbered carts, all over our authorized strength, which will enable us to move in comfort. As a precaution every wheeled vehicle, guns included, is marked with a monogram formed of the letters T.Y.T. (short for Tytler), which looks like a divisional sign, and will, I hope, obviate any awkward questions about the enormous baggage train which will follow the battery when on the march.

There has been really no news for the last week. We have had a high wind, rain, and but little hostile fire each day. On our side numerous intense bombardments, under which we sometimes advance and capture various shell-holes. Some of these we are driven out of again, but others we manage to consolidate, though as every hole or trench is full of water, "consolidation" is merely a staff myth. All around are freshly arrived batteries; as usual, we seem to be the last to leave the show. Apart from these futile attacks nothing happens, except that the country gets a little browner each day, and the few remaining woods more like a bunch of twisted hop poles, with the ruins of every farm a little harder to distinguish from the surrounding craters. The nights are varied by the usual false S.O.S. alarms, and thus this endless battle meanders on.

Judging from a letter received from England, everybody at home is still incredibly optimistic and looking for an early Peace. I am afraid I cannot agree with them. If Peace is made in the winter of 1917 it must be hopelessly inconclusive. If it is not made then the War will certainly go on for another year. Moreover, during the spring of 1918 we must be prepared to take over an additional line from the French, thus lessening our power of attack, while we can hardly expect that the Americans will be ready for offensive action before the autumn of 1918 at the earliest.

LETTER FORTY-SIX.

POTIJZE CHATEAU. (19TH SEPTEMBER, 1917.)

Much Ado About Nothing. More Fighting.

> Guns in Flanders—Flanders guns!
> (I had a son that worked 'em once!)
> Shells for guns in Flanders, Flanders!
> Shells for guns in Flanders, Flanders!
> Shells for guns in Flanders! Feed the guns!
> R. KIPLING.

TO-MORROW, the 20th, we go out of action at last, after as bad a two months as anyone could wish for. Since I wrote at the end of August there has been very little change on our immediate front. The whole attack is held up by our repeated failures to capture and hold the Ridge in front of Gallipoli Farm, and to the south of us, Inverness Copse forms an equally bad stumbling-block.

Except for one shell on the officers' dug-out behind the guns (its occupant on that occasion, Prest, escaping somehow alive), we have had no direct hits on the position. The mount in which we live is continually shelled, but the majority of dug-outs can resist anything up to 5.9, and we have only had one man killed there.

Bad luck and D Battery still run hand in hand. During this show they have had over 120 casualties, which is pretty stiff considering that one never has more than thirty to forty of all ranks up at the guns at a time. It was indeed a lucky gamble that we moved away from them on the 2nd of August to this position; a gamble, because one had to put in the pool the risk of finding the new place equally bad, while the whole of our previous work was scrapped, and with men pretty beat the labour of moving thousands of rounds is no light job. I remember it was a tough day's work getting the guns out of the old position on to the main road; though only 40 yards, it meant moving the guns inch by inch through knee deep mud, and took many hours. If but one shell had hit our new position it would have gone up like a sky-rocket, as its frontage was only thirty yards for the six guns —a continuous ammunition dump interspersed with guns. However, although we were in full sight of Glencorse Wood, the enemy there were far too busy to worry about batteries not on their immediate front, and with the guns close together the endless stray casualties which so often occur when men are moving from one gun-pit to another are avoided. In addition to the continual ordinary shelling, every third day the Hun gives us one of his area concentration shoots, which are pretty lurid affairs while they last.

There have been some minor operations at intervals during these last twenty days, none of them, however, marked by signal success. For us the chief event of importance occurred on the 3rd September, when the entire battery, with the exception of the guns and two caretakers, went out of action for twenty-four hours. The reason was that some General became obsessed with the notion that the Royal Regiment wanted washing, not of the laundry type, but in respect of the corpus vile, so each battery was offered twenty-four hours out of action to carry it out. Many batteries did not take advantage of the chance, but we accepted, though I do not know how many men actually reached the baths. However, they were all given passes to go off and play in Pop, and wash if they wanted to, while the double issue of rum and cigarettes kept the remnant of the army contented at the wagon line; it made quite a pleasant break. I remember that on the morning of this picnic we had a minor operation lasting for 15 minutes. As soon as it was over we dodged through some rather fierce retaliation shelling, and so reached the wagon lines safely, all dressed up with spurs, Sam Browne belt, and other rarely seen articles of clean equipment. Tiger Dennistoun having kindly lent us his car, Roberts, Taylor and I set off for the back areas, and having dropped them at Hazebrouck I went on for another 50 kilometres. After a long hunt through many villages I at last found the First Cavalry Brigade, then the Blues, and finally had lunch with Alastair Leveson-Gower. He has got a Squadron, and I stayed with him until tea-time looking at horses, etc. What a desperately hard life they lead! Early stables, all officers on morning parade, ditto at 2 p.m. parade (he got off that as I had to be amused), and officers' riding school for everyone after tea. Rather a change from our idle life in action!

On my way back I picked up Roberts and Taylor at Hazebrouck, both very bored after a bad lunch. The town was more or less deserted, and most of the hotels closed owing to their having been worried by a 16-inch naval gun. This to us was really too absurd, so we pushed off back to dear old Pop, where all was life and gaiety as usual. How depressing it is away behind the line!

At Pop we found the usual huge crowd in the streets, a band in the square, a few shells flying about, and both clubs filled with friends. After dinner there, having dismissed the car, we "lorry-hopped" the eight miles to our wagon line. Usually there are endless lorries and cars going up the road, but that night proved a bad one for traffic, so by intervals of walking, a ride first in a motor ambulance, and then in a G.S. wagon, and finally in a big closed car occupied by a good-natured Colonel of a Heavy Group we managed to land eventually at our home near Goldfish Chateau. This road is bombed every night, but we got in just in time. In the morning I had a dim recollection that about midnight, when I was half asleep, I heard a small body of cooks, servants and mess waiters, returning to the officers' lines, among them Hickey, who was telling some wondrous yarn of five bombs beside him, and somebody's nose being blown off and falling into the same ditch as he was hiding in. However, as all our men's noses seemed intact next day, I conclude it belonged to some stranger.

Roberts went up next morning to open the shop and start the war again, while I remained at the wagon line very busy with a re-teaming colour scheme of all the horses in the battery, no easy matter, as one had to consider the feelings of each driver who had had his horses for a long time. The horses were looking extremely well, as they are out grazing for eight hours each day on my partridge shoot. I was also full of comprehensive and rather ambitious schemes for training and re-drilling when out at rest, and as a result have nearly frightened my officers into applying to stay on in action, as being preferable to the proposed "Rest".

A few days afterwards, when up at the guns, we heard that we had once more changed our Divisional R.A. Commander, and that the new arrival, whose name is General B., was coming to inspect the Brigade in action. He is an individual well known for having a 106 fuse temper and "non-delay" language far in advance of any other general in the regiment, and worst of all, it was reported that his pet mania was the immediate clearance of all empty cartridge cases from gun positions.

The careful return of empty shell cases is no doubt very necessary, but on some positions it must pay the taxpayer best to let them lay till the next advance. Casualties to horses and men, while performing the slow job of loading them up in wagons, may thus be avoided. But this was no excuse in the General's eyes, and he slated two batteries of our Brigade unmercifully on account of them. It was to be our turn next day. Just behind our guns were two huge craters filled to the brim with shell cases, at least 10,000 of them. All seemed lost; however, that night came Inspiration. At dawn I arose, found an old notice board, and swiftly the battery painter covered its face with the following legend :—

"C. 28. c. 53. Dump."
"All 18-pdr. and 4.5 cases to be dumped here."

Result, much kudos for our very neat position and a broad smile on the face of our Colonel, standing behind the General.

Our mess at the guns is getting quite full once more, as at present we have with us all D Battery officers, whose mess was for the third time knocked in with an 8-inch shell; besides them we have had many dinner-parties for people in the neighbourhood, in particular, for the various batteries of the Lahore Division who are now beside us. Several batteries have obtained Lewis guns to deal with low Hun aeroplanes, so whenever a Hun 'plane comes over, no matter at what height, the whole Mound bursts out in a chatter of M.G. fire like a busy rookery.

We are now no longer shelled incessantly, and we even sit outside in the sun on the Mound, very different from the conditions a short time ago. For example, a few weeks since, the mess being very dark, I was outside getting my hair cut, and the barber and myself during the operation had to make five stampedes for safety when shells appeared to be coming more than usually close. With these long-range Howitzer shells, which arrive rather tired and slow, there is usually about thirty seconds' warning.

The cold weather and the rapidly shortening days make one realize that before we get back into action again we shall be in the middle of yet another winter campaign. To balance the general damnability, winter offers some advantages—shorter hours at the O.P., less effective gas days, fewer splinters owing to soft ground, less smell and fewer flies, and a glorious fug in the dug-outs with no ventilation and huge fires burning.

To-morrow, unless it is cancelled again, we go out to rest.

During all this Push, opportunities for really killing Huns were few and far between. One day I had a fair bag by co-operating with a 15-inch Howitzer. I happened to meet a Naval Officer near my O.P., and heard that he was going to destroy some cement pill boxes on the top of Gallipoli Ridge. As soon as he started, I also opened with shrapnel and fired three or four hundred rounds. The Hun, half-stunned by the terrific concussions of the big shell, rushed out half dazed and fell an easy prey. I must also have been sweeping the reverse side of the Ridge with good effect, the pill-boxes being on the summit, for I read in the neighbouring Corps communique next day an account saying how many Huns were seen to fall on bolting from pill-boxes, their observers being able to see the reverse side of the Ridge. But why was this effort left to chance? Are we never going to learn real co-operation between all natures of guns and services?

On another occasion, during one of the many attempts to capture Gallipoli Ridge, I again scored fairly heavily. It was during a daylight attack in the afternoon, so the light for observing was perfect. I could see our barrage advance up the hill and march away out of sight, leaving our Infantry far behind. As soon as the barrage had passed the Hun was visible rushing out of the pill-boxes and manning machine-guns in shell-holes near by, confident, I am sure, that no British shell would touch them and that they would have, as often as before, a glorious target in the shape of our Infantry attacking through the mud. My battery was at the moment employed in putting up a distant flank barrage, but without asking permission I switched two guns back on to the hill, and by means of high air bursts I located where they were firing. The target was, however, a fairly difficult one, as our men were surrounding the Ridge ; any shell over was out of sight, so one had to hit a small portion of the Hun-held summit. But once the range was right I had glorious sniping, picking off the nests of Huns esconced in the shell-holes. Owing to the deceptive gradient it seemed at times that my shells must be falling within a few yards of our own Infantry, but with my telescope I could see our leading men, and as they did not duck I knew that the range was correct.

LETTER FORTY-SEVEN.

THE PILKEM RIDGE. (20TH OCTOBER, 1917.)

Paris Leave. Merry Muddy Days.

With the sweat runnin' out o' shirt-sleeves, an' the sun off the snow in your face,
An' 'arf o' the men on the drag-ropes to hold the old gun in 'er place—
'Tss ! 'Tss !

R. KIPLING.

WE are in action again, but our rest from the 19th September till the 12th October was a very pleasant one. We trekked back to near St. Omer, coming to anchor in a group of large farms rejoicing in the name of Grand Paradis and Petit Paradis.

There we had a busy time training recruits, and getting horses and harness into good trim again. G Battery R.H.A. was out at rest near us, and Major Young came over and gave us some excellent lectures. We built a steeplechase course, including in it some natural fences, and had one or two successful races. I managed also to fit in another leave to England, my third this year, and on my return followed it up with leave to Paris. I had been there about three days, when just as I was dressing for dinner in my room at the Ritz, the telephone bell rang, and picking up the receiver I heard the voice of an English N.C.O. in the A.P.M.'s Office asking for me. His message was:—"All officers of the 150th Army Brigade to rejoin immediately." Then followed ten minutes of frantic telephoning to cancel all plans made for the next two days, nor were they few, so quickly does life become complicated in that city !

After a theatre I caught the 11.40 p.m. from the Gare du Nord, Hickey meeting me at the station with my kit, and by means of a few well-placed bribes I was able to retain a whole carriage for myself.

Only 48 hours passed—but it meant a change from the luxury of the Ritz to a water-logged dug-out on the Pilkem Ridge.

The other three officers of the brigade who were on Paris leave did not catch the train, so I had to launch into the pursuit alone ; it often means a long stern chase to find a unit which has moved on, especially if it is an army brigade unknown and uncared for by all.

At Boulogne, Hart, the brigade signal officer, joined me; he had been rescuing the band instruments from a store, in which they had been left over a year ago.

We changed trains at Calais, and I had time to call on Major Fraser, of Farraline, at his office on the quay. Then we journeyed on to St. Omer, where I saw my horses and groom anxiously waiting on the platform, with the news that the battery had marched early for the Herzeel Area. A 30 kilometres ride, however, in the rain did not look inviting, so we threw our kits back into the train, and by means of endless changing and a final two hours on a small-gauge farmers' line we got to our destination, hellish dark and raining hard!

We found the Area Commandant's Office at last, and the occupant of it, Colonel Gilmour, late Grenadier Guards, gave us our directions. After a weary walk of two miles, partly across country, we at last found the farm where the battery was billeted.

Next day, the 13th October, we marched to our future wagon line near Woesten, north of Ypres, reaching the place by midday in a pitiless downpour of rain. On the previous day, two officers per battery and a few men had gone straight through on motor buses to take over the guns of the outgoing army brigade on the morning of the 13th. The wagon lines were vile, nothing having been done for the comfort of men or horses. In the afternoon I rode up to the guns, a 7-mile ride, along crowded roads. From the canal at Boesinghe onwards the roads got worse and worse, until I was floundering in mud up to the girths as I struggled through Abris Wood, on the eastern side of which I at last found the gun position, a miserable spot.

In daytime by very skilful driving, it is sometimes possible to get a wagon or cart up to the position with rations and water in petrol tins, but at night this is quite impossible, and everything has to be carried the last 500 yards up a duck-board track, which luckily passes near our guns. Even in fine weather everything is more or less under water, and the pumps have to be worked every day to keep the water down in the gun-pits and dug-outs, though none of them are sunk more than a foot below ground-level.

Our dug-out and mess is fairly strong, but very small; there is only just room to put down three stretchers at night, which, supported on ammunition boxes, serve us for beds. In the morning the water is always six inches deep on the floor, so you can imagine the slime and stench we live in.

Next day, fortunately, was fine, and the Hun was quiet, so I was able to take stock of the position generally, which I had not yet seen properly, as I reached it at dusk the night before. The guns are a very job lot, with practically no tools or spare parts, but thanks to the material which Roberts had sent up at dawn, we were able to get the dug-outs somewhat improved.

On the following day I went for a walk to try and see something of the Hun front line, also to locate our own people, as owing to a recent advance here no one quite knew which particular line of water-logged shell-holes our men were holding.

There is a great improvement of the roads as compared with that of the roads in the October Somme fighting of last year. Now the roads are being made by road experts instead of being tinkered at by Battalions in reserve, also last year there was no trench board walks to get about on. Here in our area there are two streets, Hunter Street and Clarges Street, which, starting from the old front line, run parallel about half a mile apart for a distance of 7,000 yards forward, in fact almost up to our present front line. The whole world moves up and down this long snake of single trench boards—reliefs, wounded, and endless carrying parties—so progress up them is slow. Whenever one party meets another, one of them has to find a place where it is safe to step off the boards, without sinking over the knees. The Hun, of course, has got certain points registered to a nicety and takes a heavy toll daily, but one has to use the streets, as it is quite impossible to get across country otherwise.

Eventually I reached a spot called Faidherbe Cross-roads, just in front of the forest of Houthulst, and got an excellent view of the time programme which I had ordered my battery to fire for my benefit. However, although this O.P. was really excellent for observing the Hun front line, I was dissuaded from selecting it as our permanent O.P. on hearing from a Company Commander that no one ever went to that spot in daylight, because of the accurate Hun sniping. Consequently I departed in haste, making short rushes from one shell-hole to the next, and then having put a few hundred yards between the Hun and myself I called at a pill-box, and found to my surprise that Colonel Gilly Follett was inside with his battalion head-quarters. What a gallant soul he is!

On the whole I think I have never seen such an uninteresting zone, as, except for the trees of the forest, nothing is visible of the enemy's country.

Next morning at dawn there was a reconnaissance with the Colonel in order to mark out two forward positions, and a large working party started to make them. However, by noon contrary orders came in, necessitating a fresh reconnaissance, and we also heard that we were to take over the guns of a neighbouring brigade which was going out to rest for a few days, we, on our part, leaving caretakers at our own guns. It was the worst position I had ever seen, everything being filthy to the last degree, guns included.

Next morning we took over these guns, a proceeding which lasted about ten minutes, rather different from the old days, when it took about two days ! The guns were in a swamp beside the Steenbeck, and all more or less under water, the officer and the two men per gun on duty having to exist in some blown-in pill-boxes about 200 yards behind the guns, while another 500 yards back the three Battery Commanders manage to live in another pill-box, which merely consists of a cement tunnel, about 12ft. by 5ft. In these narrow quarters the three have to sleep, eat, struggle with the huge map boards which block the whole place, write orders and wrestle incessantly with the phone. Our spare officers and men had to live away back in our old position, a disjointed, tiresome bunderbust, which insured that no one was ever able to find the person they wanted.

Next day saw yet another reconnaissance with the Colonel and the other B.C.'s, to select more new positions. We waded about in the mud for a few hours, and stuck in pegs to mark the gun-pits we selected in our allotted area. The engineers were struggling to make a track, but there was still at least 500 yards of impossible country between our position and the point they had then reached.

All finesse has left the war now ; it seems to have degenerated into slinging a given weight of shell on to a certain area in a detailed space of time. Many batteries apparently never attempt to observe their own fire, and generally speaking things have got pretty slack among the bad ones. One sees heavy guns on the forward slope of Pilkem Ridge in full view of Hunland, and, in fact, guns and Howitzers, slung down anywhere and anyhow, the only deciding factor being whether it was possible to get ammunition up to them.

I rode down to the wagon line in the morning, as I wanted to see the miracle which Roberts was said to have performed there in putting up covered standings with brick rubble floors sufficient for all the horses in the battery in three days. It proved to be a wonderful effort ; as for material, some he had indented for, some he had "wangled", winning the hearts of Dump Officers and N.C.O.'s with honeyed words and much drink, but the bulk he had stolen at night from the huge timber dump next our wagon lines. His dishonest system was to load up the stuff on G.S. wagons while the sentry was plausibly engaged in conversation with some more of his robber gang.

As we are subjected to incessant bombing attacks, we endeavour to protect the horses as much as possible by piling all the available manure behind their standings between two walls of sandbags, which is gradually built higher as the time goes on, for now that the Hun is using his new instantaneous fuse, these raids are daily becoming more serious. We have certainly been lucky as compared with others, nevertheless we have lost during the last few days four drivers killed or wounded, and about fifteen horses.

Calling at Head-Quarters on my way back to the guns I heard that fresh orders had come in, and that all previously chosen advanced positions were now cancelled, and that we had only forty-eight hours to get the guns into action along the north side of the Broombeck, also to get up 6,000 rounds per battery.

We were now up against the toughest proposition that this brigade had ever encountered. One of the greatest drawbacks when arranging plans, especially when they are altered so frequently, is the long distance the wagon lines have to be behind the guns, a mounted orderly taking about three hours, and vehicles or pack-horses anything from four to seven hours, to perform the single journey.

Every day the Hun shelling gets steadily heavier and at least once a day a fleet of Gothas, flanked by a dozen fighting machines, sail slowly over the massed battery positions and fairly shower down bombs. Their leader usually fires a Vèry light as the signal for the bomb barrage to begin, and owing to their wonderful fuse one had to lie flat in a hole instead of merely the perfunctory duck with which one can usually evade a 5.9.

That night was thoroughly tiresome, 5.9's, telephone messages, and gas shells making sleep impossible. At dawn next morning we had to have yet another brigade reconnaissance to choose our new positions and start the infantry working-party and our own men on them. The road was solid with endless strings of pack animals, every beast in every brigade doing its bit getting ammunition up in the race against time. The engineers, too, were working frantically to complete the road as far as the left-hand position, which happened to be mine, but there was still a gap of 400 yards, so all the ammunition for the batteries on that 400-yard frontage had to be piled in vast heaps in the mud at the end of the road, where it lay in wet confusion. Along the finished portion of the road were ten other batteries, all of whom were equally busy packing up shell and material, so the narrow corduroy track which represented the road was soon a seething mass of activity. Every now and then one of the horses would get pushed off the track, and once off there was little hope of saving him, as they invariably seemed to slip into some crater ten feet deep and filled to the brim with liquid slime, quite indistinguishable from the surrounding mud.

The morning was misty and wet and it looked ideal, as the Hun could get no observation on to the roads, but for some uncanny reason, exactly at 8.30 a.m., they started a terrific barrage with very heavy shell on all the roads behind us. It dropped like a curtain between our old position and our future one, and all movement was stopped for the next six hours.

Fortunately for us nearly all our horses were by that time on the home side of the curtain, though very few of the drivers were able to make their third trip up with shells that day. One driver and his horses were never seen or heard of again. At our new position we could hear the heavy stuff rumbling overhead, but with the mist nothing could be seen of what was happening, except that the long queue of pack horses in front of the curtain seemed to be fixed there for "the duration". I went back along the duck-boards and reached the main road on the Pilkem Ridge; it had been a real rough house there; the road was so blocked with dead horses and overturned wagons that it was almost impossible to get a pair of pack horses along. A thoroughly wasted day, though every hour was of the utmost importance if we were to get into action in time for the next big attack.

After a short pause in the afternoon, heavy shelling re-commenced and continued till dusk; it was pretty hot work wherever one went, and just at dark a 5.9 burst on the corner of the mess at our old position, wounding Poldon, O.C. of D Battery, in four places; Prest and Wilshin, too, were rather knocked about, as our large stove was thrown up by the explosion, and landed on the top of them. One advantage however, of being perpetually wet is that on such occasions no one catches fire. After an hour the shelling slackened, and we were able to get Polden away on a stretcher, very cheery and joking about its being his birthday that day, and this his only present.

Although our mess is only a few hundred yards from one of the duck-board streets, the journey at night with a stretcher must seem an eternity to the wounded, as the bearers have to pick their way up to their knees in slime while dodging the yet deeper places.

As the Battery Commander's pill-box at the cross-roads had been more or less destroyed during the day, Polden and I had been invited to spend the night at Head-Quarters, so after an hour's struggle in the pitch darkness I reached their pill-box dead beat, having been knocked down by a close gas shell on the way.

Next morning, the owners of the guns we were looking after reappeared, so that we were able to concentrate all our men on pulling our own out of their pits and getting them to some spot where they would not sink out of sight while waiting for their limbers; we also tried our hardest to make some sort of a track by which we could reach the main road.

By noon the staff, having at last realized that the R.E. could not possibly make the road along the Broombeck within the allotted time, directed that B Battery and ourselves were to go and hunt for a place forward from where we could fire during the battle. Emsley, O.C. of B Battery, and I therefore plunged off through the mud once again, and eventually discovered a small piece of ground about 50 yards long, just off the road at Widjendrift. There we could just wedge in the two batteries, but it was full in sight of the Hun, and with the muzzles poking through a long screen erected to hide the traffic on the road behind us—an absurd place, but in this paradox of war it had to do. It meant however, handing over to C Battery all the ammunition we had packed up to the Broombeck with so much labour, and criminally hard work it had been, too, on the wagon line, as each trip meant fourteen hours at least on the road, and often longer, with but few hours' rest between trips.

I wonder if guns have ever been moved before across such impossible country? C Battery, which had its old position 200 yards behind us, started to advance early in the afternoon, but by dark had only managed to move five guns as far as our position, when every horse and man were absolutely beat. Rather slow progress in the march to Berlin!

Just before dark we had an extra bad dose of bombs, dropped by a whole herd of Gothas. Hickey, who had been my servant since 1914, was wounded, also another of the servants, the latter fatally. He was Taylor's man, and Taylor accompanied the stretcher party as far as the dressing station to see him safely off to a C.C.S. A few hours later, an N.C.O. returned and reported that the doctors had nabbed Taylor, as soon as they saw him, as a shell-shock case. He and I had got tangled up with an 8-inch shell near the mess, just before the bomb raid started, and besides, he had hardly recovered from his wounds received at Messines, but almost to my regret he reappeared soon after midnight, having escaped from the aid post when the M.O. was looking the other way.

Our gun teams were due to come up that afternoon, but just before they arrived a huge shell landed fair on the roadway and blocked it completely. It must have been bigger than an 8-inch, as half a dozen G.S. wagons could have been hidden in the depths of the crater it made.

What fiendish hard work it is for men and horses! Here is a typical example :—Six 8-horse gun teams had left the wagon line at 10 a.m. ; they reached the block on the road behind our position by 4 p.m., and getting the vehicles reversed and trekking back, only as far as our advanced wagon line, took them till 10 p.m. They started off at 3 a.m. next morning, and the crater having been filled up they reached us at 9 a.m. ; from then till noon was one long fiendish struggle to move the guns across the 300 yards to where the timber road began. It was desperate work—one gun at a time—fresh teams into each gun every 50 yards, and every man on the drag-ropes—the whole job being done under fairly heavy shell-fire. Once on the timber road, however, it was good going as far as Widjendrift, but then another desperate struggle began to get the guns hauled on to their new platforms, which were erections of scrap timber built between shell-holes, on which the guns perched like rickety sparrows. It was the best we could do, as the background all round was pulp.

We have been given an Infantry working-party of fifty men to help us in, but they had taken five hours to reach the spot and had had no food since the day before, so it was a difficult job to get eight hours' work out of them. However, it had to be done, and some searching among a big heap of dead yielded a few tins of bully beef and biscuits, which greatly heartened the weary crowd.

During the day, with the help of a hundred extra horses, we managed to get up 5,000 rounds for the two batteries, at last, by the night of the 21st, we were ready for the show next day. Like all other batteries, our men and horses were pretty blind beat, and the officers were no better. Prest, slightly gassed, Taylor suffering from his old wound and very much shell-shocked, Wilshin at the wagon line recovering from his wounds received on the 19th, and me a little fuller of gas than usual.

LETTER FORTY-EIGHT.

ON TREK. (24TH OCTOBER, 1917.)

The Attack on Houthulst Forest. We are Decimated by Gas. Our March to Fifth Army School. Our Short Stay There.

> His place forgets him; other men
> Have bought his ponies, guns and traps.
> His fortune is the Great Perhaps
> And that cool rest-house down the glen.
> R. KIPLING.

AT 5.35 a.m. on the 22nd, the attack on Houthulst Forest began. It was a horrible morning of driving rain and mist, and it was a perfect miracle that our infantry ever advanced at all, but somehow they managed to, and captured the fringe of the forest, thus robbing the Hun of observation of our immediate area. Our task in the barrage was a simple one, assisting in the forming of a second creeping barrage in front of the main barrage. Luckily for once extreme accuracy of fire was not essential, as we had not been able to register the guns, which slid about everywhere on their impromptu platforms, and now and then kicked themselves off their perches, sinking immediately axle deep in the mud.

As soon as the set barrage was over I went forward again to try and find yet another forward position, as our Broombeck site was not likely to be accessible for a good many days. The Hun was evidently angry over losing ground that morning, and we had a very stormy passage wherever we went. While trying to locate our new front lines a Hun machine-gun gave us a burst, and we went to ground in the lip of a large crater filled with the usual reddish coloured slimy water. The Hun was shelling all around, and a shell, luckily a dud, landed plump in the water beside us causing a great upheaval in the slime. Then suddenly out of the depths there arose a hideous helmet-clad head—a dead Hun with features contorted in a ghastly grin and one arm outstretched, attempting, as it were, to pull us into the mire also, and then slowly sank back into the loathsome depths from whence he came. A cheering little incident for an autumnal afternoon stroll!

That night was a real bad one, much gas, heavy shelling, and several

S.O.S. calls, and for the third night in succession sleep was quite impossible. Next morning, on calling at Head-Quarters, the Colonel ordered me to retire to the wagon line for a few days, as an extra bad dose of gas had made me voiceless and I could only see with difficulty, so after a seemingly endless four hours' walk, varied by periods of motor-bus hopping, I reached the tiny cottage, built of dried mud, which served as our wagon line mess. What perfect comfort it seemed getting to bed there, in the one tiny room entirely filled by two beds, and a table, and, joy of joys, there was a huge open fire !

Roberts went up that afternoon to take my place at the guns, and I ran the wagon line from my bed, chiefly in writing, as I could not talk at all. We were bombed regularly every night, but round the mud walls of the hut were two rows of sandbags built up to a height of three feet, so by lying flat in bed a few inches below the level of the sandbags one has the feeling of perfect security from splinters, which is all that is necessary. I always think that if the Sisters of Fate have a direct hit in store for one, either from shell or bomb, it is useless to try and avoid it, as assuredly, if thwarted, they will dispense something worse later on, but it is up to everyone to give constant thought to means of protecting himself from splinters. This comforting theory I always preach to the men, and it certainly saves life and labour, and reduces the number of avoidable splinter casualties. The Sergeant-Major invariably arrived for his evening orders in the middle or a bomb raid, so he would lie on his front on the floor, taking down the orders with much licking of pencil and blowing, for though he retains the "round button" he has lost his Horse Artillery figure !

While down at the wagon line, we heard the news that the Fifth Army were to choose one R.G.A. Battery and one R.F.A. Battery to go to their Artillery School at Abbeville, and act as the "show" depot batteries there, for the rest of the winter, and that we were in the "short leat" for the job.

Accordingly, a few days later, on being summoned to 5th Army R.A. Head-Quarters, I arose from my bed, and motored there with Major Gordon, the R.G.A. choice from our Corps. The interview must have been rather comic, as I still could not speak above a whisper. Gordon, for various reasons, was fairly certain of winning the R.G.A. prize, and he duly did, which made our chance less, as even if we dead-heated with the other battery, they were not likely to take an R.F.A. and R.G.A. Battery from the same Corps. Sure enough, a few days later word came through that we had lost. The men had heard of our chance, and had been getting up the harness to burnished condition despite the awful surroundings ; needless to say, they accepted the decision in the same cheery way that they accept all the tragedies and comedies out here.

During this time gas casualties at the guns had been piling up. Wilshin and Prest were both in hospital, and we had had heavy losses among the gunners. On the night of the 1st we heard rumours of intense gas-shelling in the Widjendrift area, and next day, two badly gassed men staggered into the wagon line with the news that the officers' dug-out had had a direct hit with a gas shell, and that there were no officers left in A or B Battery. In my battery Roberts and Taylor, and half the gun detachments were casualties. Taylor died a week later, and B Battery had had all their officers gassed except Johnstone, who was at the wagon line with me. I arose once more from bed and rode up as far as Abris Wood; from there on to the position I had to make my way on foot, as the shelling was too bad to risk taking horses.

Things were certainly pretty bad at the guns, the air still reeking of gas and the ground saturated with the mustard gas liquid and the men all half-blind and covered with mustard gas blisters. Every order had to be given in writing, as neither I nor the N.C.O.'s could articulate a word, and to complete the humour of the situation everyone was sick at every possible opportunity. More gas and much shelling that night.

Early next morning we were inspected by some R.A. General. I forget who he was, but he must have seen a curious sight. In any case, whether it was the result of his inspection or not, orders came in at noon that the Brigade was to withdraw to the wagon lines. This we accordingly did, and a week later, having in the meantime rescued our guns, we went back to Persia Camp, near Wattou, where we refitted with officers, horses and men.

The following incident may give you some idea of the strength of mustard gas. While out at rest the Q.M.S. assistant unrolled some blankets which had come down from the gun position a fortnight before, evidently impregnated with mustard gas. It resulted in his having to go to hospital for several weeks with huge blisters on his hands and arms!

It is uphill work trying to re-make a battery with new officers; Taylor is a great loss, but the others, with any luck, will re-join in a month or two.

Great news came in on the 22nd November. The Fifth Army School Depot battery had been sent to Italy and we were to set out for the school in two days' time to take their place. Luckily we had kept our harness in first-class condition, but we had a very busy two days fitting ourselves out (at the expense of the other batteries) in guns, sights, spare parts, horses, etc. Then we had an auction of all our surplus gear, chairs, tables, canteen stores, mess gear, piano, etc., and lots were drawn for all our stolen Government property—stoves, tents, timber, paint, oils and tarpaulins.

On our last night we had a farewell dinner, which I gave to the Brigade in the little restaurant in Wattou Square. It was a pretty riotous affair; the old ladies who run the place are old friends, and wisely cleared the rooms of all breakables beforehand, and are perturbed at nothing. Clifford brought his father, Colonel Clifford, who commands a brigade near, but by careful choosing of his place at the table he was but little damaged during the proceedings after dinner.

We marched next day in lovely sunshine, in fact, we almost glittered, so clean were we, and having been given two 3-ton lorries in addition to all our horse transport, the ammunition wagons were in marching order, and for once escaped looking like a string of tinkers' carts. The transport, of course, exuded dogs from every pore, but both the dogs and the transport were neat and tidy.

It was a long journey, five continuous days' marching, covering 135 kilometres of rather hilly country, but the horses stood it well, and we had only two loose shoes and two horses slightly galled during the whole time, despite the number of eleventh-hour remounts which we had received on the eve of our departure. We trekked south, stopping the night at Ecke, Wandonne, Renbrun, and Bois Jean, arriving at our destination, Flibeaucourt, on the 28th.

The lorries were of course invaluable, as each day they took the cook and billeting party forward, so that not a moment was lost on the arrival of the battery each evening, and by careful bunderbusts in every detail it is wonderful how much valuable time can be saved, each minute gained meaning more rest for horses and men. The orderly officer each day made a gradient sketch to show the hills on the next day's route, and we could therefore plan out the march as regards watering and other halts.

Among the many games we played on the road for the benefit of all ranks, a scheme evolved for conducting watering on the road was most successful. So often when an order to halt reaches the tail of the long column, precious minutes are wasted before the rear vehicles have discovered whether it is merely a temporary check or a fifteen minutes' halt for water. "Numbers One" do not know whether there is time to change a horse in their team, and everybody is asking questions and wasting time. Our game was as follows:— A water reconnaissance party rode forward, perhaps an hour in front of the battery, and finds the BEST PLACE for water, not merely a possible place. A man is posted where the head of the column must halt, and the trumpeter rides back 500 yards or so, and as each section passes him blows the watering call, and the time allowed for the halt, so that within two minutes of halting every pole is down, every girth slackened, and if necessary the gunners are away to the water with their green canvas buckets.

On the last day but one of the march, it poured in torrents all day, and owing to the hilly country and a long march we did not reach the billets until dark. However, next morning we marched at 4.30 a.m. in inky darkness, entailing much reconnaissance work on the part of the battery staff until we reached in safety the main Abbeville-Montreuil road.

We halted at a village 7 kilometres from the school at 8 a.m. Breakfast was waiting ready for us there, and during our halt till after midday we were able to get the vehicles washed and oiled and the horses, harness and men really clean before marching to the school that afternoon.

The first two days there were busy ones, getting to know the detail work of that wonderfully organized school, the Commandant of which was Colonel Davidson, R.G.A. On Sunday, 2nd, I rode in early to Abbeville to spend the day at No. 2 Veterinary Hospital with Major Hobday, of throat operation fame, and as he and his hospital were on the point of starting for Italy, I was given from his Museum a sack of bones, teeth, sections of feet, and other pieces of horse anatomy, showing every known disease or bone fracture, which I knew would be very acceptable for the instructors at the school in their lectures.

On my return to the school at 3 p.m. I found the battery were "standing by" to march to Cambrai, where the Hun had just broken through. Orders for an immediate departure came from Army at 5 p.m.; they were cancelled at 6 p.m.; but at 7 p.m. definite orders came in that we were to march next day. Very hard luck, particularly on the drivers, as they had been working like tigers on their harness, and to keep it in perfect condition during a five days' winter march is no mean effort; it was a sad blow to pull out of our comfortable quarters, and to launch ourselves once more into the unknown. However, our short stay had not been in vain; we had, after a terrific match, defeated the hitherto unbeaten School Football Team by three goals to two!

LETTER FORTY-NINE.

HUEUDECOURT. (13TH DECEMBER, 1917.)

A Forced March to Cambrai. Closing Days as a Battery Commander. Back to Fifth Army School.

> What does he next prepare?
> Whence will he move to attack?—
> By water, earth or air?—
> How can we head him back?
>   R. KIPLING.

HAVING said farewell to all at the School, we marched away on the morning of the 3rd. It was luckily a perfect day for a trek, and the men were wonderfully cheery, in spite of the dispelling of their dream of a five months' rest. A thirty kilometres march on the 3rd brought us to Cocquerel, on the Somme River; another thirty kilometres next day to St. Sauveur.

On arrival there we found, much to our surprise, that all billeting arrangements had already been made for us by a squadron of the 10th Hussars who were in the village, and on going round to thank them I found the officers were all Old Etonians—Gosling, Ednam and Gough. They were there with their horses and a few men, while the remainder were serving in the trenches at the point where the Hun had broken through. On the 5th we reached Sailly, and on the 6th Peronne.

Being still pretty bad with gas, I had gone on in advance by lorry to try and discover where the rest of the brigade were, and so reached Peronne myself on the night of the 5th. Very few of the buildings in that town were still intact, but the E.F.C. runs an officers' club in one of the few large buildings which have escaped total destruction. Everything was choc-a-bloc, and the club and town were packed with lost officers and men, officers without men, or men without officers, and gunners without guns; I heard of several gunners who got their Berlin tickets in that show.

Next day, the 6th, I went off by lorry to 7th Corps Head-Quarters, but we were not wanted there; I wish we were, as Lanyon, formerly the Brigade Major of the 30th Division, is now on that Corps R.A. Staff. Then I trekked north to 3rd Corps Head-Quarters, and heard there some faint tidings of where the rest of the Brigade might be found. Accordingly on the 7th the battery marched on to try and locate our brigade wagon line while I went again in the lorry to hunt for the Divisional Head-Quarters under which we were going to be, and after much wandering, found them. All units and divisions have been performing such kaleidoscopic changes lately that a mere item such as Divisional Head-Quarters is quite difficult to locate.

We spent the night in a very wet wood near Nurlu. Orders came in soon after midnight that we were to be in action by 10 a.m., so we pushed off with the guns before dawn, on a horrible morning of rain and mist, and came into action near the rest of the brigade at Boars Copse, in front of Trescault.

Our Colonel being still away, I had to run the sub-group. The other sub-group was under Colonel Gisburne, of the Meynell Hunt, an extraordinarily stout old veteran who seems to take a delight in walking through the hottest barrage. He lives in the next cell to me at the bottom of a 30-ft. staircase. We both have a room about the size of a small bathroom and two yards of passage. In our suite, Almond, the adjutant, Hart (signals), and I sleep, eat and work, while at one end is the office and the switch-board. At night the suite is well occupied, three of us in the bunks, the floor littered with a snoring mass, consisting of one runner, one clerk, and the signaller off duty, while the seventh inmate is the telephonist on duty.

There is not much news, merely the typical "push conditions", mud, ammunition dumps and transport, the usual slogging away by both sides, entailing the usual S.O.S. panics at dawn and dusk, when both sides barrage each other for a few aimless hours. On the 13th we moved out and came into action again, a few miles further south near Hueudecourt. In the former position we were in the newly-captured Hun country, but in the new one we were facing the sector where the Hun made his deepest counter-invasion into our lines, and the battery was in an area formerly devoted to Divisional Head-Quarters, rest camps, etc., so there was plenty of accommodation to be had, although of a somewhat unprotected nature.

Soon after our arrival there, Fifth Army rang me up to ask if I would go back to their School as an Instructor there. I accepted. It is sad, as my old desire to slay is as strong as ever, but the gas has taken more effect than I had thought, so there is no alternative. Accordingly, a few days later, on the Colonel's return, I handed over to him, said good-bye to my battery and horses, and wended my way back through a December snow-storm to Peronne and thence by train to Abbeville. So ends for the present the happy days of Hun Shikar.

LETTER FIFTY.

NEAR ABBEVILLE. (FEBRUARY, 1918.)

At the Red Fox School.

DURING the last two months, as instructor at the School, I have been so incessantly busy that it has been difficult to write much. The school itself runs delightfully smoothly and with perfect unity, every instructor being a fervent believer in the "Red Fox" (Fifth Army Emblem) and the "Red Fox" spirit. The three patron saints of the School at Fifth Army R.A. Head-Quarters combine to see that the School lacks nothing, and is certainly the best equipped in France.

I have a class of officers, usually about 25, including a few American Battery Commanders. I never realized, till I started to instruct, the depth of my own ignorance, a discovery doubtless shared by all others when they start lecturing. Between the courses, which usually last for a month, one has a few days' "break". One of these I spent at Etaples with the Forestry Head-Quarters, where Lovat, Alhusen, and about fourteen other officers live in great comfort, and during the others I visited G.H.Q., to see my many friends there.

We are so civilized at the School that we have even sent home for our blue kit to wear in the evening. It was a shock at first to have to wear an instructor's hat, complete with red band, as when with one's battery one never dreamed that one would have fallen so low during the War.

A great part of our spare time is spent inventing "gyms" for oneself and ridiculing other people's efforts in the same direction. The output of these is at least one per day—they chiefly consist of intricate mathematical studies purporting to direct the wanderings of a shell so that it may arrive at a given spot. Personally my strong point is picking holes in other people's efforts, being still firmly convinced that the best method of Artillery War is to jam one's nose against the target and then to wade in and slay.

LETTER FIFTY-ONE.

VERS, NEAR AMIENS. (2ND APRIL, 1918.)

With Fifth Army during March.

HILLS, Butler-Stoney and I had just finished the gunnery course when the news arrived about the great Hun push against the Fifth Army. To be quite accurate the School of Gunnery had closed for a fortnight, and Hills and I were really in London the day the first reports came out. We arrived at Calais from Folkestone on the evening of the 23rd of March. It was a perfect evening, with an east wind, which brought the thunder of the bombardment on the Belgian Coast surprisingly close.

We immediately realized the seriousness of the situation, for we knew only too well the hopelessly unprepared state in which the French had handed over their lines to the Fifth Army in January.

Up till then it had been a quiet sector, so the French had done little to it, and we knew that in spite of ceaseless work at strengthening it, which became a virtual race against time, the lines were still far from complete.

We had only fourteen Divisions to cover our long front, while the Third Army to the north of us had 19 on a $26\frac{1}{4}$ mile front; comparatively, therefore, the Fifth Army should have had 30 Divisions instead of 14, and even that would make no allowance for the partially protected state of this front.

We knew the unceasing efforts which General Gough had made to get G.H.Q. and the nation generally, to realize the menace that had been hanging over our heads since the New Year, but the "invasion of Britain terror" appeared to blind completely the powers that be to the danger with which we stood face to face here on the battle front. Everything possible and impossible had been done, so far as our resources permitted, to meet the attack, but our numbers were too few to hold up the overwhelming forces which were launched against us.

Twice as many German Divisions attacked the Fifth Army as were employed in the attack on the Third Army, and yet people in England and even in France wondered why the line gave way.

Some said that we had been "caught napping", though I happen to know that the 19th Corps foretold the exact day, hour and minute of the German Zero hour, and many other predictions were as exactly right.

I think one of the chief factors was the dense morning mist of the 21st and 22nd; it blinded every gun, M.G. and rifle on the front, and beside this the mist upset all the carefully made plans of our Artillery Commanders. Their pre-arranged counter-preparation barrages, which were planned to search out all the likely assembly points from which the enemy could launch his infantry after the preliminary bombardment was over, all came to naught. As it turned out, practically all communications with the front line were cut by the opening barrage, and in many cases the infantry imagined that they were being attacked hours before it really happened, so S.O.S. messages were sent back to the Artillery, compelling them to cease their all-important counter-preparation work and to drop their fire back into No Man's Land where, for the time being, every shell was wasted.

It is a well-known fact that if you have time to study closely a fixed barrage across a certain area, it is always possible to detect the weakest parts in it. In some cases the Hun must have been able to watch this barrage for three or four hours before the scheduled hour of the attack, and in consequence probably got through without heavy casualties, and moreover had not been shaken by our shelling of his assembly points.

The speed of the Hun attack was extraordinary. He certainly advanced twice as quickly as we ever did in any of the Allied attacks since the beginning of the War, the reason being that he "anticipated success," and with his irresistible numbers was able to ignore and leave behind him any specially stubborn strong points which did not yield to his first onslaught. The result of his speed was that our men, retreating from the front system, had no time to settle down in the second line of defence before the Hun was on top of them.

These are only the rough ideas which struck one at the moment. Doubtless hereafter endless bitter controversies will rage over the rights and wrongs of this retreat, and it will afford a glorious target for self-complacent arm-chair critics, politicians, and other loathsome things.

To go back to our arrival at Paris. Soon after we landed the inevitable bomb raid commenced, so we took shelter in a deserted café dining-room. Everyone there had gone to the cellars, so by walking round the various tables we managed to collect swiftly quite a respectable dinner, after which we went off to find quarters with the ever hospitable Fraser of Farraline, who had the job of landing officer at Calais.

Next day the nerves of the civilian population were much shaken by the news of the long-range bombardment of Paris—to them it must have meant that the Hun was thundering at the very gates of the capital.

Leaving Calais by the midday train we reached the station for our old school in the evening, the only incidents of the journey being the various attacks of Hun 'planes which forced the train to stop, a frightened French lady who insisted on holding Hills's hand in the tunnels, and an excellent lunch on the train. We arrived at the school to find Penrose holding the fort alone, and much serious news awaiting us.

Looking at the horses, sorting out one's kit for war once more, and routing up the forgotten "battle bowler," occupied the evening, and early next day we started off in a lorry for Abbeville. We meant to go by train to Amiens, but the railway station did not look inviting or progressive, and no one knew "nothing more about no trains nowhere." Hence we are driven to call on the A.Q.M.G. and M.T.O.C. and many other worthies, and by assuring them that the War could not possibly be waged successfully unless we reached Army Head-Quarters at once, we got permission to take the lorry as far as Amiens. Needless to add, it required much persuasion, since the breath of war had not yet ruffled the officialdom of Abbeville.

On reaching Amiens soon after midday, we found the town packed with people looking for their units, and as the lorry refused to move a yard further, we dumped our servants and kit in a bedroom at the Hotel du Rhin. After an exciting hunt I managed to snaffle a Ford car from a Y.M.C.A. hut into which Hills, Diggle (B.M., 21st Division R.A.) and I packed ourselves and fled to Villers Brettonneux. There we found in the Chateau the Fifth Army Head-Quarters after their fourth move since the attack.

Standing outside I met General Gough as cheery as ever, but rather scornful at our late arrival for the picnic. The Chateau walls were covered with the usual maze of telephone wires which Signals had erected in wonderfully quick time, and inside the Chateau were many vast empty rooms in which the various branches were working.

Having found R.A. we got our orders from Col. Broad. Briefly they were to look after the area between the Somme and the River Luce, to organize it as regards rations, catching stragglers, helping the siting of fresh batteries coming up, and a hundred and one other duties. We then collected a car and several riding horses, and divided up the school officers and N.C.O.'s between our show and the R.A. Rest Camp. The latter was being run by Waite, the School Adjutant, who was in charge of all the lost R.A. personnel. We had a busy night of it, as movements from point to point were much hindered by the seething mass of retreating traffic.

On the previous nights Huns, disguised as British officers on motor cycles, had got through into the back areas. They caused one or two serious panics by ordering villagers to clear out at once, shouting that the Hun Cavalry was at hand. As may be imagined, when once a mass of motor lorries starts stampeding down a road it is not the easiest matter in the world to check them, especially when the darkness is such that it may be felt. So at several cross-roads we posted piquets with a lorry or caterpillar beside them to be ready in case a motor vehicle panic started to block the road and thus check the panic effectively though perhaps somewhat abruptly.

Some staff officer asked one of my piquets what orders I had given them. The N.C.O. replied: "The Major said we were just to shoot everybody making alarm or spreading despondency, and most particularly to shoot officers." Some were shot, but life was too busy to go into further details.

Late that evening the (25th) Army Head-Quarters moved back to Dury, and the general position of the front seemed more threatening than ever. Just before dawn I motored forward to the great La Flaque Dump to hurry on the evacuation or destruction of its contents. It was a vast dump covering acres of ground, the R.E. portion of it, chiefly timber and iron, had, of course, to be left, but the gun park, I.O.M. works and ordnance stores were nearly cleared, and the ration dump was reduced to 50,000 rations instead of the million or so usually there. I tried to hasten the clearance of the gun park, but the labour company men who were loading the lorries were nearly dead beat. There was also 10,000 gallons of aeroplane petrol A. We took as much as we could for our own private lorries, as it almost doubles their speed, but I fear the bulk of this dump had later to be set on fire.

On returning to Villers Brettonneux I found that the 19th Corps Head-Quarters (very old friends) had just moved into the Chateau. As the morning wore on things began to get more hectic than ever, as it became impossible to keep in touch with the flank Divisions or Corps. We were very busy all day with all sorts of work, chiefly collecting rifles, S.A.A. or lorries, forming stragglers into digging parties or companies for defence, finding lost batteries or guns, anything from 9.2 Howitzers to 18-pdrs., and getting them into action to shoot point blank down roads. These and numerous other details involved much motoring and telephoning to find various mislaid units, from an Army Corps downwards.

It is difficult to give a description of the hopeless jumble of such a day or the quaint mixture of scenes witnessed on the main road. A torrent of traffic, thousands of refugees, in most cases pushing their worldly goods in a wheelbarrow, a pathetic stream it was, chiefly composed of very old and very young people, ever flowing westward.

In the garden beside me two small girls in clean pinafores played shuttlecock in the bright March sunshine, while just over the paling on the road stood a deserted handcart, with a very old woman strapped upon it, dead and abandoned. On the other side of the road we were getting an 8-inch Howitzer into action to shoot down the straight road into Warfussee, and near it a company of our lost gunners were making a stockade for the future blocking of the road.

Late that afternoon we received orders from Army to move back to Longeau, an eastern suburb of Amiens, taking with us all the personnel of the R.A. Rest Camp and to join forces with Colonel Davidson, who had moved his gun park back there.

At dusk, therefore, Spragge, Hills and I motored back. It was strange indeed to see the flicker of bursting shrapnel on the hills above Corbie, spots which in 1915 and 1916 we used to regard as the height of civilization and peacefulness.

It was a horribly clear night, ideal for bombing, and with our tents less than 200 yards from the main railway junction, the prospects for the night did not look healthy. Our fears were certainly justified later, for we came in for one of the severest and most protracted bomb raids that has ever happened in France. Bombs are so much worse than shells. One can sleep with a feeling of perfect security when the Hun is pounding away with 5.9's at a battery 200 yards to a flank, but with bombs it is very different. There is always the eternal "make and break" hum of the German machines, easily distinguished by ear from our own, the disgusting noise of the "Archies" yapping like a pack of toy Schipperkes, then the final circle round with engine shut off, followed by the four, six or eight bombs, according to their size.

I had turned in at 10 p.m., and soon after the bombing started. As bad luck would have it, just as the Colonel and Hills were standing outside my tent on their way to bed, a 120-pound bomb swished over the tent pole and burst exactly $4\frac{1}{2}$ yards from the head of my camp bed. Hills and Davidson, our Colonel, were lucky to escape with their lives, the former being wounded in two places and Davidson in about twenty. The bill was a pretty heavy one, six officers and 22 men killed and wounded. After we had got the worst case off to hospital I retired to my bed bag, as sleeping head-on to such a crash does not improve one's walking or thinking powers. All the others retired to spend the night either sitting in the open fields or in some safer locality, but feeling disinclined to move from my wrecked tent I spent the night there.

All night, until 3 a.m., with only short intervals between each raid, the bombs continued to fall. During these intervals gallant bands of would-be helpers regularly discovered me inside the remains of the tent, and invariably insisted that I must be a casualty, and frustrating their well-meant efforts was somewhat trying to the temper. In the morning light my tent certainly did look rather disreputable, the flies all blown away, the sides riddled, and 28 splinters in the pole alone, while my old tin hat on my pillow had three holes through it. However, with the help of a strong charge of rum and tea I arose quite recovered, and motored up to see Army at Dury.

During the night one of our officers had met Grieg hunting for the mislaid 12-inch Howitzer Battery, and he had said that if I showed signs of life by morning I was to take on Colonel Davidson's job. I met General Gough at the Chateau in his usual good spirits, and very grieved about our Colonel getting laid out.

At the R.A. Office I heard that the gun park was to be cleared out of Longeau and moved back to Nampes, about twenty miles further West. An army gun park, however, even in peaceful times, is not a very mobile thing. Including damaged, new, or repaired guns we had at Longeau some ninety 18-pdrs., forty 4.5 Howitzers, twenty 6-inch, a few 8-inch, large morsels of 9.2 Howitzers, several thousand Lewis and Vickers machine-guns, about two train-loads of stores, spare parts, machine-gun drums, belts, etc., and complete workshops of various grades, medium, light, and heavy. Hitherto, of course, no artillery officer had ever been allowed to breathe the sacred atmosphere surrounding the departments under the control of the Ordnance Services, but in this crisis, for certain reasons which I will not put on paper, Army had decided to give absolute plenipotentiary powers to R.A. Officers throughout the whole branch, hence the Colonel's job, which after two days, fell to my lot. It was a curious position, as one had to deal with several Ordnance Colonels.

Having got my orders at Amiens I whirled round various villages collecting 120 horse-power caterpillars, four-wheel drives, and lorries from various super-heavy Howitzer batteries which had managed to escape, or which had not been in action at all. All this mixed pack of heavy vehicles I sent racing down the road (if a caterpillar can be said to race at two miles an hour) all the way to Longeau. I also collected many lost and wandering lorries and about 200 equally lost Labour Company men with a few officers, and they, too, were sent to work in our vineyard.

Then on to Nampes to select the site of the gun park, but seven casualty clearing stations had got there before us, and the station was filled with 4,000 walking wounded, so Nampes was impossible. Having inspected various other stations on that branch line, I went back to Army to see General Hambre and Colonel Craik (Transportation). and it was decided that the gun park should move to Poix. On my return to Longeau I found that the bulk of the carts and lorries had arrived and that during the day Spragge and the others had managed to dispose of a lot of new guns to batteries applying for them; they also got rid of a thousand Lewis guns.

We now started evacuating in earnest; long strings of guns were tied behind each "cat." and a party of walking men were detailed to help to guide the tail round corners in the road. One or two guns were also tied behind each loaded lorry, and the whole lot were sent off that evening on their 26-mile march to Poix. An engine being luckily available at Amiens station, a heavily-loaded train with one of my officers and a hundred men in it was sent off forthwith, so that the shop at Poix might be opened straight away.

Before dark I tried to get some faint idea of what my ever-changing commando really did consist of. I found I should have 5 officers and 6 N.C.O. school instructors, all of whom could be relied on to apply the necessary hustle and ginger to the remainder. The latter consisted of a fluctuating quantity of labour men, perhaps 300 in all, with four officers, a lost trench-mortar battery with three officers and some men, the ordnance staff, some light workshops, and an unknown quantity of vehicles, which, with about three acres of ground covered with stores and guns, completed my flock. One can never trust the stray vehicles very far, as, should they come across their own unit, they usually bolt off and rejoin, never to be heard of again by us.

The bombing of the previous night had hastened the evacuation of Amiens by the civil population, and as we had no wish to repeat our experiences, we moved our kits into a very comfortable deserted villa, in the garden of which were hens, and still better, plenty of eggs. I remember that at dinner that night, Ash, while searching in the cupboard for more plates, produced a very large pickle bottle, inside which was a small baby preserved in spirits! I enjoyed here the first real meal and the first sleep of any sort I had had since I left the school three days before.

The evacuation of the gun park continued all the next day, which was the 28th. A very long train loaded with equipment of every sort turned up at our station, where it was certainly not wanted, but we managed to increase its load with a good many tons of our stores, and it was sent off to find its way to Poix. It was a busy day; endless batteries poured in asking for everything under the sun; men and horses were the only things we could supply easily, as Waite had plenty of them coralled in his rest camp. We reduced paper work and signing to a minimum, so batteries could come in and get new guns, stores, horses and men, and be off again in a few hours.

On calling at Army Head-Quarters before noon I found that our General had gone, thanks to the black hand of political influence, and that the Fourth Army was taking over. The afternoon was indeed a busy one, trying to get everything away and at the same time keep back enough to supply the wants of our many customers. As we have stores of every sort of guns, from 13-pdrs. to 12-inch Howitzers, you can imagine the complexity of these acres of stores. We had the luck, however, to catch another railway engine, and with the help of many trucks got another big train-load away that night, which greatly cleared the congestion.

I also had to cope during the day with what was to me an entirely new species of the genus "Soldier". A large car stopped at the gun park and disgorged a glittering Colonel wearing the red and blue armband of G.H.Q. He asked every imaginable question, which at first rather nonplussed me, but I soon discovered that, provided some answer was given, he wrote it down happily in a very neat hand-writing in his still neater pocket-book. Exactly how many tons of gear had I left in the camp, how many were on the road to Poix, how many had arrived, exactly how many coaches, and how many trucks I would require to complete the evacuation, and he finished by taking a comprehensive list of all my wants from an 18-pdr. dial sight to a firing pin for a 12-inch Howitzer.

Later on in the evening, when at Army, I had to ring up G.H.Q. about some equipment, and mentioned that I supposed it was unnecessary for me to repeat my requirements as I had already given them to Colonel X.Y.Z. The "G.H.Q. end of the telephone" laughed and said, "Oh, he's been round to you, has he ? Give me the whole list again, as nothing ever gets further than his pocket-book." Truly a newcomer into the sphere of Army and G.H.Q. staff life had much to learn.

In the evening I handed over the remains of the gun park to Major Crowe, Commandant of the Fifth Army Trench Mortar School, and then motored to Poix via Army, reaching my destination after a long, slow drive in pouring rain. As we had no lamps we had a few collisions and other mishaps on the road, but after a search I found the barn in which our advance guard officers had installed themselves, in time for a late meal of roast chicken, not an unusual dish at this period.

Next morning, the 29th March, was real wet, and Spragge and I went down early to the station to relieve the night officers. Five trains from the Base, or from our old gun park, had arrived, and besides all

FIELD GUNS IN FRANCE

the stores that had come by road there was on the platform a pile of stuff 15 ft. high and 60 ft. long, all in glorious confusion, having been unloaded in the dark. In addition, there were at least 700 pairs of wheels, with either guns or wagons on them.

Of course, the station was not complete without its very excited R.T.O., who was almost off his head, and was threatening, in the fiercest style, everybody, including Grieg, of Fifth Army, who had turned up to see how things were going. However, with the help of a hundred fresh men and additional transport which was collected in the neighbourhood, we were able to get the station clear, but it was a slave-driving morning, as quite half the men were dead beat.

In the course of many motor dashes collecting men or lorries I found a large ration dump in the process of moving, so I assisted in their move by lifting 40 gallons of rum and 2 cwt. of sugar, the rum in particular being invaluable to our weary contingent.

The day was, however, not without its humour. An Artillery Colonel turned up with the mistaken idea that his area of command covered our gun park, so the position was somewhat strained till, in response to my S.O.S. message to Army R.A., Colonel Broad sent explicit instructions defining our respective commandos. By evening our camp was something like a gun park, but there was still a strong touch of the jumble sale about it. The Ordnance people, however, were beginning to learn that twenty-four hours' work was expected out of them per day, so that the worst of the confusion was soon over.

That night, Longeau having been cleared, only just in time, too, Crowe joined us at Poix, and again took over from me. My next job was to go forward fifteen miles to Vers, and open a new gun park there for all horse-drawn batteries, in order to save them the long trek back to Poix. I also was given jurisdiction over the area and villages around, as far as billeting, rationing and re-equipping horse-drawn batteries were concerned.

Fifth Army R.A. Staff are ideal to work for. They give one a job and leave one entirely to oneself to carry it out, with the result that anyone who has worked for them swears by them and their methods.

Spragge left at dusk with a column of lorries, each pulling two 18-pdrs. or Howitzers, ready for issue, and reached Vers with the bulk of them by dawn. The remainder got lost or temporarily broke down, but they all turned up safely next day, while I stayed on with Crowe to hand over the show to him by daylight.

LETTER FIFTY-TWO.

VERS. (APRIL, 1918.)

Re-equipping the Army. Many Changes.

ON the morning of the 30th March, having handed over the gun park to Crowe, I collected my little band of Officers and N.C.O. instructors, and by lorry and car we moved to Vers. We found that our advance party had done splendid work; they had taken over a large factory yard with excellent offices and store rooms, which made an ideal site for a gun park and issuing departments for ordnance stores, besides that they had taken over a very nicely furnished house with a bathroom complete to real hot water, which belonged to the owner of our factory.

As the job was entirely novel to us we had to make up our own rules and a system for book-keeping, and the signing for, and issuing of, all the guns and stores. Happily we were able to set off against our many difficulties the blessed fact that there was not a single ordnance officer on our premises !

In order to advertise to the world in general that our shop was open, Barraclough, a portrait-painter and sculptor by trade, made beautiful notices which were stuck up in all the villages, and at all cross-roads for miles around, for the information of all R.F.A. and 60-pdr. batteries belonging to the 18th and 19th Corps.

On calling at Army in the afternoon, I found our R.A. busy handing over to Fourth Army R.A., and in the evening Colonel Napier, of Fourth Army, came down to see us with Colonel Broad. Next day, Easter Sunday, was spent chiefly in motoring about, first to the 18th Corps, and then on to the 19th Corps. At the latter place I ran across Colonel Weston Jarvis, Corps Camp Commandant, as cheery as ever in spite of the incessant moves of his Corps Head-Quarters, then back to Army for lunch with Buxton, of Fourth Army, who is opposite number to Grieg.

There was already quite a change in the air and all sorts of curious people were about. To keep in with the politicians certainly seems a good recipe if one wants to be known to posterity as a successful Army Commander.

FIELD GUNS IN FRANCE

By dint of much persuasion I got Signals to instal a telephone in our office, so that we can now talk to Poix and the various Corps Head-Quarters. Each Corps is, of course, firmly convinced that they are our special favourites, and that they are getting thereby more than their share of stores and guns.

Next day, the 1st April, was another glorious spring day. Buxton visited us in the morning and saw us at our busiest, detachments from forty batteries all clamouring at once for guns, wagons and stores.

We have to issue guns on a priority list which is given us by each Corps, so often three or four teams with only a senior driver in command belonging to some battery on our list arrive and decide to wait two or three days until their turn comes round. We have horse lines erected in the yard, and we always keep a thousand rations on hand as our ration strength fluctuates from our little staff of fifteen up to many hundreds at a moment's notice. Waite has supplied us with cooks from his rest camp, so that at whatever hour of the night men and horses arrive from the line for equipment, they find everything ready for them in the way of hot food and rum and rations for themselves and for their horses. They appreciate this consideration very much instead of being met with "no guns available, call again to-morrow."

Waite also runs an officers' rest-house, as many officers come with orders to stay until they had collected all their requirements. Whenever a convoy of lorries arrived with stores all these waiting people would swoop down like vultures, and watch every article being unloaded and then proceed to renew their importunities.

Our one safeguard against these brigands is Major Lang, R G.A. The history of him and his battery is rather comic. We found him lurking in the wood near Villers Bretonneux with a brand new 12-inch, Howitzer Battery, which had only left England three days before and had not yet been in action. As such heavy Howitzers were not wanted in this kind of warfare, Lang has been acting as Carter Paterson for our show, following us on all our wanderings with his 16 lorries and six 120 h.p. "cats." I also have the use of his fine new Vauxhall car, a priceless boon. At the same time he supplies us with N.C.O.'s and guards to help to control the mass of humanity and horses that surge in upon us. All are welcomed into the yard, but none can pass his lynx-eyed sentries without a "pass-out" slip which prevents people absconding with stores. With the help of his lorries, and other lost ones which we have annexed, we are able to run a frequent lorry service from here to the railhead at Poix and back. Fortunately, Lang is one of the best, and quite sees the humour of his present position, and his help is absolutely invaluable.

Every evening I have to visit Army to report the demands made by the different Corps for 13, 18, and 60-pdrs. and 4.5 Howitzers, during the day, also to report what loads of stores are most wanted up from the base by rail and movements of units in our area. This visit takes over an hour now instead of ten minutes of orders at machine-gun speed, to which one became accustomed when dealing with Grieg or Broad.

And so the days fled past. Meanwhile Fifth Army R.A., or rather Reserve Army, as we are now called, had taken up their quarters at the old school. Grieg visited us once or twice to give us news of our home and our horses, also to discover how the band of "Red Fox" exiles were faring under the new regime, and what prospects there were for us to disentangle ourselves and get back to our own army.

Early on the morning of the 5th April an urgent summons to come at once to Army Head-Quarters roused Waite and me from sleep, but on inquiry elicited the fact that the "crisis" was not acute enough to necessitate our motoring off there before breakfast. Really, now that the War is becoming the world's sole occupation, one had to be firm about having definite hours for indulging in it.

On arrival at Army we found them all of a "Hou-hou," in the middle of a sudden move back to Flixecourt. We commenced our interview with Buxton in his well-furnished office, but before it was over, the R.S.M. and his minions had emptied the whole room except for a Bell telephone sitting forlornly in the centre of the floor. As usual there was no time to ask how the War was going, but from the suddenness of their departure one gathered that the Hun was being tiresome. Often, after having visited several Corps Head-Quarters, on returning home, when asked for the latest news, one remembers that not a single word has been uttered about the recent operations. But our job at present is to supply guns and equipment, and there is quite enough chat flying about without increasing it.

I returned to Vers to make bunderbust in case we had to move out, and as a precautionary measure moved the 12-inch Howitzer Battery back about four miles, as if things did get serious we should require all their lorries.

However, later in the day, on visiting 18th and 19th Corps Head-Quarters, I found perfect peace reigning once again. As Flixecourt is such a long way off, Waite and I are spared our evening visit to Army and do our business by 'phone instead.

Men who had been on leave from units involved in the retreat had a desperate time trying to rejoin them, every base, official and R.T.O. seeming to conspire to prevent people leaving the base ports, so that it took many two or three weeks to re-join. One day recently, while motoring through a village, I heard my name called frantically, and on stopping I found a very old friend, Golding, a warrant officer on the 30th Division R.A. Staff. A terrible tale of woe then followed, how he landed on the 22nd March and had been wandering about ever since. He had also under his wing a very young officer and 20 men from his Division. I knew luckily where the brigades were, and on my way to Poix delivered him to the fold of the 30th Division Head-Quarters, who had quite given him up for lost. Lunch there with General Geoffrey White, Gregory and Webb, was quite like old times.

That morning, the 6th April, Fourth Army had told me that as soon as I could conveniently hand over my job, Reserve Army wanted me back. Feigning great surprise, I said that I would see what could be done. On going to Poix I saw General Hardy-Newman, who has the command of the whole area, and he said he had no objection to some of us leaving, provided the various shows we were running continued to function. Accordingly next morning I left Vers early and called at Flixecourt to report my departure, and then sped swiftly back home.

The horses were all looking splendid in their summer coats, and the whole place as pretty as spring could make it. The Chateau itself was decorated with many dummy notices, the padre's sitting-room door was labelled D.A.Q.M.G., other rooms G.S.O.1, etc., all this to repel the many horrid people who creep stealthily round to spy out the land, and prevent them from going to G.H.Q. and secretly claiming the whole establishment on the strength of it not being fully utilized at the moment.

On our way homeward, while passing a lot of lorries parked beside the road, rather a humorous incident occurred. There was suddenly an explosion on the bank above our heads, and before we had time to take cover five more small bombs landed. The lorries were rather knocked about, but no one was hurt. Our passing through Amiens was also unhealthy, as a H.V. gun was throwing it about all around.

Our rest at the school, however, was a short one, two days after our arrival there we were sent off to plan out the Artillery defence of the G.H.Q. line, one of the many lines of defence which were being hurriedly prepared to the North of Amiens.

It is not until one has wandered in the back areas of France, alone with one's servant and unattached to any unit, with no mess transport or horses, and often with no rations, that, unloved by all, one realizes the utmost depths of the horrors of war. My companion in adversity was a Siege Artillery Colonel, on the same job as mine except that he was looking after the heavy artillery. For a week we eked out a miserable nomad existence in various villages in our sector of about 14 miles.

The R.A. General in charge of this work was Brig.-General Knapp, and on my first interview with him he looked at me and said, "Why are you improperly dressed?" A hasty glance showed me that every button was fastened, and that those *rara avis*, spurs and Sam Browne, were both in action on my person. However, to my still greater astonishment, he told me that a fortnight before I had been given a bar to my D.S.O. The papers had got lost in some office, hence a year's delay.

Our job was to mark down on the map suitable positions for each Artillery Brigade echelonned in depth, to find O.P.'s and wagon lines, etc. This work was at times rather impeded by the habit our front line had of jumping fancy-free from one hill-top to the next until the R.E. had definitely decided its site.

However, having completed the northern sector from Pas to Authie, I was able to finish the southern sector while staying in comfort with Crowe at his Fifth Army Trench Mortar School at Valheureux, and as soon as my work was done we heard that our school was to re-open in earnest, taking in officers and N.C.O.'s from every army. Accordingly, on the 24th of April, all the wanderers returned to the school, and the happy life of the "Red Fox School" was once more a reality. The classes were of a fortnight's duration, with only a break of two days between each, so that for the next two months life there was a very busy and happy one. We were concentrating chiefly on open warfare tactics and tried to make young officers realize that F.A.T., the gunner's Bible, was still as correct and as up-to-date as the day on which it was written. No easy matter trying to dispel the clinging miasma of siege warfare conditions.

General Uniacke spent much of his time at the school, and under his guidance you may be sure that the instruction was thorough and up-to-date. With our own horses, and with one or two borrowed from the depot batteries, we managed to get up a polo team, using part of the golf-course and part of the football grounds as our pitch. The 52nd and the 74th Divisions, both fresh from the east, spent a fortnight or so in our neighbourhood, many of the B.C.'s and junior officers attending the school in order to learn the peculiar horrors of artillery warfare in France, and we played some matches against them, Brig.-General Hext, the C.R.A. of the 74th Division, and Day, his Brigade Major, being the shining lights of their team.

On the whole we soon found that, apart from their natural ignorance about gas and other things peculiar to France, there was not much we could teach the B.C.'s, and their batteries were quite a treat to see. Thus passed very pleasantly the early summer of 1918.

LETTER FIFTY-THREE.

BOMY TRAINING AREA. (28TH JULY, 1918.)

Interesting Work. Gas Trouble and Hospital.

Who recalls the twilight and the rangéd tents in order
(Violet peaks uplifted through the crystal evening air ?)
And the clink of iron teacups and the piteous, noble laughter,
And the faces of the Sisters with the dust upon their hair ?
R. KIPLING.

DURING the month of June there were many happenings, and unfortunately the bulk of them were unpleasant. Firstly, of course, the school, like every other unit on both sides of No Man's Land, was decimated by "flu," so that the classes wilted away under the scourge and several of the courses had to be prolonged for another ten or fourteen days. In the next place, General Uniacke left us to take up his new post as Inspector of Training R.A., in the new I.T., as it is called, which has just sprung into being. He has long been desirous of starting one great central school for Colonels and Battery Commanders in which every Artillery subject is taught, and also a Northern and Southern School for junior officers.

By doing away with Army Schools, uniformity of instruction would at last be secured, and that is greatly needed. Only too often instructors will not stick to THE BOOK, but teach fancy systems of their own—very fancy they often are, and confusing to young officers going from one school to another. The ideal, I think, should be rigidity of executive orders coupled with boundless imagination and initiative in everything else.

In the month of June we also heard that another army was plotting at G.H.Q. to take our school from us. Intrigue and counter-intrigue followed in breathless succession, and there was much betting at every Head-Quarters whether we would be able to stave off the determined attack that was being made to capture our citadel. But at last the end came, our final course dispersed on the 10th of July, and the school was given over to another Army. Three of us instructors had been applied for by the incomers to remain as instructors with them, but the *esprit d'armée* that exists in the Fifth Army R.A. and the fanatical worship of the "Red Fox" was far too strong to let us think of remaining at the old school, however much we loved the place, so a few hours after the dispersal of the course the three of us escaped swiftly by car and sped northwards to join Fifth Army Head-Quarters at Therouanne, south of St. Omer. Things blew up for trouble as soon as the incoming people discovered we had left, and their army got on to G.H.Q. about us, but fortunately we had phoned through an S.O.S. to warn Fifth Army, so that they got in their say first, proving that we were wanted for a hundred and one jobs with them.

We spent two days of pleasant idleness in a comfortable new camp near Coceque till the whole of the staff of Fifth Army Artillery School and Trench Mortar School gradually gathered together, including even our excellent band, the delight of all units near us. Our future was then decided. I was given the very pleasant job of chief staff officer of training for all units out at rest, having Penrose, Spragge and some other officers and N.C.O. instructors to help me.

The remainder of the Red Fox instructors were to look after all the R.A. reinforcements who, instead of being kept lingering at the base, were now sent up direct to our camp for training and distribution. Briefly, our task was to see that the spirit of the Army Training Instructions for units when at rest was adhered to, without unduly interfering with the ideas and schemes of the Division and Brigade Commanders. A careful mixture of steel and velvet is required to avoid any friction.

Besides all this we were required to give lectures on any subject, to organize field-day schemes, to make a practice range for Field Artillery, to run classes for specific subjects, such as air recuperators, Lewis guns, etc., so that our time will be occupied in the immediate future. At present we have seven brigades in our area, five Field Artillery Brigades and two Siege, widely scattered in the neighbouring villages.

I have enough instructors to be able to send one to live with each Army Brigade or Division. I live at the camp and spend ten hours a day motoring round, visiting the various units and coping with their endless demands, lecturing at intervals and taking demonstration battery gun-drills. When organizing the stretch of country which we use for our practice camp, I may mention that we had great difficulty in persuading the French agriculturists to believe that if they would continue to work close beside the targets when the red flag was up, they were quite likely to get hurt.

It is rather curious that twice in six months I should get an entirely new job without any precedent to work it on. The first one was when I was put in charge of the Army gun park, and now this running the new intensive system of Army training.

FIELD GUNS IN FRANCE 245

The new I.T. are very keen on our show here, and help us in every way they can, as they regard it as their pet experiment. Last Friday, at the end of our first training period, we stage-managed a great Artillery Field Day for R.F.A. and R.G.A. Brigades. We borrowed several hundred men from the reinforcement camp to form the German and British Infantry, and had hostile tanks represented by lorries cunningly camouflaged to look like the real thing; there was even a flight of aeroplanes sending frantic wireless messages, and quite a successful congestion on all the roads with so many batteries on a small front, furnishing quite realistic push conditions.

It was a complicated scheme entailing several very rapid retirements followed by an advance. The hill-tops were smothered with Generals from G.H.Q., I.T., Army Corps and Divisions. The average combined field day is usually a sheer waste of time for Artillery, and a field day purely for the benefit of gunners was a complete novelty to most of the onlookers, and on the whole the day went smoothly as far as the staging and scenery went.

We used to have many such days at the old school, so we are up to the tricks of the trade, in fact, it was only the good practice we had had there in the way of intensive Artillery instructing that made it possible for us to carry on our high pressure existence here. It is rather like being perpetually in a shop window; at one moment one may have to take gun drill or driving drill, at the next to deliver a lecture, so it keeps one well tuned up all the time.

The front is very quiet, and there are a surprisingly large number of divisions out at rest, so numerous horse shows and military tournaments are held. How annoying it must be for the Hun to hear of such doings in an "Army on the verge of collapse!"

From the high hill above the camp there is a marvellous view looking east, first Cassel Hill in the distance, then Mont des Cats, Mont Noir, Mont Rouge, and on very clear days Kemmel and even Messines Ridge.

We live in luxury in bell tents dug down 4 feet, the earth walls lined with canvas, wood floor, and the tent pole elevated 5 feet on a big wooden post, thus giving head-room everywhere. Four wooden steps lead down from the door, and what with bedsteads, chairs, and cupboards, one is very much at home. General Birdwood is, of course, at Fifth Army, and he rode over one day for breakfast at our camp, and to inspect the morning parade of the reinforcements.

NOTE BY THE AUTHOR.

Towards the end of July the evil effects of continued doses of gas again asserted themselves, and after carrying on for a week on a diet consisting mainly of chlorodyne, I went off for a rest, having been invited by Millicent, Duchess of Sutherland, to stay as a guest at her "Casualty Clearing Station" near St. Omer. What a wonderfully well-run show it was! There I remained for three weeks, but got no better, so was officially admitted to hospital and evacuated to England at the end of August. When I reached London I was taken to No. 9 Park Lane Hospital, and eventually given several months' sick leave by medical board.

Happily this verdict was reversed within a fortnight, when I was lucky enough to get the job of D.A.A. and Q.M.G. on the military section of the Supreme War Council at Versailles, and a special medical board was assembled to see if I could be passed fit enough for the job. I managed to convince them, although one of the board did suggest that a light deal coffin would be as handy as a suit-case, and would also serve for another purpose. Accordingly, on the 5th October I set forth for Versailles, disguised as a staff officer, where, as an onlooker, I was present at the closing scenes of the War, during the Armistice negotiations and later the Peace Conference.

> But to-day I leave the galley. Shall I curse her service then?
> God be thanked! Whate'er comes after, I have lived and toiled with Men!
>
> R. KIPLING.

> The moril of this story, it is plainly to be seen:
> You 'avn't got no families when servin' of the Queen—
> You 'aven't got no brothers, fathers, sisters, wives, or sons—
> If you want to win your battles take an' work your bloomin' guns!
>
> R. KIPLING.

THE END

INDEX

INDEX

NOTE.—Military rank as at time letters were written ; for Infantry Battalion see under Battalion for Artillery Brigade see under Brigade.

Abbeville, 222, 225, 227, 231
Abris Wood, 214, 223
Alhusen, Lt.-Col. F., 228
Almond, Capt. E. A., 227
Amiens, 34, 71, 99, 137, 231, 233, 234, 235, 241
Anderson, Major-Gen., 105
Antoine, General, 206
Army, 2nd, 175
Army, 3rd, 229
Army, 4th, 65, 71, 236, 238, 241
Army, 5th, 143, 148, 222, 225, 228, 231, 241, 242, 244
Armstrong, Capt., 55, 56, 57
Arras, 143, 169
Arrowhead Copse, 90, 96
Artillery School, 5th Army, 222, 225, 227, 228-229, 244
   5th Army Trench Mortar School, 236, 244
Ash, Capt., 235
Auchonvilliers, 27
Authie, 242
Australians, 128-131
Australian Artillery, 131, 136

Banks, Lt., 109
Barraclough, Lt., 238
Basseux, 144
Battalion Guards Entrenching, 65
   1st Grenadiers, 206
Battalion 4th Grenadiers, 206
   2nd Scots Guards, 206
   Welsh Guards, 206
Battalion Lancashire, 180
   Manchesters, 40, 41, 44, 89
Battalion 10th Manchesters, 40
Battalion 18th Manchesters, 59, 141
Battalion 2nd Royal Scots, 42, 141
Battalion Irish, 203
Battery G, R.H.A., 213
Battery Renfrew, 52, 55
Battery 65th (How.), 45, 52
Battery C/148, 141

Battery A/149, 56, 73
   B/150, 146, 149, 151, 176, 177, 185, 190, 219
   C/150, 176, 177, 219
   D/150, 149, 177, 190, 191, 197, 218
   150 B.A.C., 185
Battles by date :—
   1916.
   28th Jan. (Frise), 43
   1st July (SOMME), 81
   Mid July (Trones Wood), 84-86
   14th July (Longueval), 89
   18th July, 93
   20th July, 95
   30th July, 99
   27th Sept., 106
   Mid October, 107-124
   1917.
   9th April (ARRAS), 154
   23rd April, 162
   3rd May, 166
   19th May, 171
   7th June (MESSINES), 181
   31st July (3rd B. OF YPRES), 195
   16th August, 201
   18th August, 203
   22nd August, 205
   22nd October, 221
   December (CAMBRAI), 226
Beach Thomas, 123
Beaumetz, 142, 144
Beaumont Hamel, 28
Bellicourt, 151
Bengal Lancers, 146
Bennett, Lt. E. A., 136
Bernafay Wood, 84, 89, 97, 99
Bethune, 105, 106
Bevan, Lt. N. M., 119
Billon Wood, 104
Birch, Major-General Sir Noel, 42, 65
Birdwood, Gen., 245
Blaireville, 143
Blues, The, 209
Boar's Copse, 227
Boesinghe, 214
Boiry Becquerelle, 145, 166

INDEX

Bois des Tailles, 37, 65, 71, 104
Bois des Vaches, 49, 53
Bois Jean, 224
Boisleux-le-Mont, 146, 151
Bray, 34, 36, 37, 40, 50, 71
Bretencourt, 144
Brigade, 149th, R.F.A., 34, 36
Brigade 150th, R.F.A., 65, 93-94, 125, 149-172, 213, 222
Brigade 1st Cavalry, 209
Brigade 90th (Inf.), 82
Brigade 3rd Guards, 206
Broad, Lt.-Col., C. N. F., 231, 237, 238, 240
Broombeck, 217-219
Bull ring, 176
Bullecourt, 173
Burke, Lt., 109
Bussy Les Daours 137
Butler-Stoney, Major R. B., 229
Butte de Warlencourt, 132
Buxton, Major, 238, 239, 240

Cairns, Lt., 162
Calais, 214, 229, 230
Cambrai, 225
Canadians, 160
Cappy, 37, 41, 53, 56
Cassel Hill, 245
Caterpillar Valley 82, 86, 127
Cavan, Lord, 34
Chipilly, 66
Clarges St., 215
Clarke, Lt. Garnett, 176, 181, 183, 190
Clifford, Lt.-Col., 224
Clifford, Major E., 224
Coceque, 244
Cocquerel, 226
Cojeul River, 146, 151, 156, 173
Combles, 100
Corbie, 50, 52, 233
Corps, Anzac, 131
Corps, 3rd, 226
Corps, 7th, 226
Corps, 11th, 105
Corps, 14th, 34
Corps, 18th, 238, 240
Corps, 19th, 230, 232, 238, 240
Corps, 20th (de Fer French), 65, 70, 85
Courcelette, 28
Craik, Col., 235
Croissilles, 163
Crowe, Major W. H. F., 236, 237, 238, 242
Curlu, 37, 38, 41, 44, 49, 50, 59, 68, 128

Davidson, Lt.-Col. C. G. F., 225, 233, 234

Day, Major, 242
Delville Wood, 86, 93, 108, 128
Dennistoun, Lt.-Col. I. O., 206, 209
Derby, Lord, 34
Dernancourt, 106
Dickson, Major Gordon, 158
Dickebusch Lake, 175
Diggle, Major, 231
Division, Guards, 34, 199, 206
Division, Irish, 121, 204
Division, Lahore, 211
Division, 2nd Colonial (French) 58, 85
Division, 18th, 55, 59, 81, 89
Division, 21st, 154, 155, 156
Division, 30th, 81, 85, 116, 119, 143, 154, 156, 201, 226, 241
Division, 35th, 97
Division, 36th, 203
Division, 39th (French), 81, 109
Division, 49th, 143
Division, 52nd, 242
Division, 56th, 154
Division, 74th, 242
Divisional Ammunition Column, 30th, 135
Dixon, Lt.-Col. F. A., 65, 125, 137, 141, 159, 167, 170, 175, 176, 181, 197, 199, 211, 222, 227
Doullens, 24, 137, 174
Duerden, Lt., 201, 202, 203
Dury, 232, 234

Ecke, 224
Eclusier, 53
Ednam, Lord, 226
Edwards, Capt. Hon. E., 6, 27; 34
Edwards, Q.M.S. Wheeler, 168
Ellice, Major E., 65, 72
Elton, Brig.-Gen., 31, 42
Emsley, Major, 219
Essars, Lock, 105
Etaples, 228

Faidherbe Crossroads, 215
Falfemont Farm, 100
Farnham, Major Lord, 140, 172, 199
Faviere Valley, 90, 92, 100
Feuillères, 59
Folkestone, 229
Follett, Lt.-Col. G., 215
Fontaine, 157, 163, 172
Forestry H.Q., 228
Fourth of June, 71, 178
Flers, 106, 107, 108, 117, 131, 136
Flibeaucourt, 224

INDEX

Flixecourt, 240, 241
Fraser, Major, 214, 230
Fraser-Tytler, Capt. P. S., 99, 102
French Army, 49, 53, 56-58, 61, 65, 75-78, 85, 93
Frezenberg Ridge, 200, 201
Fricourt, 135
Frise, 37, 41, 45, 46, 65, 85
Fry, Major-Gen., 24
Fullerton, Major, 73

Gallipoli Farm, 205, 208, 211
Gas, 178, 188-190, 191, 205, 223
Gavrelle, 173
G.H.Q., 228
Gibbs, Major, 103
Gilmour, Col., 214
Gisburne, Col., 227
Glencorse Wood, 208
Goldfish Château, 210
Golding, R.S.M., 241
Gordon, Major, 222
Gordon's Farm, 175, 177
Gort, Lt.-Col. Lord, 206
Gosling, Capt., 95, 226
Gough, Lt., 226
Gough, Gen. Sir Hubert, 229, 231, 234, 236
Grandcourt, 28
Gregory, Major, 76, 141, 241
Grieg, Major A. D., 234, 237, 238, 240
Grinlinton, Major, 37
Grouches, 137
Guards (see Division of)
Guemappe, 146
Gueudecourt, 110, 117, 121, 131
Guillemont, 84, 90, 93, 94, 97, 201

Hambre, General, 235
Hardecourt, 97, 98, 99, 100, 104
Hardy-Newman, Gen., 241
Hart, Lt., 214, 227
Havre, 23, 29
Hazebrouck, 174, 209
Henin, 146, 147, 150, 151, 161
Henin Hill, 154, 155, 156, 165
Heninel, 146, 155, 156
Herbecourt, 59
Herzeel, 214
Heseltine, Lt., 37
Hext, Brig.-Gen., 242
Hickey, Gunner, 70, 94, 151, 210, 213, 219
Hill, Lt., 178, 179
Hills, Major, 229, 231, 233

Hindenburg Line, 146, 151, 152, 156, 157
Hobday, Major, 225
Hotel du Rhin, 34, 231
Houthulst, Forest of, 215, 221
Hunter St., 215
Hussars, 10th, 226

Inspectorate of Training, 243, 245
Inverness Copse, 208

Jack, Major J. C., 146, 152, 176, 190
Jarvis, Lt.-Col. Weston, 238
Jelf, Lt.-Colonel Wedd, 141, 142
Johnstone, Lt., 69, 223

Kemmel Hill, 177, 245
Kills, good, 50, 55, 60, 70, 90, 92, 94, 96, 112, 117, 120, 132, 154, 156, 157, 161-163, 164, 167, 212
Kirkland Major, 36, 38
Knapp, Brig.-Gen. K., 241

La Flaque, 232
Lang, Major, 239
Langemarck, 201
Lanyon, Col. O. M., 71, 113, 226
Leckie, Major-Gen., 35, 56, 61
Leuze Wood, 101
Leveson-Gower, Lord Alistair, 209
Lloyd, Capt. Kemes, 65
Lloyd George, 185
Long, Lt.-Col., 41
Longcroft, Brig.-Gen., 206
Longeau, 233, 234, 235, 237
Longueval, 84, 86, 98, 106, 107, 129
Lotte, Commandant, 53, 58
Lovat, Lord, 228
Luce River, 231
Luchieux, 174
Lupton, Major, 60
Lyon, Lt.-Col., 26, 31, 34, 57, 63
Lyon, Brig.-Gen., 140

Macdonald, Capt., 31, 36, 50, 63, 71, 72, 89, 95, 98
Maclean, Lt., 27, 35, 63, 73, 74, 77, 86, 92, 93, 111, 112, 119, 121, 136, 138

INDEX

Mailly Maillet, 26, 30, 34
Maltz Horn Farm, 91, 95, 96
Manchesters (see Batt.)
Maricourt, 34, 38, 40, 59, 61, 65, 70, 75, 84, 87, 93, 95, 104
Maricourt Valley, 36, 65, 70, 73
Maurepas, 56, 101
Méaulte, 118
Mehal Shahal, 171
Merville, 105
Mesnel, 28
Messines (see Battle of)
Messines Ridge, 175, 176, 184, 245
Monchy Hill, 146
Monchy, 144, 155, 173
Monkhouse, Brig.-Gen., 181
Mont des Cats, 244
Mont Noir, 244
Mont Rouge, 244
Mont St. Quentin, 37
Montreuil, 225
Montauban, 82, 84, 85, 86, 89, 99, 118, 126, 131
Moulin de Fargny, 37, 38, 55
Musson, Lt., 93, 100, 101, 104, 119, 137

Nampes, 234
Napier, Lt.-Col., 238
New Zealanders, 106
North Irish Horse, 140, 173, 199
Nourisson General, 109
Nunn, Major J., 56, 60, 66, 73, 77, 79, 151
Nurlu, 227

150 mm. Valley, 37
O.P. (observation post), 27, 28, 63, 96, 138, 153, 177, 203
Oppy, 173
Ormerod, Lt.-Col., 27
Oxford Row, 197

Park Lane No. 9, 246
Pas, 242
Pask, Capt., 45, 52, 109
Paul, Capt., 67, 68
Peace Conference, 246
Penrose, Major J., 231, 244
Peronne, 37, 85, 226, 227
Persia Camp, 223
Pilkem Ridge, 213, 216, 218
Plug Street, 178

Plum Farm, 202
Poix, 235, 236, 237
Polden, Major A., 218
Pongo, 182, 206
Pont Noyelles, 36
Poperinghe, 199, 200, 209
Potigze Château, 189, 196, 197, 198, 199, 203, 204
Poyntz, Col., 76
Prest, Lt., 190, 202, 208, 218, 220, 223
Prussian Guard, 101, 106
Puchevilliers, 26

Rawlinson, General, 71
Renbrun, 224
Richthofen, 148
Ridge Wood, 184
Riley, Capt., 37
Roberts, Lady, 82
Roberts, Capt. C., 185, 199, 203, 209, 210, 215, 216, 222, 223
Ross, Brig.-Gen. Sir Walter, 34, 35
Ross-Johnson, Major-Gen., 140
Rougemont, Brig.-Gen. de, 72
Royal Dragoon Wood, 40, 57
Royal Irish Rifles, 27
Rupprecht Farm, 201
Ryding, Gunner, 71, 76, 78, 139

Sailly, 36, 226
St. Boiry Marc, 145
St. Julien's Farm, 203
St. Julien, 197
St. Martin, 146
St. Omer, 213, 214, 244, 246
St. Ouen, 24, 26, 30, 31, 36
St. Pol, 141
Sandys, Lt.-Col., 206
Sarson, Major, 145, 152, 190
Seligman, Lt.-Col., 25, 26
Serre, 30
Shaves, Close; to myself, 76, 111, 144, 150, 152, 176, 178, 200, 203, 206, 218, 219, 233
  To others, 30, 47, 73, 78, 82, 88, 94, 100, 102, 135, 218
Skindles, 199
Smith, Capt. M. Beckwith, 108, 136
Snow, Lt.-General, 140
Somme (see Battle of)
Somme Farm, 203
Somme River, 34, 37, 41, 106, 231
Southampton, 23

INDEX

Spragge, Capt. F. B. B., 233, 235, 236, 237, 244
Stanley, Lt.-Col. Hon. G., 34, 36, 44, 76, 95
Stanley, Major, 119, 124, 142
Steenbeck, 216
Stevens, Major, 98, 103
Straubenzee, Brig.-Gen. Van., 59
Supreme War Council, 246
Sutherland, Millicent, Duchess of, 246
Sutton, The Hon. R., 71
Susanne, 36, 37, 38, 40, 42, 43, 45, 46, 48, 50, 56, 57, 75

Talmas, 36
Taylor, Lt., 161, 178, 206, 209, 219, 220, 223
Telegraph Hill, 154
Terry, Major I., 73, 79
Therouanne, 244
Thiepval, 28, 204
Trench Mortar School, 5th Army, 236, 244
Trescault, 227
Trones Wood, 84, 86, 87, 88, 89, 90, 91, 92, 93, 94, 96, 97, 99, 104, 132
Tudor, Lt.-Col., 34

Uniacke, Major-Gen. Sir H. C. C., 242, 243
d'Uzé, Duchesse, 174

Valheureux, 242
Vaux, 37, 38, 39, 40, 41, 50, 59
Vaux Valley, 36, 47, 70, 128

Vaux Wood, 37, 39, 59, 68
Verdun, 82
Vers, 237, 238, 240
Versailles, 246
Villers Bretonneux, 231, 232, 239
Vignacourt, 34, 35
Vlamertinghe, 187, 200

Waite, Capt., 231, 235, 239, 240
Wales, Prince of, 136, 206
Walrond, Capt. V., 102
Walsh, Lt.-Col. R. K., 67, 69, 105
Wancourt, 146, 156
Wandonne, 224
Warfussee, 232
Wattou, 187, 223
Waterhouse, Gunner, 178
Webb, Capt., 241
West, Capt. A. P., 34
Westoutre, 174, 175, 185
White, Brig.-Gen. G., 65, 71, 72, 113, 128, 241
Widjendrift, 219, 220
Wilshin, Lt., 145, 150, 163, 164, 177, 178, 185, 195, 203, 204, 218, 220, 223
Wilson, Lt., 27, 89, 94, 113, 116
Wine House, 197
Woostan, 214

Young, Major, 213
Ypres, 34, 178, 187, 214

Zonnebeke, 198, 200
Zouaves, 73, 99

GAMEBOOK OF GERMAN CASUALTIES FROM PERSONAL OBSERVATION

Page
50	20 Huns	
51	M.G., probably crew escaped	Battle of Frise and pre-Somme
55	3 Huns	
61	1 Hun	
71	M.G. and crew and 2 snipers	
91	Say 50	
92	Say 10	
93	Ration party (6)	
94	Say 15	
96	1 killed, 3 wounded, with rifle	
100	Say 10	
101	Say 10	Battle of the Somme
116	Say 120—A Company, less 10 men (confirmed), on p. 116	
117	Say 20	
120	Say 30	
123	Various days, say 30	
147	77 m.m. gun and crew (4), as they had not bolted out of the cave	
147	20, confirmed when we captured the place two days later	
148	1 officer, 6 men (confirmed)	
149	6 (confirmed)	
156	20 (observed)	Battle of Arras
158	Say 30 at least (2000 rounds fired)	
161	Say 20 (no record kept)	
162	Say 20	
164	21 (seen)	
167	Say 8	
172	Say 10	
211	Say 15	Third Battle of Ypres

Total, 412 Huns

(From April till October, 1917, inclusive, an average of 20,000 rounds per month was fired by my Battery. Query—How many casualties?)

255

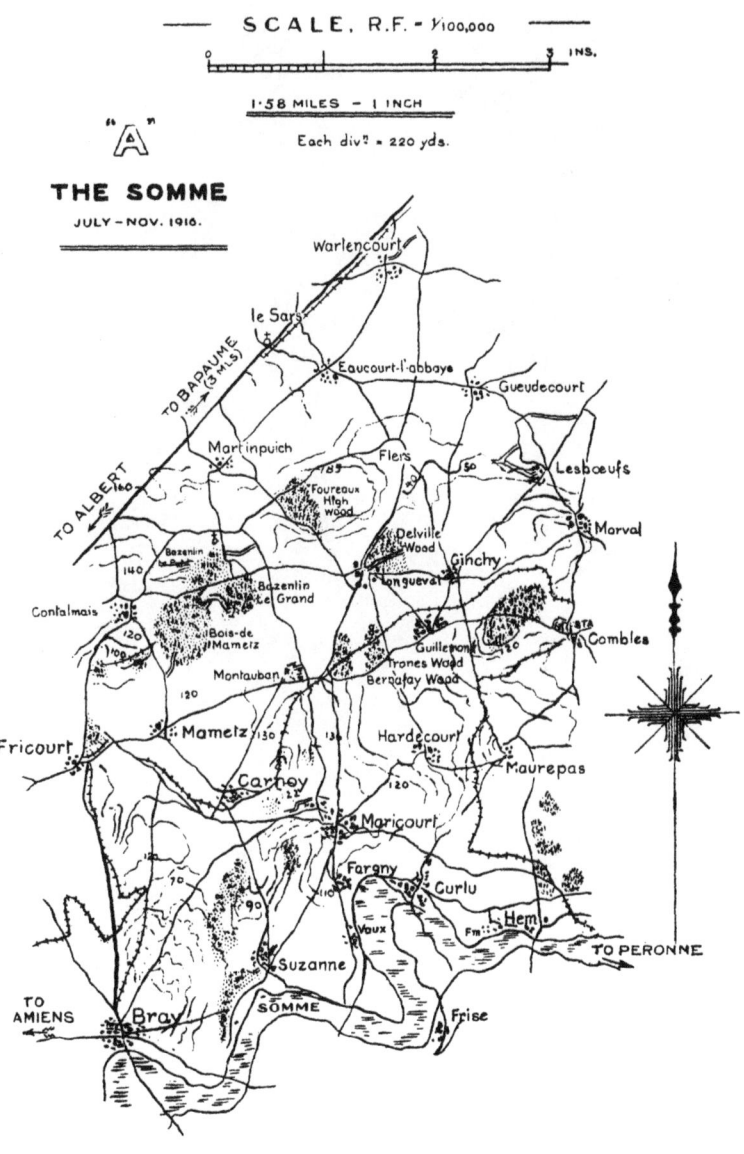

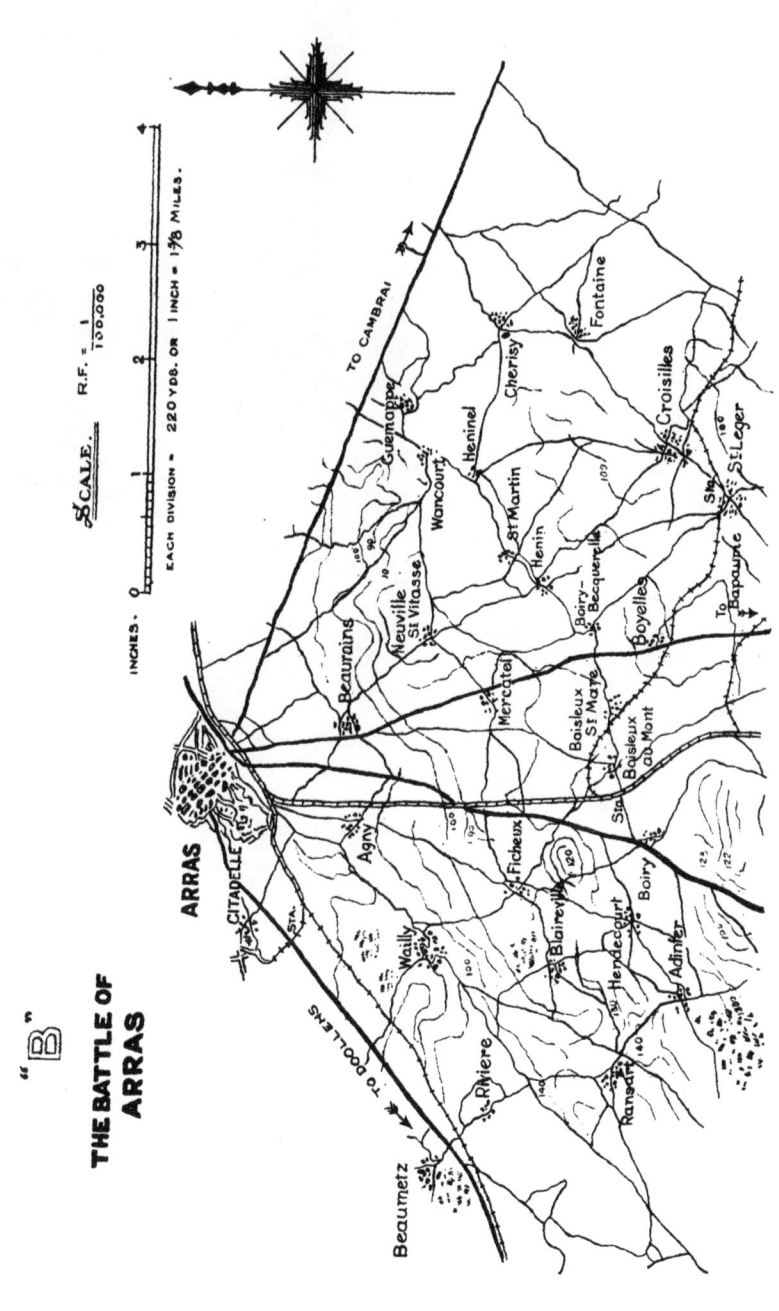

"D"
3rd Battle of "YPRES"
July–Octr 1917.
"C"
Battle of
"MESSINES RIDGE"
June 7th 1917.
Forest of Houthulst
CANAL
Koekuit
Poelcappellé
Langemark
Woesten
Pilkem
Boesinghe
St Julien
Elverdinghe
STA
Zonnebeke
Wieltje
Brielen
St Jean
Potyte
Vlamertinghe
YPRES
Hooge
TO POPERINGHE
Zillebeke Lake
Zillebeke
Gheluvelt
TO MENIN
Dickebusch
Lake
Voormezeele
St Eloi
Hollebeke
Mille Kruysen
Groote Vierestraat
La Clytte
Mont Scherpenberg
Oesttaverne
Wytschaete
Kemmel
Locre
Mont Kemmel
Messines
SCALE = R F = 1/100.000
1 2 3 4 INS
1·58 MLS = 1 INCH

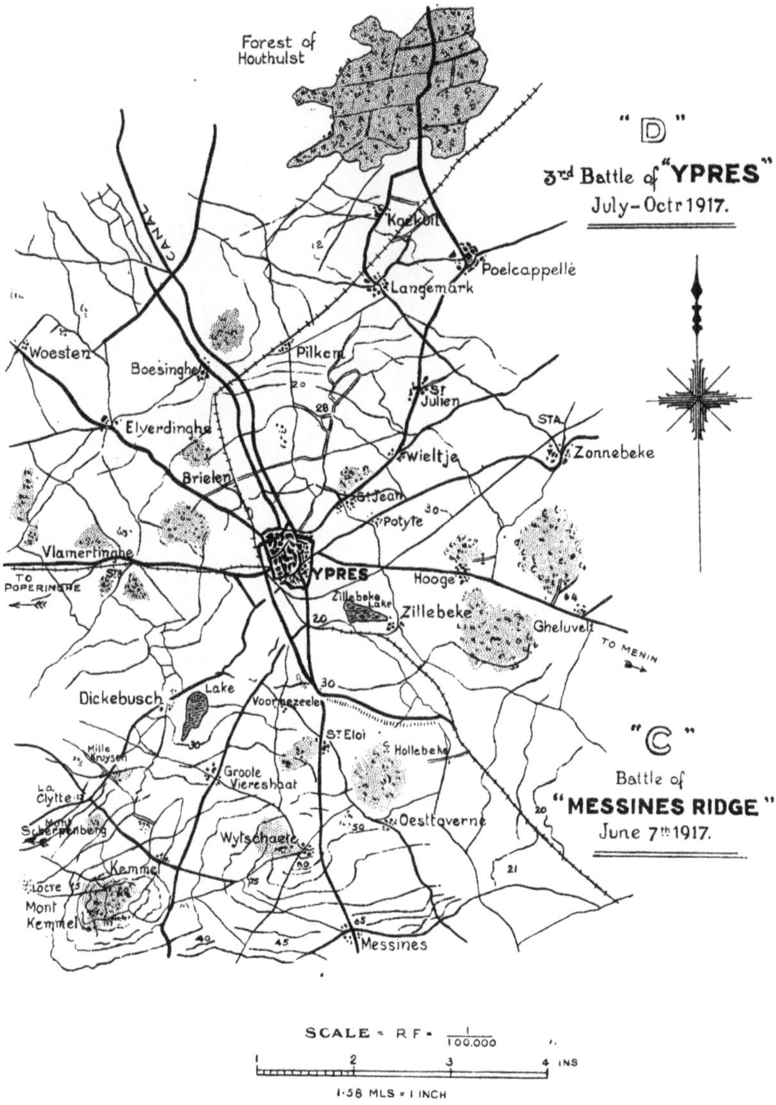

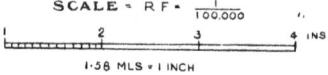

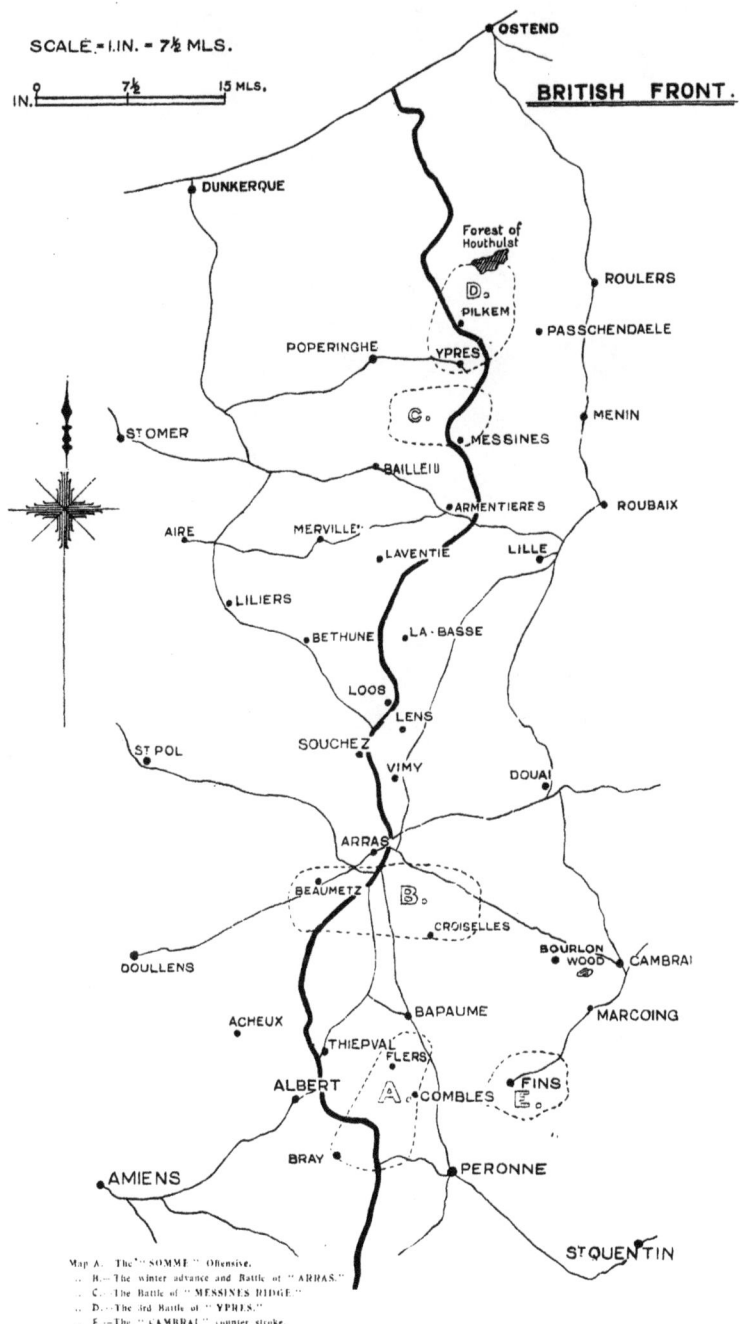

Map A.—The "SOMME" Offensive.
" B.—The winter advance and Battle of "ARRAS."
" C.—The Battle of "MESSINES RIDGE."
" D.—The 3rd Battle of "YPRES."
" E.—The "CAMBRAI" counter stroke.